The
Good Daughter

The Good Daughter

A Memoir of My Mother's Hidden Life

JASMIN DARZNIK

GRAND CENTRAL
PUBLISHING

NEW YORK   BOSTON

Grand Central Publishing
Hachette Book Group
237 Park Avenue
New York, NY 10017

www.HachetteBookGroup.com

Printed in the United States of America

First Edition: January 2011

10 9 8 7 6 5 4 3 2 1

Grand Central Publishing is a division of Hachette Book Group, Inc. The Grand Central Publishing name and logo is a trademark of Hachette Book Group, Inc.

Library of Congress Cataloging-in-Publication Data

Darznik, Jasmin.
  The good daughter : a memoir of my mother's hidden life / Jasmin Darznik.—1st ed.
      p. cm.
   ISBN 978-0-446-53497-0
1. Women—Iran—Social conditions—20th century.   2. Iran—Social conditions—20th century.   3. Mothers and daughters—Iran.   4. Darznik, Jasmin, 1973—Family.   I. Title.
   HQ1735.2.D37 2011
   305.48'891550092—dc22
   [B]
                                        2010003722

For my mother and grandmother

ACKNOWLEDGMENTS

So many friends, family members, and colleagues have supported, guided, and (more than occasionally) prodded me along in the writing of this book.

Linda Watanabe McFerrin gave me the courage to begin and for this I owe her my first thanks. In addition to leading me to Linda, Book Passage in Corte Madera, California provided me a wonderful community in which to read, learn, and write, and it's impossible for me to imagine *The Good Daughter* without that community.

Kelly Sonnack devoted early enthusiasm and unwavering attention to this memoir. I am grateful also to David Groff for his astute guidance. Sandy Dijkstra and the whole Dijkstra team—Elise Capron, Andrea Cavallaro, Natalie Fischer, Elisabeth James, and Taylor Martindale—have been enormously helpful to me at every turn.

For her uncommon patience and keen insights, I thank my editor, Caryn Karmatz Rudy. Thanks also to my publisher, Grand Central, and to Amanda Englander, who helped me send this book into the world. I've been very lucky, too, in my editors at Random House UK, Vanessa Neuling and Drummond Moir, who read draft after draft.

I'd like to acknowledge the wonderful organizations that supported this book: The Marin Arts Council, San Francisco Foundation, Intersection for the Arts, A Room of One's Own Foundation,

Community of Writers at Squaw Valley, Norman Mailer Writers Colony, and the Steinbeck Fellowship Program at the Martha Heasley Cox Center. In addition to the financial resources they extended for the project, they put me in contact with many of the mentors and fellow writers I've mentioned here.

Endless thanks go out to Rebecca Foust, whose friendship makes me believe in fate. She and my friends Shahdeh Shooshdary, Amy Motlagh, Sue-Ellen Speight, Mahta Jahanshahi, Marie Ostby, and Eileen Kane were my first devoted readers. Jahanshah Javid, editor of iranian.com, gave me my first writing "gig." Persis Karim and the members of the Association of Iranian American Writers continually inspired me with their camaraderie.

I am also particularly grateful to my son, Kiyan Darznik-Banaee. His inimitable spirit gives me joy every day.

And thanks, finally and profoundly, to my mother for the honesty, wisdom, and generosity with which she shared her story with me.

The
Good Daughter

Prologue

Like all the photographs that came with us when we left Iran, this one was as supple and as thick as leather. Its edges were tattered and a long white crease coursed through the image. I might easily have mistaken it for just another old photograph, but this one was nothing like the others.

The girl in it was my mother, Lili, and though she couldn't be older than fourteen, someone had rimmed her eyes with kohl and darkened her mouth with a lipstick so deep it looked black in the picture. Her dress was satin, pulled taut across her torso and pinched at the waist, and her shoulders turned in awkwardly where a wedding veil skimmed her body. The man at her side was not my father. I'd never seen him before. He wore a gray fedora with his tuxedo and his right hand encircled my mother's waist with surprisingly elegant fingers.

A bride, I realized with a start, she'd once been this stranger's bride.

Nearly as astonishing as this revelation was my mother's expression in the photograph. Eyes fixed on the distance and lower lip pouting, she looked as if the next shot would have shown her crying. I had never known my proud Iranian mother to look like that.

I sat stunned, gripping the photograph between my thumb and forefinger, unable to look away. I was sitting in my mother's house, a house to which I'd never imagined I'd return. It was late in the afternoon, five weeks after my father's funeral; I was helping her go through his things and this photograph had fallen from a stack of letters whose Persian script my eyes could no longer follow. A photograph hidden, forgotten, and now found.

Iranians would likely shrug at such a discovery, lift their eyes toward the heavens, and sum up its meaning as *qesmat*, or destiny. This was a word I'd hear often in the days following my father's death. *Qesmat*, my mother told me, had brought me back to California. I hadn't seen her in nearly a year when she called to tell me my father was in the hospital and that I had to come home...*now*. I left my apartment on the East Coast without even packing a suitcase. He died before my plane landed in San Francisco, but I returned to my parents' house still unready for tears.

My mother and I grieved at a distance, each of us in her own way. Lili's friends encircled her, crying with her and soothing her and praying with her day after day. I kept to myself. I did not cry. Then, three days after the funeral, I drove my mother to the airport. Together we watched my father's body, housed now in a black-ribboned coffin, being hoisted onto the plane that would carry him across the ocean to Germany, the home he'd given up when he moved to Iran in the sixties to marry my mother. The sky that morning was a rare December blue and nearly cloudless. "*Qesmat*," she whispered as the plane arched out of sight, and at this, finally, I cried.

We'd been a world of our own once, my mother Lili and I, a constant, intimate twosome beyond which I could imagine nothing, least of all myself. Then we came to America and I started turning into an American girl. That's when she began telling me about The Good Daughter. The Good Daughter lived in Iran. She didn't talk back—as I had learned to do in this *kharab shodeh*, this broken-down place. Actually, she didn't talk much at all. The Good Daughter listened. She understood—always—about manners and modesty. She didn't wander off to play in the streets by herself. The Good Daughter sat by her mother's side and heeded her mother's words. When a man looked at her, she lowered her eyes at once. And she was very, very pretty, with a sweet face and long, flowing hair just like the maidens in Persian miniatures.

Over the years The Good Daughter became a taunt, a warning, an omen. When I spoke immodestly, when I wore my skirts too short or let boys flirt with me, I was not my mother's real daughter, her Good Daughter. "If you become like the girls here," she'd say, "I'll go back to Iran to live with my Good Daughter."

The Good Daughter I knew back then was just a story she'd made up to scare me and make me into a good daughter, too. It was like my mother to tell such stories to keep me close and to keep me good. But I didn't want anything to do with The Good Daughter of my mother's Iranian world. The less I resembled her, the better it suited me. By the time I found the photograph of my mother as a young bride, I'd left home, as girls in this country always do and no true Iranian daughter ever would.

And yet for forty days after my father's death I stayed in my parents' house, smiling and nodding like The Good Daughter of my mother's stories while her friends dropped by in the afternoons in their lace-trimmed veils and carefully made-up eyes. "What will she do now?" they whispered to each other, and for forty days I served them tea and quietly watched them eyeing her for clues.

The house was finally empty the day I found the photograph, the funeral rites complete and the visitors gone. The platters of dates and pastries and fruit had all been cleared away and cardboard boxes lay scattered on the floor of every room of the house. I worked long into the afternoon, packing up my mother's clothes, bills, letters, and leather-bound photo albums. In one of the spare bedrooms I came across my father's books of Rilke, Kant, and Khayyám and also my grandmother Kobra's prayer shawl, rosary, and gilt-trimmed Koran. In my old bedroom closet I found the Gypsy dolls my grandmother sewed me years ago in Iran and a Persian picture book defaced by my own childish scribbles.

My mother and I were alone in the house where she could no longer afford to live, and when the photograph slipped loose from a bundle of letters she was upstairs sleeping with an open bottle of Valium on the table beside her bed.

I carried the photograph to the living room and sat cross-legged on the floor for a long time, staring up at the large black-and-white portrait of my parents on their wedding day. Tehran, 1962. She, raven haired with Cleopatra eyes, plays Elizabeth Taylor to my father's blond and slightly sheepish Richard Burton. I grew up with this portrait and all the stories my mother loved to tell about her wedding to my father. Every pair of eyes, she'd told me, had trailed her on the day she married her *damad farangi*, her European groom. As proof of who she'd been, of what our country had once been, she hung this picture in every home we ever owned in America: the tract house in Terra Linda, the five-bedroom house in the Tiburon hills, the villa on Richardson Bay. If, for many years, someone had asked me to tell them about Iran, I would have pointed to this photograph of my parents, as if every story began there, in that moment.

Now I'd found a photograph that had survived revolution, war, exile, and something else besides: my mother's will to forget the past. Although I couldn't yet imagine the stories it would tell, I slipped it between the pages of a book and carried it three thousand miles away.

Six months later I was back in California, sitting in the new in-law unit my mother had managed to carve out from her Spanish-style villa. The rest of the house was rented out by then, and she was living in two small rooms cluttered with everything she'd salvaged after my father's death. She'd given up entertaining her friends, said the space was too cramped to serve a proper tea, so what was the point of inviting anyone over anymore?

By then I'd looked at the photograph so many times I could have drawn its every detail from memory. Who, I'd wonder again and again, was the man at her side? What had happened to him? And why had my mother never told me about their marriage?

For a long time her grief over my father's death, and my own, had made it impossible to ask her these questions. Six months had passed and still I didn't know how to begin. But the photograph lingered in my mind. I had to know the truth, no matter how painful it would be for me to ask about it or for her to answer my questions.

I cleared my throat. *"Maman,"* I said at last, and held the photograph out to her.

She glanced down at it and then scanned my face, trying to decipher what, if anything, I understood and what she could still stop me from knowing. She shook her head and continued drinking her tea. "No," she murmured finally, averting her eyes. "This has nothing at all to do with you." She set her cup down, snatched the photograph from my hand, and left the room.

I didn't mention the photograph again. The next days passed awkwardly, each of us holding herself apart from the other, and I was grateful to return to the East Coast. We didn't speak again for some weeks, but a few days into the beginning of the new university term she called me and accused me of rifling through her things. I'd stolen the photograph from her, she said, and there was just nothing else to say.

Then she started sending me the tapes. The first one arrived in springtime, a few weeks after No Rooz, the Iranian New Year. Eventually there would be ten of them. That year my mother Lili would sit alone in her house in California, speaking the story of her life into a tape recorder for me. The tapes always came marked up in Persian, and I couldn't make out much more than my name when I opened the envelope and found the first one. As I traced my mother's inscription with my fingertips, it occurred to me that I didn't even own a cassette player. The next morning I headed into town to buy one, and with that her story began to pass like a secret life between us.

One

Avenue Moniriyeh

"If you want to know my story," my mother Lili began, "you have to know about Avenue Moniriyeh, about your grandmother Kobra and your grandfather Sohrab, and what Iran was then. Because we couldn't just do what you do here—forget your name and who you belong to. Our lives were not like that. No."

WHEN SHE NAMED HER ninth child, Pargol Amini indulged her own fancies at last. "Kobra," she announced to the midwife, and smiled from the bloodstained sheets. The "great one."

At this, the midwife looked up and considered her face.

Pargol Amini had black eyes and cheeks so fair and flushed they were like snow blotted with blood, as was said back then. In a room that had grown warm and damp with her exertions, she met the midwife's gaze with a heavy stare.

"Kobra," Pargol said again, her voice softer but still sure. Even the newborn—a tiny raging bundle with a shock of black hair—was silent at that moment. The scent of cinnamon and cardamom rose from the kitchen and threaded its way through the house. The midwife took in a single sharp breath, bit her lip, and then resumed her task of dusting my great-grandmother's loins with ashes.

When Pargol was a girl she and her family had left their village in the south, journeyed a hundred miles across Iran's dusty, red-rimmed central plateau, and settled in the then-walled capital city of Tehran. Though she could not read and had never been to school, she could recite the Koran by heart from beginning to end in Arabic—God's tongue—and she knew most of the hadith as well.

The names of Pargol's other eight children had been chosen under the watchful gaze of her father-in-law. Together they made up an unremarkable roster of Muslim names: Ali-Reza, Qasem, Fatemeh, Abolfazl, Mohammad, Ali-Ahmad, Khadijeh, Zahra. But by the time of this child's birth, Pargol's father-in-law was dead and she, barely thirty, was already called old, and so on that day in 1921 the list of her children's names settled finally on one born of her own imagination. Kobra.

Later it was commonly suspected that Pargol had lost her mind. Everyone feared for the child. But Kobra grew up to be the prettiest girl of the family, with the only pair of honey-colored eyes in the house. And with her beauty came a temperament so gentle that it dispelled every rumor about her mother's willfulness and her own virtue.

Around her neck Kobra wore a black string from which a single tiny blue eye hung and nestled itself in the hollow of her throat. The amulet was meant to protect her from the Evil Eye that since the day of Kobra's birth had bedeviled Pargol—so fearful was she that jealous eyes would alight on her favorite child.

In Iran they call such children the pearls of their mothers' fortunes.

The Aminis' house sat in an alleyway barely wide enough for two people to walk side by side, and along the middle of it ran the *joob*. These were the open waterways that once traversed the entire length of Tehran, north to south. The *joob* water started out clear and cold at the foot of Damavand, the snowcapped volcano to the north of the capital, but by the time it reached Pargol's house near the old southern gates of the city the stream had become thickly clogged with refuse and dirt. Every day there were stories of boys who'd wandered far from home, fallen into live waterways somewhere in the city, and returned in damp clothes—something for which they'd surely be beaten, since the *joob* was known to carry ringworm, typhoid, and diphtheria and they'd been warned many times not to play near it.

When women ventured into the streets at all, they did so always with the fear that their veils would dip into the waters of the *joob* and render them *najes*, or impure. But peddlers wended their way daily through the alleyways, their wooden carts piled high with onions, herbs, vegetables, and fruits. When their wheels ran into the *joob* or ruts and bumps—of which there were many then throughout the capital—the clatter of pots and pans stopped briefly, then started up again once the peddlers hauled their carts onto a smoother patch of road. Long-haired, cloaked dervishes were also known to traverse the city, hawking poems, soothsayings, and tonics as they went. It could be said that the streets belonged to the peddlers and dervishes and also to the beggars who lined the stone walls of all such neighborhoods.

The house itself was built of hand-hewn bricks, with honeysuckle and jasmine spilling over the high walls that enclosed it. The large colony of sisters and aunts and mothers and grandmothers within never left except to attend a wedding or funeral close by or else to make a pilgrimage to a martyr's shrine. And for that they always traveled with their men.

Every seven days from behind the walls of her house, Pargol heard the plaintive cry of the *namaki*, the salt-seller. Humpbacked and toothless, he roamed the city with his salt borne on the back of an ancient donkey. Every few blocks he'd cup his fingers around his mouth, tip his head to the sky, and call out, *"Namaki! Namaki!"* When she heard his cry, Pargol would throw her chador about her and poke her head out the door for her weekly slab of salt.

Pargol had married a rug merchant by the name of Qoli Amini, known better as Qoli Khan, or Sir Qoli. He stood a full head shorter than his wife, a predicament that, true to both his nature and his outlook on life, he regarded with a mixture of disbelief and amusement. Every day Qoli Khan set out for the great canopied bazaar in the center of the city. Once there, he'd take his place next to the fruit-seller's pyramids of melons, pomegranates, oranges, bundles of mint and parsley, and crates of dried figs and mulberries. Perched on an enormous gunnysack of salted almonds, his complete inventory of rugs beside him, he waited in the bazaar from morning to night so that people could consider his wares and pay him the modest sums with which Pargol managed their lives.

As Kobra grew, Pargol favored her in a thousand quiet ways, but the strength of her affections was never more evident than when the Bloodletter came calling. This happened twice a year, once at the end of summer and once at the end of winter. Bloodletting was thought to keep a body healthy and strong, proof of which could be found in the rosy tint it lent to even the most sallow complexion. But no matter how many times they were reminded of the treatment's benefits, nothing kept the children from running at the sight of the Bloodletter's blistering cups and the jar of slithering black leeches she harvested from provincial riverbanks.

Pargol brooked no resistance. Hands on hips, jaw set, she routed her children out of their hiding places throughout the house. She sent her sons in first, and then one by one she pinned the girls' plaits to the tops of their heads. When the Bloodletter finished with the boys, she sliced the girls' backs with a razor and pressed her cups to the cuts or else planted her leeches onto their bare backs. Kobra's siblings hollered or whimpered, each according to his or her disposition and the vigor of their respective treatments. Pargol always suffered their torments without blinking, but she could not bear to hear her youngest daughter so much as whimper, and so year after year Kobra was left unmolested in her hiding place behind the water cistern in the basement.

Still, when Pargol decided to send eleven-year-old Kobra from the house to learn a trade, not even a long history of such indulgences could stop mouth after mouth from falling open. A girl stayed in her father's house until her marriage, and even the less pious would have agreed that formal education was wasted on females. But soon after Kobra turned eleven, Pargol predicted that as the last of so many children it was unlikely Kobra would ever marry. For this reason, Pargol explained, it would be necessary to send Kobra to a school that prepared young girls to become professional seamstresses.

Many secretly believed that Pargol wished to keep this one child for herself, and that it was for this reason that of all her daughters it was Kobra whom she sent forth to study and work. But whatever the reason, from then on Kobra could be seen each morning stepping into the streets of Tehran, kerchief knotted at her chin, with a basket of fabric and needles in one hand and a small iron pot filled with rice and stew in the other.

There were twelve other students in her class, all of them from families poorer than her own, but she made her first friends sitting side by side on the floor with those girls. Their teacher, Malekeh Khanoom or "Mrs. Queen," was a round-faced widow with long hennaed hair and two thick rows of gold bracelets dancing at her wrists, and she laughed easily with the girls. In the mornings she taught them to sew and in the afternoons she taught them to embroider. From the fabrics—silk, velvet, georgette, voile, crepe de chine—Kobra guessed that the garments she would be sewing were meant for the fine ladies of the city, and it thrilled her to run her fingers along the glorious bolts of fabric stacked along one wall of Malekeh Khanoom's basement and to imagine the materials skimming a woman's body here, clinging to it there.

Malekeh Khanoom showed the girls how to measure with their hands, spreading her fingers wide like a fan and counting off from the tip of her thumb to the tip of her pinkie. One, two, three. Ample figures would still be in fashion for another few years, and a waist the width of three outstretched hands was considered ideal in the days that Kobra sat in Malekeh Khanoom's basement learning her trade. The girls watched their teacher and then, shyly at first, spread their own fingers against the fabrics she set at their feet. One, two, three. They looked up to make sure they had measured well, and when Malekeh Khanoom had nodded and smiled at every one of them they took turns cutting the fabric with Malekeh Khanoom's only pair of brass scissors.

The girls themselves wore cotton pantaloons with *sheleeteh*, the short, flounced skirts of a curious provenance. The story went that once, during the nineteenth century, a Qajar king had been shown a photograph of some ballerinas on a Paris stage and was so taken by the sight that he set out for France posthaste. During the trip he became an avid patron of the ballet, coincidentally running up stupendous bills at the Paris brothels. These he settled by selling the French government rights to carry out archaeological expeditions in Iran and to retain whatever artifacts they unearthed. On his return, the Qajar king decreed that all the ladies of his court should henceforth appear dressed in tutus. Out of modesty the Iranian princesses wore their silken skirts with long tunics and flowing trousers or white tights underneath. The skirts were given a Persian name, *sheleeteh*, which suggested the rustling sounds they made when the ladies of the Qajari palaces danced in them.

Now that the Qajars had been overthrown in favor of the Pahlavi dynasty and Western clothes had become a matter of not just fashion but also royal mandate, only poor women still dressed in *sheleeteh* and their skirts were made of plain cotton, not silk, and issued no pleasing rustles when they walked. My grandmother's only *sheleeteh* was apricot colored, and it had belonged first to Pargol, who had worn it to cross the desert so many years ago.

Sometimes Malekeh Khanoom let her students keep remnants from the dresses they sewed. In her first month at the school, Kobra chose two squares of voile and with them she sewed two scarves. One was blue like a robin's egg and the other crimson as a pomegranate seed. She had no pearls or golden coins, and so she embroidered them with a handful of tiny turquoise beads. She took the two scarves home to Pargol, who wore them constantly—one day the blue one, the next day the red one—with great pleasure, and more than a little pride.

The first year Kobra went to Malekeh Khanoom's school as a student, but she was so clever and hardworking that the second year she went as an assistant and the third year as a teacher herself.

Then one night Kobra's brother Ali-Ahmad, the gambler, put forth a proposition that altered my grandmother's fortunes forever. One evening, after losing a great sum of money—his greatest loss yet in what would be a long and infamous career—Ali-Ahmad turned to his gambling opponent and said, "You can take my sister in marriage." He did not name her at all but added simply, "The youngest one."

Ali-Ahmad knew his friend Sohrab had reason enough to accept the offer, but most likely neither of them spoke of it that night or any other. Whether Ali-Ahmad regretted this later no one in the family could ever say. They'd only remember that when he returned home that night with news that he'd found Kobra a suitor the news was met with unbridled glee.

Kobra's sisters, themselves all recently married, tittered and giggled; her aunts clucked their tongues and smiled. Sohrab was so handsome and cut such a fine figure in the neighborhood that even

Pargol took Ali-Ahmad's news as a stroke of incredibly good luck.
By the next morning Kobra's aunts and sisters had already begun
to sew and embroider a crimson tunic and flounced wedding skirt,
and by week's end they'd pooled their monies to buy Kobra a pair
of wooden platform shoes at the bazaar. Malekeh Khanoom, Kobra's
sewing instructor, lent out her string of tiny blinking lights (a trea-
sure from *farang*, or Europe, it was rumored), which Pargol, in a fit
of creative inspiration, nestled into Kobra's wedding veil. And with
Kobra so outfitted and Ali-Ahmad's debts neatly covered by what
would have been Kobra's bride price, my fourteen-year-old grandmother became, for a time, an *aroos*.

In those years a young bride had no name. Known simply as the
aroos, or "the bride," she truly took her husband's name only when
her mother-in-law died. When Kobra was called *aroos*, her hair fell
in two black braids, thick as coiled ropes, down to the middle of
her back. She was shy, neat, and modest, which Sohrab knew would
endear her to his mother, a woman known to all as Khanoom, "Missus." But however beautiful Kobra's eyes and plaits of black hair, she
was simple, provincial, and as unlikely a match for my grandfather,
with his elegance and airs, as, it would seem, she was for her own
fantastical name.

Sohrab was the first son born to Khanoom after two daughters,
and as such he was also her *cheshmeh cheraq*, the very light of her eyes.
By the time Sohrab was two years old, his father had already quit
their house on Avenue Moniriyeh and taken three other wives. He'd
also long since stopped sending his first wife any money. Khanoom
lived by her hands, sewing and knitting, and raising Sohrab and her
other children on her own. When, one by one, her husband's other
three wives showed up at her door, passed over just as she herself had
been, she took them in, too, and they lived in her house like sisters
and worked alongside her.

Since his earliest days Sohrab had been spoiled with the attentions of the many women of his mother's house. As a boy he was known as the little dandy in their midst, and they sewed all his clothes themselves and ironed them for him, too, even when he was no more than three or four years old and they would not have thought to do the same for their own best garments. Between their endless rounds of sewing and knitting and cooking and cleaning, they plucked the seeds of pomegranates and fed them to him from a bowl. They saved him the soft-bellied figs from their garden and popped them into his mouth whenever he came to sit with the women in the kitchen. And Sohrab took in their attentions just as easily as he had once taken his mother's milk.

He would not stay at their side for long, though. By the age of seven Sohrab was already the acknowledged leader of the pack of neighborhood boys who wiled away the afternoons in the alleys riding bicycles and shooting homemade slings. By eleven he had the run of the whole city and would often linger in the streets or the *qaveh khaneh*, coffeehouse, where men recited the *Shahnameh*, Ferdowsi's eleventh-century verse epic, for one another. Sohrab would linger in the city long after school ended, leaving his mother to curse her fate and pray, hour after hour, for his safe return.

As a young man of twenty Sohrab had somehow secured a high post in Iran's national textile bureau. No one quite knew how this had happened. He had neither money nor connections, and it was a job for which he had no qualifications besides his charm and his taste for finery, but these had proved sufficient. On their way to Europe and America, many of the country's most opulent carpets passed under his hands and exacting eye and could be shipped off only with his consent. His salary was generous by standards of the day, but to satisfy his luxurious tastes he supplemented his income with gambling, a favorite diversion since his teenage years. Within a few years of his marriage to Kobra, Sohrab had done well enough to dress in perfectly tailored Western suits, then still rare in Iran, and also to drive a black Chrysler of which he was no less vain than of his own brilliantined hair.

It was no secret that even after he married Kobra my grandfather's eyes still lingered on the smartly dressed ladies who had recently begun to appear on the streets of Tehran. It was also a fact known to many that for several years before his marriage Sohrab had courted a lady so chic and lovely it was said she could pass for an *aroos farangi*, a European's wife. But this woman, Simin, was twice divorced and unable to bear children; Sohrab knew that until he produced heirs to his family name, he could never marry her. So when his friend Ali-Ahmad had offered Sohrab his sister, whom he'd once seen at Ali-Ahmad's house and still remembered as a plump and pretty girl, Sohrab had not thought long before saying yes and bringing her to live in Khanoom's house on Avenue Moniriyeh.

Sohrab's sisters and three stepmothers took Kobra in with smiles and compliments. "Look at her pretty hands!" gushed one. "And her lovely eyes!" added another. She was given her own small room in Khanoom's house, and in her first months there Kobra sewed herself a quilt and embroidered a cloth on which she set her prayer shawl and rosary and also her hand mirror and hairbrush. All day she worked in Khanoom's kitchen, cleaning and chopping herbs for the *sabzi*, picking pebbles from the rice, and tending the grains over a charcoal brazier. At night she went to her room to wait for Sohrab. In the first years of their marriage, he came to her a few times a week, and it wasn't long before a baby appeared in a basket by her feet in the kitchen, and her breasts and belly were still swollen when two months later a second child began to grow in her.

They were her pride. As a boy Nader was especially prized by the family, but Lili was a beautiful child, plump and rosy cheeked, with sparkling black eyes, dimples, and an exquisitely tiny nose. The neighborhood women cooed and fussed over her whenever they dropped by the house on Avenue Moniriyeh. Even Sohrab, little given to children as he usually was, seemed charmed by her.

Kobra loved the courtyard of Khanoom's house and the deep blue tiles of the *hoz*, the shallow pool that stood there in the shade of a large persimmon tree. Khanoom's persimmon tree was also a favorite of the neighborhood birds, who would gather to feast on the fallen fruit under its branches. While her children napped in the afternoons, Kobra would steal away from her work to sit on the edge of the *hoz* and watch the birds as they pecked greedily at the seeds embedded in the fruit's rotting flesh.

In the years leading to the 1941 Allied invasion of Iran, when Soviet soldiers commandeered the northern provinces and British soldiers roamed the capital and controlled the oil fields to the south, the bread at Khanoom's house was often dotted with pebbles and splinters and the stews they ate were only rarely prepared with meat. Sitting under the persimmon tree one afternoon in late fall, Kobra was cracking the shells of sunflower seeds between her teeth when she suddenly had an idea. She dusted the seeds from her skirt and went back into the house. She returned with a large wicker basket, which she set at the base of the persimmon tree. She scattered a fistful of sunflower seeds under the tree and then she held her breath and she waited.

She trapped five small brown birds the first day, and Khanoom clapped her hands in surprise, smiled with genuine pleasure, and praised Kobra's cleverness.

As a child of three, her daughter (and my own mother), Lili, would sometimes come across Kobra hunting birds in the courtyard. A sly smile would spread across Kobra's face as the creature's wings fluttered between her fingers. Later when Lili took her place on the floor of Khanoom's parlor for supper, she'd find a stew set out with bones so tiny and thin they were eaten along with the meat and she would cry and refuse to take a single bite, even though she knew there would be nothing else.

Most nights Sohrab went out with his friends to parties where the ladies were very slender and wore Western dresses and were much more beautiful than Kobra. When she asked to go with him, he told her she looked old and slovenly in her chador and that he would be embarrassed to take her along. She offered to go without her veil or even a simple head scarf, even though this would have made her barely less uncomfortable than roaming the streets naked. Still he went out alone.

Every night after putting her children to bed, she sat cross-legged in her room, propped her mirror against the wall, and set a candle on the floor beside it. She lined her eyes with a stick of *sormeh*, eyeliner, first outside and then inside along their rims, and then she darkened her mole with its tip. She swiveled up her only tube of lipstick, dragged its crimson grease along her lips, and next blotted her fingers with lipstick and set about rouging her cheeks. She dabbed rose water behind her ears and between the cleft of her breasts, and then she sat peering at herself in her mirror until at last she heard the brass knocker crash against the door.

He always returned well after midnight, his impeccable suits and silk cravats scented by liquor, cigarettes, and the perfumes of other women. Kobra would ask him why he'd come home so late, saying his dinner had grown cold and she had been so worried, and if he answered at all, it would be to tell her that it was none of her business and why did she stay awake at all if it was only to annoy him? But if she ever fell asleep before his late-night arrivals and therefore failed to open the door for him after a second or third banging of the knocker, he would storm into the house and strike her, demanding to know where she had been and why she had not come at once, as any decent wife ought. Lili and her brother, Nader, often woke to the sounds of shouting and crying, and if they left their rooms and came forward Sohrab would beat them, too, though sometimes he would only raise a hand to strike them and stop just before it came crashing onto their heads.

"*Besooz-o-besaz*," Kobra would have been enjoined if she'd sought out anyone's advice. Burn inwardly and accommodate; burn inwardly and accommodate. But Kobra sought no one's advice. Too ashamed to confide her suffering to her family and too proud to unburden herself to her in-laws, Kobra lifted her eyes and her palms to the sky and confided only in God.

In spring and in summer Sohrab left for months at a time for the cooler provinces. In Karaj or Hamadan he and his friends would recline on carpets thrown across a riverbank, passing around a gold-trimmed *qalyoon* (water pipe) and drinking *araq*, a Persian vodka, late into the night. One year he rented a cottage in the foothills of the Alborz Mountains, and toward the end of the summer he sent for Lili to spend a week with him there. She had never spent such a long stretch of time with her father, and it was difficult for her to reconcile the smiling, easygoing gentleman in the countryside with the fierce, formal patriarch she knew at home. Even his clothes were different. Here he wore cream-colored linen slacks and during the hottest parts of the day he rolled up his sleeves and undid the top buttons of his shirt as well, habits unheard of in the city. There were many pretty women about the cottage, but to Lili none seemed prettier than the fair, blue-eyed lady who linked her arm in Sohrab's and whispered in his ear as they walked together in the garden.

Since she was the only child among the party, Lili idled away the hours outside. What she liked especially was to pluck fruits from the trees—mulberries, sour cherries, and plums—and to hoard them in her pockets so that whenever Sohrab took her in his lap and stroked her hair she could present them to him like treasures. And in the mornings, when her father and his guests were still asleep, she helped the servants set honeydews and watermelons in the crook of the stream that ran behind the cottage.

The fruits would be left to cool in the water all day, and when Lili returned to retrieve them at dusk she'd find the women bathing together there in the stream. Beech trees lined the banks and their leaves shone like silver when the wind tousled them and they caught the last of the sunlight. Because the stream was shallow and the stones of its bed were flat and smooth, she could wade out to the center all by herself, but sometimes the current twisted her skirt around her legs and sent her tumbling. The woman with the blue eyes bathed in the river, too, but there was always a female servant to dip a pitcher into the water for her and pour it over her lovely shoulders and her long black hair, and when she caught Lili watching her she seemed neither surprised nor disturbed by such wide-eyed attentions.

The following spring Sohrab and his cohorts journeyed across the border to Iraq, where he indulged his hosts by consenting to have a portrait taken of himself wearing an Arab headdress. Lili wished desperately that he'd take her with him. He would not consider it, but he promised to bring her back a gift, and so when he changed trains in Ahvaz he stopped at a flower stall and bought a bunch of narcissus flowers, their buds still tight and not yet fully fragrant, and he gave them to Lili when he returned to Tehran.

Kobra had spent the spring of Sohrab's trip to Iraq burning and accommodating, burning and accommodating. One day she went down to the basement of Khanoom's house where all the sacks of grain and flour were kept. As Kobra bent down and reached for a bag of rice, a large black scorpion raised its stinger and plunged it into the heel of her hand. She cried out at once, but before one of Sohrab's sisters could reach her the poison was already coursing through her blood, hot as fire. Her arm tingled and went numb, and she was sure that she would die.

But Khanoom, a seventh-generation *Tehrooni* with an intimate knowledge of the city's thousand perils, knew the cure. She hunted down the scorpion in the basement and killed it with one whack of her garden shovel. That night Kobra was put to bed with her hand facing up toward the ceiling and the dead scorpion bandaged to the site of its sting. The creature's legs, still stiff, dangled from her wrist.

"The sting of a scorpion comes not from ill will, but from its nature," Khanoom counseled, by way of soothing Kobra.

Kobra did not sleep that night, not a minute. She sat bolt upright hour after hour, drenched in her own sweat, crying for her mother and unable to look away from her hand, but by morning her fever began to break and slowly she understood that she would survive.

Although it was my grandmother Kobra who prayed five times a day, taking care each time to fold her prayer mat and veil into neat squares afterward, in the end it was Sohrab who found deliverance from his marital woes. In the ordinary course of his days, Sohrab had little use for the rituals of faith, but his religion extended him several important privileges then in place for men, one of which would prove especially useful: he could divorce his wife without documents or witnesses. To free himself of Kobra, he had only to speak his desire.

The argument started like any other of their arguments. He'd come home late from a party. In the circles in which he then moved, it had lately become fashionable to take a puff of opium with liquor, a combination that had brought him home even more bleary-eyed and unsteady on his feet than usual. The old curses and recriminations flashed between them, though this time he didn't strike her with his open hand but instead made a fist. He struck her just once this way, but even in his state he managed to do it with such perfection that the room went black and she fell to the floor. When Kobra opened her eyes it was to the sight of her own blood, streaming so profusely onto the tiled floors that it had formed a small pool beside her.

She left the house on Avenue Moniriyeh with nothing that night—not a single coin—and no clothes but the nightgown she was wearing and the veil she drew around her to hide her bloodied and swollen face. The next morning she would awake in her mother's bedroom to find that the flesh of her nose had collapsed and spread across the middle of her face. The local bonesetter could do no more for Kobra than slice out the crushed bones from her face and bind her nose with gauze to quell the blood, and you might have said (as many did) that from then on her honey-colored eyes were wasted on her.

"Who can understand the ways of God?" Kobra's aunt remarked coolly. "It is her *qesmat*, destiny."

Her mother, Pargol, was enraged by this callousness. "Bite your tongue!" she hissed.

On the night of Kobra's wedding six years earlier, Pargol had kissed her on both cheeks and whispered the warning with which Iranian mothers had always sent their daughters into marriage: "You are leaving in a white dress—come back home dressed in white." By this it was meant she should not return home until she was covered by a white funeral shroud. To do otherwise signified the worst fate that could befall a woman: divorce, and all that it meant to live without the protection of a man. When Kobra appeared before her that night in not a funeral shroud but a bloodied veil, Pargol would not have thought to turn her away, but in truth not even she knew what would become of Kobra now.

One thing, at least, was clear: the children belonged to their father, as Iranian children always had. Neither of them would call Kobra *maman*, or Mother, again. When Sohrab sent her from the house, Lili and Nader stayed on to be raised by Khanoom and Sohrab's sisters and stepmothers. Kobra was forbidden from seeing her children, but she missed them terribly and so some afternoons she would draw her veil over her face and stand outside the gates of their school, waiting to catch a glimpse of them. She'd call out their names, slip a handkerchief filled with little candies through the bars of the gate, and warn them not to forget her.

Now that Kobra was gone, Khanoom would have to be mother to Sohrab's children. She had much to do and was therefore always the first to rise in the house on Avenue Moniriyeh. She'd wake before dawn, when the streets were still empty and quiet. Downstairs in the courtyard she rinsed her face three times from her hairline to her chin, washed the length of her bony, white arms, scrubbed her feet from the tips of her toes to her ankles, and then she ran a trickle of water down the part of her hair. She was a fastidious woman— had never been known to miss a single *namaz* (prayer) and was so thorough in her ritual cleansings that her palms were perpetually mottled and chafed. By the time she was done performing her ablutions and had turned back into the house for her morning prayers, the first dark figures would be hustling down the alleys outside her house—husbands and wives on their way to the *hammam* (bath) to purify themselves of last night's couplings before the muezzin's voice pealed through the half-lit sky.

Her prayers complete, Khanoom began preparing the samovar. Urn-shaped, wider than a tree trunk, and wrought of pure brass, the samovar sat in the center of Khanoom's parlor, and from dawn to dusk it would be kept at a boil so that anyone who came to the house could always be offered a freshly brewed cup of tea. Khanoom struck a match and tossed it over the coals, and while she waited for the water to boil she rolled a few leaves of lettuce between flatbread for her breakfast and pulled out one of the dozen hand-rolled cigarettes she always kept in her pockets. She held the cigarette to the coals until it lit and then, cigarette dangling between her lips, she steeped the day's first fistful of tea leaves in her small china teapot.

Then, once she'd finished drinking her first tea of the day—which she took black in thimble-sized draughts from a tiny crystal teacup—Khanoom pulled on her shawl and took her morning walk through the walled garden behind her house. Khanoom's father had been a scribe who went by the name Mirza Benevees, or Mirza The Writer. Although she herself could neither read nor write, even in such private moments she always carried herself with the same proud and graceful bearing as that learned forebearer.

From Mirza she'd also inherited her great passion for flowers. She kept little vases in all the rooms, morning glory and honeysuckle and whatever else she found in bloom, but she loved jasmine flowers best of all. Each morning she placed a saucer full of the star-shaped blossoms beside her samovar and then she tucked a few sprigs under the folds of her breasts as well. As the day wore on and Khanoom smoked her cigarettes and poured teacup after teacup and performed her prayers and set about her work, the scent of jasmine rose with ever-deeper sweetness from her chest.

The first month, Lili asked after Kobra every time she sat at the samovar for her first tea of the day. "She's gone to visit her mother," Khanoom would tell Lili. "Don't worry, *madar-joon*. She'll come back." And then Khanoom would pour Lili a small cup of weak tea and with a silver spoon stir in a lump of crystallized sugar until it had dissolved completely. If the tea was too hot, Khanoom would tip some of it into a saucer for Lili and let her drink it from there.

From the time she was four years old, Lili could drink as many as five little cups of sugared tea from Khanoom's samovar in a single sitting. Lili loved everything that was sweet—candies and pastries, cherry-rice and orange rind–rice—but best of all she loved *kha-geeneh*, the thin pancakes Khanoom drenched in honey, saffron, and rose essence and served each morning along with hunks of sheep's milk cheese and fresh sheets of seeded bread from the bakery down the street.

While her appetite seemed only to have grown with Kobra's absence, Lili's brother, Nader, had become nervous and very thin and his eyes seemed always to be searching the rooms of Khanoom's house for their mother. When he cried at night, Lili took him into her own bed and tucked her quilt around him. He had a face as white as the moon and black eyes fringed with eyelashes even longer and thicker than her own. Since Kobra had disappeared, Lili's beatings had grown less frequent, but for Nader they seemed only to have gotten worse. Lili knew that if their father heard Nader crying in the night, he'd hit him for it, and so she'd acquired a mother's ear for even his softest whimper.

One day she came home from school and found her brother dressed in a pair of white cotton pantaloons and a crimson sash knotted at his middle. A large party of women had gathered in the parlor. She saw presents stacked up high along one wall, and when she reached for one her aunt told her she should not touch because the gifts were all for Nader. When he descended the staircase in the strange pants, naked from the waist up and crying like a forlorn kitten, Lili puzzled over what they had done to make him so unhappy and why they'd bought him so many presents to make up for it.

Nader had been circumcised that day and the white flowing pantaloons had been sewn especially to ease his recovery. Kobra had been gone two months by then. Khanoom would regret her absence at such an auspicious event, but the celebration had been long in the planning and so there was nothing to be done for it. As he sat in the center of the room with a pile of new toys next to him that afternoon, her little brother's eyes were full of all he'd learned, and lost.

★   ★   ★

But before the end of three and a half months Kobra appeared before the wooden doors of the house on Avenue Moniriyeh wearing her old black chador, a weathered suitcase by her side, looking not so much relieved as exhausted.

Sohrab had divorced her on a whim, without any formal procedure whatever, but just as surely as marriage under traditional Islam comes in several forms—ranging from the temporary and transient to the formal and final—so, too, does divorce. In the days of Sohrab and Kobra's marriage, a woman living outside her husband's house could be claimed back within three and a half months, thereby nullifying the divorce. Ostensibly this was to ensure that she'd not left bearing his child—an act tantamount to theft—but in Kobra's case the rule would serve a different purpose.

Over the next years Sohrab would cast Kobra out many more times, though on occasion she'd grow so miserable that she would leave of her own accord. Each time she found refuge in her mother's house. Kobra would weep for her children and she'd weep for herself and no one, not even Pargol, was capable of coaxing her from her misery.

However, Kobra's exile always proved temporary. For the first few weeks following Kobra's departure Khanoom would be glad to have an end to the midnight rows on Avenue Moniriyeh, but eventually she and Sohrab's sisters would tire of caring for Kobra's children, so they'd all head out together to Pargol's house to claim Kobra back.

Sohrab said nothing whenever Kobra reappeared, but he hardly ever came to her room anymore, and his sisters were never as kind to her as they'd once been. After Sohrab first turned her from the house, Kobra's stews were deemed too salty, the grains of her rice too short, and her puddings far too bland to eat. Weeks or months would pass, Sohrab would again send her away, and then, before three and a half months had gone by and the divorce could become final, Khanoom would once again pull on her veil and bring Kobra back to the house on Avenue Moniriyeh.

At first these abrupt departures and reclamations set neighborhood tongues wagging, and this shamed Khanoom into hastily fetching her daughter-in-law from Pargol's house. But over the years so many unmarried cousins and widowed sisters were eventually absorbed into the house that its rooms were always noisy with the voices of women—gossiping and bickering, confiding and accusing. Except for the two hours of the afternoon when everyone went down to the basement to nap, it was impossible to tell who would be coming and who would be going and what would be said about it all, and in time Kobra's disappearances and reappearances were folded into all the other stories of that house.

Sohrab's room had five wooden doors, each carved with intertwining vines and many-petaled blossoms. It was the largest room in Khanoom's house, the only one with a water closet, and it took up nearly all of the second story.

As a gesture of respect, Lili began each day by purifying her father's hands. She would creep into Sohrab's room and fetch the jug beside his bed, then go down to the courtyard and pump water from the cistern beside the *hoz*. Back in the room she quieted her breathing and watched her father as he slept. His eyelashes were so long that they rested on his cheeks when his eyes were closed. She longed to brush her fingers along them, but she dared not touch him for fear of waking him.

She dipped a fresh cloth into the jug and then she began slowly to wash her father's hands. Soft and exquisitely tapered, Sohrab's hands were white and unblemished except for where cigarettes had stained two fingers of his right hand a deep yellow. Sometimes he stirred and sometimes he slept right through her ministrations. Because the ritual was her only opportunity to observe her father closely, she always stretched out these moments at his side each morning, washing and rinsing his hands many times over before stealing finally from the room.

At times there seemed to be no end of money in their house and Khanoom worried about where it had come from, but she was happy all the same, always busy buying things for the parlor—new vases, candlesticks, cushions, and carpets. One day Lili came home from school to find a suitcase in her bedroom stuffed with bills. "Do you like this money?" Sohrab had asked her. She glanced at the suitcase and said that surely she didn't need it. At this he nodded and smiled warmly at her. "Some people will do a lot for this money. But you answered well. You are a good girl." Then, before closing the suitcase and locking it, he pulled a single crisp bill from the pile and pressed it into her palm. She kept it in a box with her earrings and bracelets and never dared to spend it.

No family of means would ever allow a daughter to walk in the streets alone, even for just three paces, so when Lili started school at age six Sohrab ordered his young manservant, Mamm'ali, to walk her there and back every day. Knock-kneed, skinny, and pimply, Mamm'ali did not speak to her at all, not a word the entire way, but just stared into the distance with her books and notebooks tucked under his arm. She was not at all sorry when Mamm'ali disappeared and instead a driver came for her each morning at seven thirty with her father's black Chrysler. His name was Saeed and he was a young man of twenty-three with wavy brown hair, dimples, and sometimes a sweet smile for her, too.

Then there were months when Sohrab gambled away all he had and the house on Avenue Moniriyeh became a different house altogether. Khanoom's trinkets would disappear one by one from the parlor, and at night the family sat down together with only a bowl of unbuttered rice before each of them. If there was any meat, it all went straight to Sohrab's bowl, though he was known to drop some into Lili's and Nader's bowls as well. Saeed the driver disappeared and not even scrawny, pimple-faced Mamm'ali came round to fetch Lili from school. Instead it would be her own smartly dressed father standing by the gates of the School of Virtue with his silver-tipped cane and black fedora. When his debts grew truly substantial, Sohrab went out less often and was surlier than ever. Lili did not mind. It pleased her to have him walk her to and from school, even though his temper was far worse than even Mamm'ali's. And at home she fluttered around him with tea and sweets, washed his hands each morning, and massaged his brow each night if he let her.

Such intervals of poverty always threw Kobra's resourceful-ness into high relief. With a handful of flour, a cup of water, and a sprinkle of sugar she conjured a stack of pancakes that, while plain, kept her children's stomachs from rumbling through a whole day at school. An old housedress became a pleated skirt for Lili and three pairs of knickers for Nader. Clippings from their haircuts became the wig for a hand-sewn doll or the mane for a lion puppet. And at such times Sohrab's guests rarely left the house without Kobra send-ing Nader after them to ask for a few *tomans*. Mostly the gentlemen obliged, though one of them was in the habit of tossing a handful of coins at Nader just for the fun of watching him fish them out of the dirty waterways along Avenue Moniriyeh. Whenever that particu-lar gentleman called, Nader returned from his mission bawling, his leather shoes heavy and dark with *joob* water and his pants sodden to the knees with it.

But soon enough Sohrab's fortunes would be replenished by a good night of gambling and he'd emerge from his room with a smile, sometimes even singing to himself and snapping his fingers as he skipped down the stairs, and once again he'd be gone from the house until late in the evening. It was then that Saeed the driver would reappear, his own smile a little bolder each time he returned.

★　　★　　★

Even when Sohrab managed to gamble away all of his savings (and much of his mother's besides), he'd somehow borrow enough money so that each morning Lili could dress in her dark gray pinafore and take her place among the other girls at the School of Virtue. Modeled on the schools of the French lycée system, this was an institution as stern as both its name and the expressions worn by its two headmistresses, a pair of middle-aged sisters known to the girls as Mistress the Elder and Mistress the Second.

In the mornings two hundred pupils—all girls—assembled by the gates of the school on Avenue Pahlavi. The ones with the cashmere coats congregated near the front of the line, and the ones with shabby coats or no coats at all stood to the back. Lili's coat was made of soft gray lambskin, and she always stood toward the middle and kept her eyes trained to the front. When the Mistresses Elder and Second called out good morning, the girls promptly formed a line and then, at the Mistresses' signal, belted out Iran's new anthem. "O Iran, jewel-studded land!" the girls cried, and only after this would they be let inside.

Most everything at the School of Virtue was learned by rote, and questions of any kind were met with sour looks or else a quick rap against the knuckles. Long before they'd mastered the rudiments of reading and writing, the girls began reciting classical poems by heart. Fountain pens in hand and pots of ink at the ready, they proceeded to take pages and pages of Persian dictation. The study of mathematics, geography, and history advanced through similar feats of memorization and willed incuriosity.

Lili enjoyed nearly all her classes, but one subject, Arabic, proved a perpetual torment. Before starting school she had known it as the language of her grandmother's prayers and could never read the letters without hearing the sweet tenor and cadence of Khanoom's voice in her head, but at the School of Virtue Lili was judged not on her memory of these prayers but on her knowledge of their meaning. In this and also in her penmanship Lili was found lacking. Whenever the Arabic instructor reached Lili's desk, two deep creases sprang up between the teacher's eyes. She'd bend over Lili's shoulder, close enough for their breaths to mingle, and proceed to guide Lili's hand through the letters with her own crushing grip.

The girls wore gray pinafores with round-collared white blouses. Twice a week they stripped off their uniforms and pulled on knee-length black shorts and marched in formation in the school's court-yard and performed the calisthenics that the Ministry of Education deemed necessary for their bodies. They were accompanied in their movements by military marches streaming from a gramophone—a marvel achieved by the energetic pumping of the machine's hand crank by their gymnastics teacher. The girls with cashmere coats had special exercise shoes, but everyone else just wore regular shoes to exercise.

Even more than their cashmere coats, Lili coveted the patent-leather dress shoes of the rich girls at her school. Khanoom had always bought Lili's shoes, and she usually chose a brown leather pair nearly identical to her own. They were presented to Lili once a year at No Rooz, the Persian New Year, along with a party frock and newly stitched underclothes. She'd never quite grasped the ugli-ness of her shoes until the day she first fixed her eyes on the shiny dress shoes at the School of Virtue. Lili begged and pleaded until at last Khanoom agreed to take her to the bazaar to search for her own pair of patent-leather shoes.

"A hen's milk or man's life"—it was said that anything could be bought at the bazaar. Lit only by gas lamps and candles, the market-place was dim even in the middle of the day. Gripping her grand-mother's hand, Lili walked through the entrance, past the turquoise domes of Shah's Mosque, and on toward the teeming belly of the market. Together they threaded their way past stall after stall, past the goldsmiths and silversmiths, carpet-sellers, livestock, donkeys, beggars, castabouts, tricksters, and thieves who made their homes within the bazaar's narrow passages.

Khanoom and Lili walked on until at last she spied the shoes she wanted. Graced with tiny bows at the front, they were shiny and did not have even a single scuff on the bottoms. Best of all they were red, a bright tomato red she'd never even seen any of the girls wearing at school. The shoes were too tight by at least a size, but she had wanted them anyway, and would wear them until blisters bloomed on all her toes and her heels grew thick with calluses.

On the day Khanoom bought the red shoes, they celebrated with a lunch at Shamshiri, the bazaar's kabob restaurant. They retreated to the back corner, away from the passersby, so that Khanoom could enjoy her meal without troubling too much about her chador sliding off her head now and again. Stomachs rumbling in anticipation, they waited for the server, whom they privately called Mr. Kabobi. Over six feet tall, with a luxurious mustache that curled up at the ends, Mr. Kabobi could shove the meat from as many as three skewers onto their platter between two of his thick fingers. That day Mr. Kabobi appeared, as ever, with a smock smeared with grease and streaks of blood. Khanoom ordered four foot-long skewers, two for each of them, and even in the dark back room of the *kabobi* the meat still glistened with butter and the rice looked glorious with its orange and yellow swirls of saffron. It was the best kabob in all the city, and Lili, with her new red shoes already on her feet, ate with relish.

In the afternoons she was forbidden to play in the alleys close to the house, but the next day after school she lingered there to show off her pretty new red shoes. All at once a boy came running, shouting out that he'd just seen her father in the streets, just a block away from Avenue Moniriyeh. She ran into the house and hid herself among the pile of mattresses in the basement. One of the children had squealed on her, and when Sohrab found her that day he beat her so severely that she went to bed with a fever that would not be cured by even ten cups of her grandmother's sugared tea.

Fever or no fever, Kobra or no Kobra, Lili never missed the *hammam*. Once a week the women of Khanoom's house bundled their towels, copper bowls, sweets, and fresh clothes into large embroidered cloths, then walked together to the low limestone building that housed the quarter's communal baths. They splashed themselves with cold water from the fountain early each morning, before the first prayers of the day, but the *hammam* was their only full bath of the week and therefore also a holiday.

From her bundle Khanoom pulled pomegranates so ripe with juice, they were heavy as stones. "Don't spill the seeds," she'd whisper, and press one gently into Lili's hands.

Then Khanoom and the others disappeared into the steam and the sweet, damp scents. Inside the bathhouse they eased themselves onto low benches, drew water from the fountain, and loosened their tongues with talk until the heat puckered and wrinkled their fingers and toes. Wet thighs slapping against tiles, pitchers and bowls clattering against stone, they scrubbed themselves with coarse rags until their skin raged pink and their heels were raw. They took turns dunking themselves in the warm, elevated pool. They combed and plaited one another's hair. And then all but the oldest ones lay on tables to be smeared with the warm, sticky paste that ripped loose the hair on their legs and groins.

Lili sat on the steps by the *hammam*'s entry, her pomegranate balanced between her knees, watching the women come and go. The sky would begin to darken and finally one of her older cousins would come fetch Lili. Her own body would be hastily scrubbed in one far corner of the *hammam*, and as her hair was washed and combed and wound into braids she'd steal glances at the older women.

"Tsss!" her aunts scolded. "Don't open your eyes so wide, *dokhtar* [girl]!"

One year when Khanoom was braiding her hair in the *hammam* a lady called out to them, "What a pretty girl! Her skin's as white as alabaster!"

Khanoom gave Lili a quick, furtive scratch on the buttocks to ward off the Evil Eye and then called back a cheerful, "*Merci, khanoom!*"

"Will you marry her off?"

"She's only just turned nine...."

"Well, in that case she can grow up with her husband!" the lady replied. To this Khanoom gave no answer but to laugh and consider Lili with a strange, and then very tender, look.

By this time in the afternoon it would be late—Sohrab would be home, impatient for his dinner—and when the others rushed to gather their belongings and began hustling back toward Avenue Moniriyeh, Lili would follow along behind the train of women with her small bundle of juice-stained linens pressed against her chest.

In summertime, when the sky was bright and thick with stars, they all slept on the rooftop. At sunset, after Khanoom hosed down the tiles, piles of mattresses were hauled up from the basement and huge swaths of white netting were strung up to keep the flies and mosquitoes from tormenting them in the night. Divans, cushions, and carpets were assembled in the garden where Sohrab would hold court with his friends late into the night. Lili was forbidden from coming close to them, even just for a peek, but from where she lay on the roof she could see the smoke from the men's cigarettes snaking its way into the night air and could hear their voices as they told stories and jokes.

Often Lili would fall asleep before dinner, which could be served as late as ten or eleven on a summer evening, and then Khanoom would shake her from sleep. "Wake up, child!" When she opened her eyes she would find her grandmother crouched beside her under the netting with a bowl nestled in her lap. "Eat this and then go back to sleep," Khanoom would whisper, and heap rice and stew onto a spoon for Lili. Some nights as she chewed, sleepily, in the darkness, she could hear the men in the alleyways that ran along Avenue Moniriyeh, trilling poems as they stumbled back from the *meykhaneh,* the wine tavern.

Khanoom sewed Lili a prayer shawl festooned with pale pink rosebuds, and at Khanoom's side she learned to whisper her prayers, press her forehead to the *mohr,* a holy stone, bend and straighten herself at the proper intervals. At Ramadan everyone except Sohrab woke before dawn to eat the rich foods—dates, porridges, stews—that would fortify their bodies through the day's fasting, but there would always be a little something for the children to tide them over until sunset: a chunk of halvah wedged between bread, a handful of soaked walnuts, and a few yellow sultana raisins.

Every few months a *rowzeh-khan* (reader of homilies) came to Avenue Monireyeh to recite passages from the Koran. Lili marveled at how the women's faces, just moments before alive with chatter and gossip, fell slack and mournful at the *rowzeh-khan's* first words. They rocked their bodies back and forth, slowly at first and then faster and faster, and then they'd raise their hands up to the sky and begin to moan and cry and beat their chests with their fists. Listening to these parables of human suffering, they released their own emotions with a fervor that drowned out the *rowzeh-khan's* own impassioned readings, but at the end they invariably emerged calm and happy, their worries washed suddenly clean for the day.

Once or twice a year the women of the house boarded the *masheen doodi,* the "smoke machine" or train that connected Tehran to the ancient town of Rey, to make a pilgrimage at the shrine of Shah Abdol-Azim. Because there was no place for them, as women, to stay once they reached their destination, they always spent the night inside the mausoleum. It was for this reason they always set out from home with their bedrolls and blankets tucked under their arms.

Inside the train's cabin they napped and gossiped and snacked on huge quantities of watermelon seeds and dried mulberries and pistachio nuts. Slowly the city, with its tangle of buildings and smoke-smudged sky, gave way to views of arid plains, orchards, villages, and great cloudless sweeps of blue. In the spring wildflowers blanketed the desert, and occasionally a cavalcade could be seen inching its way across the buff-hued slopes, the colorful kerchiefs, tunics, and long skirts of its women visible even across a distance of many miles.

In Rey they got off and walked the rest of the way—another half an hour along a crowded dirt road—until they glimpsed the golden domes of Shah Abdol-Azim. Not far from the gates of the cemetery stood a *bazaarcheh*, a small, tented marketplace that catered to pilgrims and funeral parties. There Khanoom would reach into the folds of her chador and pull out enough coins to buy several skewers of kabob, bread, and fresh herbs, which would be bundled into a cloth and taken into the mausoleum along with their bedclothes and other provisions.

The mausoleum consisted of a single large room with marble floors and tiled walls, and even on the hottest summer days the air inside was cool enough to draw shivers. As the others filed in behind her, Khanoom would strike a match against the wall and proceed to light all the candles. The fire flickered and then blossomed to orange, and as light began to fill the chamber Lili would squint up at the portraits hung all around the mausoleum walls. These were oil paintings of the family's male ancestors—old men with heavy eyebrows, Qajar-style cloaks, caps, and lances, and a few handsome young men in similar garb. No pictures ever adorned the women's plaques, and so Lili set her blanket under a portrait of one of the comelier youths, unaware that under the bed she was making for the night lay a corpse that had once matched the portrait she'd claimed as her own.

Then, just like at the *rowzehs* (preachments), Khanoom and the others would begin to cry, softly at first but with a gathering intensity that echoed through all the chambers of the mausoleum. As a young girl she did not yet understand the reason for their crying and would look at her grandmother and aunts in disbelief and wonder at how all the bickering and gossiping of the journey could so suddenly be forgotten once they entered this strange, dark place. But then, just as suddenly, their mourning would be done, and they'd unfurl their blankets and set out the kabobs for lunch.

Khanoom minded Lili without complaint, including her in all the rituals of the house on Avenue Moniriyeh, but long periods of care-taking exhausted her. To ease her burdens when Kobra's absences coincided with the children's school holidays, Khanoom frequently sent Lili to stay with Zaynab, her eldest and only married daughter. Zaynab's husband, Ismail Khan, had been chosen to serve in Reza Shah's cabinet soon after the fall of the Qajar dynasty, and his house was situated close to Parliament, in Sar Cheshmeh, Spring's Source. To Lili it seemed a palace. Visitors first passed through a handsomely appointed foyer. Cushions lay scattered alongside a marble fountain, and perched along its rim were several *qalyoon*. When Ismail Khan's diplomatic friends and military comrades appeared at his iron-studded wooden door, a servant would lead them to the foyer, where a second servant would soon alight with a plate of fresh tobacco, and then the visitors would sit by the fountain and take a few puffs from the *qalyoon* before proceeding through the rose garden and then into the main house.

All her life Lili's aunt Zaynab loved to tell the story of how she'd once presented herself to the shah. By the time of this fateful meeting, Reza Shah had already torn down the city walls, razing old palaces and mud huts alike to make way for broad boulevards, modern houses, schools, hospitals, government buildings, hotels, and numerous palaces of his own. As a finishing touch, he surveyed his army of 150,000 and sent troops of uniformed officers into the streets with seedlings and watering cans. "If the trees die, you die," he'd told them, and few doubted the threat.

On the day the shah officially outlawed the veil in 1936 and ordered all the wives and daughters of his government ministers to appear before him unveiled, Zaynab accompanied Ismail Khan to the ceremony wearing a brand-new two-piece skirt suit and a large feathered hat. Women were known to faint from terror in His Majesty's presence and on the day that would become known as Women's Emancipation Day many of the ladies in attendance sobbed in each other's arms and cowered behind walls. Zaynab, however, had drawn herself up to her full height, looked directly into Reza Shah's eyes, and shaken his white-gloved hand with her own.

Zaynab was Ismail Khan's second wife. His first wife was said to be old and sickly and had long since retired to a separate residence on the outskirts of the city. And yet, as soon as Ismail Khan left in the mornings, Zaynab would fall into a chair and begin her fretting. Would he return that night or would he choose to stay at his other wife's house? Did he love his first wife better, or was she his favorite? And, most worrisome of all her worries, would Ismail Khan take another wife now that several years of marriage had proved her infertile?

At her most feverish, Zaynab would send a servant to bring her neighbor Touran Khanoom to the house. A Shirazi woman with pillowy lips and a curvaceous figure, Touran Khanoom had a smile that revealed a fetching gap between her teeth. She'd come to Tehran at seventeen to marry a wealthy and sweet-tempered man who was a distant relative of her father's.

Zaynab adored Touran Khanoom, not least of all because she was also one of the few women in the neighborhood who knew how to read and could therefore tell the Fortune of Hāfez. Among the many volumes of Ismail Khan's library was an exquisite leather-bound *Divan-eh Hāfez*, the collected poems of the fourteenth-century lyric poet Hāfez. The book was thought to contain fortunes for all who perused it, and its gilt-lined pages and lavish illustrations enchanted Lili. She'd settle close to Zaynab and watch as her aunt began finger-ing its pages. The calligraphy was so stylized that Lili could make out only the occasional word. Zaynab would stop several times, fur-row her brows, thumb through the book again, draw a deep breath, and finally rest on a poem. At this point Touran Khanoom would lift the book to her lap and read to herself from the page Zaynab had chosen.

"Will he come tonight?" Zaynab would ask breathlessly, leaning toward Touran Khanoom. "Tell me, will he come back to the house tonight?"

"Patience, sister, patience!"

Interpreting the Fortune of Hāfez was known to be an exacting art, one that called upon both a reader's creative and critical facul-ties. Ever mindful of the poem's portent, Touran Khanoom always took her time before delivering her divinations.

One afternoon when she was ten years old and Zaynab had called Touran Khanoom to her house, Lili asked to have her own Fortune of Hāfez read.

"Why not?" allowed Zaynab. Her own fortune had been promis-ing and her spirits were high that day.

Touran placed her glasses back onto her face and let Lili choose a page from the book.

"One day," Touran began after several minutes of silent study, "you will be sitting in a garden on a day just as beautiful as this one, and a bird will come sit on your lap. It will lift you up into the sky and carry you to another garden across the sea, and there, in that other garden, a prince will come and marry you."

Touran Khanoom settled back in her chair and regarded Lili with a smile. "That will be your destiny, my child," she said finally, and flashed Zaynab a conspiratorial wink. By then Lili was so busy imagining the beautiful bird and the prince that it did not occur to her that Touran Khanoom might not have been reading her a fortune from the book but telling a story entirely of her own invention. In the coming years, however, Lili would turn this fortune over in her mind many, many times, measuring its beauty and promise against the truth of her life.

Two

Aroos (The Bride)

"I was eleven years old when he chose me."

So far my mother's voice on the tapes had remained steady, but here the story came out like an unbroken cry. Even after fifty years, when she spoke of Kazem it was in a voice so unlike her usual voice—so choked and yielding—that it didn't seem to belong to her at all.

D RESSED IN HER DARK gray pinafore, a pair of white satin ribbons braided through her pigtails, Lili would have been too busy chatting with her girlfriends to notice the man who came every morning and stood watching her from the street across from the School of Virtue. But he came every day for several weeks, always arriving at the exact hour that the girls lined up outside the gates of the school. He wore a fedora (dove gray felt with a black band), smoked a cigarette or two, and watched Lili until she passed through the gates and disappeared into the schoolyard.

She will be my bride, he decided at last, and set off toward home and the woman who could make it so.

The year was 1949 and Kazem Khorrami, the eldest son of an upper-middle-class businessman and his schoolmistress wife, was twenty-six years old. Like my grandfather Sohrab, the members of Kazem's household were partial to Western ways and fashioned themselves accordingly. The women of his family had not worn veils for many years, and the men had long since abandoned their tunics and turbans in favor of European-style jackets, ties, and hats. The Khorrami family was headed by Kazem's maternal grandmother, whom they all called Ma Mère—this despite the fact that none of them spoke more than ten words of French, including Ma Mère herself.

But the pull of tradition could be felt even in the chic and modern quarters ruled by Kazem's grandmother. For years she had been anxious that Kazem take a wife and start his own family. A parade of suitable candidates appeared in the Khorrami compound, the length of their skirts shorter with each passing year. Kazem had warmed at once to their attentions. He'd even chosen several girlfriends from among Ma Mère's offerings, some of them quite pretty and from good families. But in the end he'd refused every one, insisting on finding his own wife and doing so only in his own time.

When at last he could no longer quiet his grandmother's pleas, Kazem looked past the permed and perfumed ladies of his own circle and told his Ma Mère to fetch him an eleven-year-old girl from a tribe of *chadoris*.

Long before Kazem first saw Lili, Reza Shah had also trained his eyes on the girls of Iran. Soon after he'd been hustled into power by the English and Russians in the early twenties, the shah had put in place a series of laws intended to catapult Iran simultaneously into the modern age and away from foreign influence. Over the next twenty years Reza Shah would go so far as to outlaw the photographing of camels, those timeworn symbols of Oriental backwardness, and to all but defrock the country's mullahs. But the most contentious of his laws and edicts would concern the women and girls of the kingdom.

Reza Shah would not be the last of Iran's rulers for whom engineering his country's future meant remaking its women, nor would he be the last to meet resistance on this front, but he'd done much to enflame the battle by outlawing the veil in 1936. That year veiled women were summarily banned from schools, cinemas, and public baths. Bus and taxi drivers were ordered to refuse them passage. When soldiers began tearing veils from women's bodies that year, cursing and beating even elderly matrons who persisted in stepping out in their chadors, many claimed that Reza Shah was keen to fill every street and alley of the country with whores. Until mandatory unveiling laws were eased some years later under the shah's son and successor, Mohammad Reza Pahlavi, this contingent would respond to the royal edict by keeping their women and daughters behind the walls of their homes, and in some quarters of the city it was not unknown for unveiled women to meet with curses, threats, or even a shower of stones.

Khanoom and Lili's aunts were exceedingly religious and by their own choice never went out at all once the shah outlawed the veil, but until the age of eleven Lili's upbringing had fulfilled the king's vision for modernizing Iran's girls. This was because Sohrab expected no less than a proper Western-style education for both his children— his daughter as well as his son. He'd simply waved away Khanoom's warnings and pleas, and with that Lili had become the first girl of her family to pass her tenth birthday without donning a head scarf and also the first one to be sent to school.

About this no one, except for Lili herself, would be as pleased as Kobra. Limited as Kobra's own schooling had been, it still set her apart from most women of their circle, and she would always take special pride in her daughter's education.

But when the first suitor came for Lili, Sohrab's attentions had been thoroughly diverted to Simin, the blue-eyed mistress with whom he'd recently set up house in a new uptown apartment. Sohrab was now sending Khanoom a fairly regular monthly allowance and he still made regular trips back to Avenue Moniriyeh to check up on Nader and Lili, yet his new living arrangements had left his mother, step-mothers, and aunts not only pained but also baffled. Reza Shah had instituted civil marriage, but it was still against the law for a man to live with a woman without at least performing a *siqeh*, a temporary Muslim marriage ceremony. Khanoom and the others guessed that Sohrab would not have had any use for such customs, and the situation had the women of the house sick with worry. Lili's aunt Zaynab had met Simin once when she'd gone to call on Sohrab at his new uptown apartment and she'd rushed back to tell Khanoom and the others about Simin's light blue eyes, high cheekbones, and splendid figure. It was the same woman Lili had met that summer she'd spent with Sohrab in the countryside, but Lili chose to keep this to herself. The woman had bewitched him, Khanoom and Lili's aunts decided, and for that there was no known cure.

In any case, when word reached Sohrab that a suitor had appeared for Lili at Khanoom's house, he extended no advice whatsoever. Khanoom interpreted his silence as a decision to allow the girl's destiny to unfold as it would, and in this way Lili's future fell into the hands of the family elders, her grandmother and two spinster aunts. Better that Lili should be married, they concurred, than for the girl to go bareheaded another year toward God-knew-what was waiting for her in the streets.

"We have guests today," Kobra announced one morning as she placed the *nooneh sangak* (flatbread) and fig jam on the breakfast table and set about tightening the ribbons of Lili's braids.

A messenger had come with the news earlier that week: the Khorramis wished to visit with the family on Wednesday afternoon. The young miss of the house should be in attendance at their arrival. Khanoom had divined their purpose at once, and all the next week she had busied herself in the front parlor, polishing her teacups and her finest brass trays and dessert bowls in preparation for the Khorramis' visit.

When considering how to best broach the subject to her grand-daughter, however, Khanoom did not think it necessary to elaborate on the purpose of the appointment. No need to frighten the girl. What would she know of marriage, anyway? Khanoom thought it sufficient to tell Lili that she should not linger after school but come home straightaway to serve the afternoon tea.

They came as a group, all women. Five or six together. The oldest woman of the party, Kazem's Ma Mère, appeared dressed in a flowing white dress cinched at her ample waist. Her hair, completely white, had been assembled into a chignon, and the white scarf at her throat was secured with a large rhinestone clip. The youngest guest to appear that day was a girl of sixteen or seventeen. In her gingham dress she seemed too shy and awkward to be a married woman, but she was introduced as their *aroos*, the new bride of a cousin.

"*Masha Allah!* Praise God!" cried Ma Mère when Lili entered the parlor with the tray of tea and sweets. "How pretty you are! Come here to me, child!"

Lili searched the room for Khanoom, and when she saw her grandmother nod and smile at her she took a seat next to the visitor.

"Do you braid your own hair?" Ma Mère asked, fingering the tails of Lili's braids.

"Yes—except after it's been washed," Lili answered. "On those days Khanoom-*joon* or my cousin Soudabeh braids it for me."

Ma Mère nodded and considered Lili's hair a moment longer. From across the parlor, Khanoom cleared her throat. "She hasn't learned to cook yet," she ventured.

"But my dear lady!" Ma Mère protested. "We have a band of cooks and servants for such things!"

"Her father...," Zaynab began.

"Yes?"

"Her father will want her to continue her studies."

"Of course she may continue her studies," Ma Mère replied with a smile. "We would want nothing else for her ourselves." She turned to Lili and gestured for her to come closer. "But let's have a look at your teeth now, my dear girl."

Lili opened her mouth slightly, and with that the woman stuck two of her fingers inside in order to make a more thorough inspection.

At last Ma Mère returned her hands to her lap. "And your feet."

Ah, a game, thought Lili, and drew her toes out of her house slippers. When she looked up, she saw that the old woman's brows were now knit in contemplation. Even though Lili was just eleven, her feet were already the size of a grown woman's and larger than was thought desirable in those years.

"We will give you notice," Ma Mère announced at the end of the visit, and then shot Lili one last look.

"Who were they?" Lili asked when the visitors had left Khanoom's house that afternoon.

"Guests of your father's," Khanoom replied. She said nothing more, but later, when she performed her final *namaz* of the day, she would prostrate herself over her Koran, press her forehead to the cold, gray holy stone, and pray that the party had found in Lili an acceptable match for their son.

One day passed. Then two and three. By the fourth day, Khanoom, knowing as she did that a long interval of silence was customary, had not yet lost her hope or her good cheer, but Lili herself had grown quite anxious. Had the visitors not thought her pretty? For this, principally, seemed the question afoot, the reason for the afternoon's game.

Whenever she saw that Khanoom was busy in the kitchen, Lili slipped away to Kobra's bedroom and studied herself in the small handheld mirror that belonged to her mother. She bore a striking resemblance to Sohrab and had always been much fussed over for this reason. She had his almond-shaped black eyes, full lips, and fair skin. She had two fetching dimples and her hair was a deep chestnut, a shade that is lovingly, if fancifully, described as *talayee* or golden in Iran. She was, she knew, uncommonly pretty.

Lili considered her reflection many times and concluded that the problem had something to do with the big feet that her aunts claimed she'd inherited from Kobra's family.

But ten days later the word finally came. The Khorramis had accepted Lili. She would be a bride. An *aroos*.

"Che shansi!" one of her aunts exclaimed. "What luck! A suitor!" A second aunt hauled out the *tonbak* (a goblet drum) and began playing a wedding song. Many *mobaraks* went round the house, followed by a chorus of ululations.

"We must sweeten our tongues!" Khanoom exclaimed.

When a chickpea cookie was pressed into her hand, Lili began to think of the lovely brides she'd often seen being led through the streets and the musicians and singers following in their wake. She popped the cookie into her mouth and then, imagining herself as an *aroos* in her very own pretty house and pretty, grown-up clothes, she smiled.

Meanwhile, Kobra seethed. She pursed her lips and thought of Sohrab and his blue-eyed whore across town. It had been at Sohrab's insistence that Lili go round without a veil or even a flowered kerchief to cover her hair. Kobra was sure that no suitor would have come for several more years if her daughter's head had been covered. And it was a sorry match; Kobra was certain of it. Although as a family the Khorramis were wealthy, Kazem himself earned only a modest salary and owned no house of his own. What security would Lili find in such a husband? But on the matter of Lili's marriage, Khanoom and Lili's aunts would have no less deferred to Kobra than to their servants, and all that was left for Kobra was to curse her own lot and set about accepting her daughter's destiny.

In the next few weeks the household launched itself into preparations for the *khastegari*, the day when Kazem's family would appear to formally ask for Lili's hand. There was a good deal of debate about whether the girl herself should be in attendance and, if yes, whether she should appear with or without her hair covered. In the end it was decided that she should appear briefly to serve the first tea of the afternoon and that she should be wearing a pink scarf over her head. This wisp of chiffon would not only preserve the solemnity of the occasion but have the further advantage of calling up the pretty pink blush of Lili's cheeks.

This time there were men among the party, and so Lili kept her eyes fixed on the tray she was carrying in her hands. Khanoom infused the afternoon tea with the essence of rose water and cardamom and assembled a tower of plump and glistening dates on her best china plate. Lili's hands trembled as she entered the *mehmoon khooneh*, guest parlor, with these delicacies, but somehow she managed to serve the party in the proper order: first the oldest gentlemen (the grandfathers of the Khorrami clan), next the fathers and uncles, then the young man in the gray fedora sitting by himself at the far end of the parlor, and finally the women of the family. She had a vague notion that the young man in the hat was her suitor, but she did not dare look at him more closely.

Never before had she felt so many eyes on her. Her cheeks burned and she kept her eyes cast down on the carpet, but she soon found it was not altogether an unpleasant thing, this being looked at by so many people at once.

But then, just as her nervousness began to ease and she felt herself warming to the party's attentions, she was suddenly called out of the *mehmoon khooneh*. She had been in the room less than ten minutes and would spend the rest of the hour behind a door outside the parlor, taking turns peeking through a keyhole with her cousin Soudabeh. It was a vantage point from which Lili could see no more of her suitor than his black dress shoes and the hems of his brown gabardine trousers.

And yet within the space of a week she'd fallen in love. The object of her affections was not her suitor, Kazem, but an enormous emerald set between two diamond-studded bows. It was Kazem's grandmother Ma Mère who'd brought the ring to Khanoom's house on a day following the *khastegari*.

"You are like my daughter now," she said as she slid the ring onto Lili's finger. "I will love you as well as if you were my own daughter."

Lili thought this emerald ring with its diamond bows was the most beautiful thing she had ever seen. At her first sight of it, she'd immediately flung her arms round Ma Mère's neck and kissed her many times over.

Some mornings Lili would even sneak the ring into her schoolbag, and at recess she would pull it out to show the other girls at school. They would crowd around her, all of their eyes suddenly wide. There were several girls at the school with *namzads*, fiancés, but they were all in the older grades, close to their graduation dates, and in any case none of them were allowed to wear their engagement rings to school.

That year Lili was the youngest one with a suitor, a fact that duly impressed all her friends—especially when she showed them the exquisite jewel that had been given to her.

"Is he handsome?" one of the girls asked dreamily one day.

Lili was taken aback by the question. It occurred to her she had not even seen her suitor's face.

"Of course," she lied. "Like a movie star."

Kazem did visit Khanoom's house once more before the *aqd* (wedding). The girl's question at school had upset Lili enough for her to insist on seeing him once more before the wedding ceremony. It was therefore agreed that one evening she and her aunt should appear outside the window of Khanoom's front parlor at an appointed hour. Kazem would be sitting in the room by himself, and from the courtyard Lili would be able to inspect him discreetly through a window.

At seven o'clock in the evening, the sky was already nearly dark, and the room in which Lili sought a glimpse of her suitor was illuminated by a single paraffin lamp.

"Well, do you see him?" asked her aunt impatiently.

Lili squinted, peered again through the glass, and said she thought she could make out a man in a coat and a fedora.

"But *ammeh* [Auntie], why is he always wearing a hat?"

"What a foolish girl!" replied her aunt. "This is the new style. Your suitor is a modern young man!"

But she was not convinced—not at all. That night she asked her grandmother to pay a visit to the Khorramis herself and inspect Kazem on her behalf.

"Please, Khanoom," Lili begged. "You must tell me what he looks like without his hat!"

Khanoom laughed.

"*Bacheh-joon* [My dear child], is this what marriage is to you? What lies beneath a man's hat?"

Her grandmother's tone was more good-humored than disapproving, but even so Lili's lips began to quiver, and for the first time she began to cry about what she could not yet imagine.

Now there was nothing to do but wait.

Several years earlier, Reza Shah had raised the age at which girls could be married from nine to sixteen. There was, however, a

Aroos *(The Bride)*

provision by which families could handily circumvent this law. If a doctor or midwife examined a girl and found her body "mature," she could be married at thirteen—three years earlier than the law formally allowed. The examination often included confirmation of the girl's virginity, a detail without which the marriage preparations would not have proceeded.

Lili had been checked before. The year she turned ten and found a spot of blood in her underpants, she had rushed to Kobra's side. "Am I sick? Will I die?" she asked through quavering lips. Kobra took one look at the blood and slapped Lili hard and quick across both cheeks. "But why?" Lili whimpered. "I didn't want to do it, *azizam* [dear one]," Kobra replied, her own eyes smarting with tears. "It's only a custom. It will keep the blush on your cheeks until your wedding!"

One of her aunts had been troubled, though, by this early onset of menstruation, and had hauled Lili to a midwife to confirm that the all-important "curtain of chastity" was still intact. On the midwife's finding Lili whole (and therefore still marriageable), her aunt and Lili returned quickly to the house and there all her aunts and stepmothers had gathered around her to sweeten their tongues. "You are a woman now!" they'd declared, beaming.

This time, for her marriage, the examination would be repeated with just a single point of difference: since the word of one female relative would be insufficient proof for the groom's family, Zaynab and two of Lili's other aunts would bear witness, too.

Lili was forbidden by her grandmother and aunts from seeing Kazem until the *aqd konoon*, the first nuptial ceremony, but he would often convey candies and small presents to her through a messenger. At No Rooz that first year Kazem sent her an enormous bouquet of tuberoses.

It was, however, the emerald ring that was her best proof of coming happiness. Except for the few times she'd managed to sneak it into her schoolbag, the ring stayed locked in a bureau at home, but whenever she began to ask about Kazem or the marriage she was allowed to retrieve it from its hiding place and slip it on her finger for a few hours.

The ring would cost her dearly. Sohrab had extended just one condition for his daughter's marriage: that the Khorramis allow her to continue as a student at the School of Virtue. But a few months shy of the final marriage ceremony, it was discovered that Lili had been showing off her emerald ring to the other girls at school, and the transgression would swiftly upend Sohrab's decree.

She'd been sitting in one corner of the schoolyard, surrounded by her girlfriends, when Mistress the Second descended upon the group, seized Lili's engagement ring, and, for good measure, slapped her several times across the face.

"This is a serious school!" she screamed. "A modern school!"

With a good deal more composure, Mistress the Elder would later explain to Sohrab that the School of Virtue did not wish to have any child brides among its charges. It did not speak well of the school's mission, and Lili was not to return the next day. Sohrab was furious. He rose to his feet, banged his walking stick against the floor, and then proceeded to curse the lady with a lavishness that failed to unsettle her even slightly.

The next day Sohrab began to cast about Tehran for another school, but he soon learned that the other private schools in the city shared the philosophy of the School of Virtue with respect to his daughter's situation.

During this period, talk of Lili's impending marriage would be eclipsed by news that Kobra had finally managed to conceive a third child, a development that, to Sohrab's family at least, seemed only scarcely less incredible than the virgin birth itself.

Whereas a family with five and six children was thought quite ordinary and as many as twelve would have not have aroused comment or speculation, a family with just two children was regarded as an oddity. Clearly Kobra, still in her twenties, was fertile; her failure to become pregnant was therefore judged yet another sign of her husband's lack of regard.

Over time this very lack of regard had only managed to augment Kobra's love for Sohrab. As both her spirits and her standing in the family sank with each childless year, Kobra sought different strategies for wooing Sohrab back from the blue-eyed jinn who'd ensnared him. Kobra always set aside the most succulent pieces of meat and the very thickest pieces of crisped rice for him. By day she laundered and pressed his suits, and by night she painted her face, plucked her brows, and groomed her nails for him.

Such ordinary wifely duties were supplemented with supernatural devotions. She patronized back-alley spiritualists, called *jadoojambals*, who charged one fee to fend off plain mistresses and another, much higher fee to fend off beautiful ones. Every time, Kobra paid the maximum fee and returned with her head swimming with fresh hope and elaborate spells. She whipped up concoctions involving such things as cat urine, dill weed, and rose petals, recited the spiritualists' recommended incantations, and proceeded to sprinkle her love potions along the doorways and windowpanes of Khanoom's house.

One year on *Chahar Shanbeh Soori,* the first of the New Year festivities, Kobra grabbed a handful of golden coins, pulled on her veil, and picked her way through the bonfires in the streets. When she reached the Jewish baths, she disrobed and threw her lot in with the unmarried, the infertile, and the generally accursed who flocked there on this night for the Jews' famed cures. As she was led from corner to corner of the bathhouse and doused with purifying waters, Kobra offered up prayers to Moses' mother, Jochebed, then dressed without toweling off the precious moisture. Kobra passed back over the threshold of the house on Avenue Moniriyeh whispering the name of Moses' father to herself over and over, just as she'd been instructed. "Amran, Amran, Amran..."

Nothing she did had any effect whatsoever on Sohrab.

Indeed, he might never have returned to her but for his ever-shifting fortunes. Kobra's third child had been conceived during one of Kobra and Sohrab's "reconciliations"—one of those interludes when Sohrab's finances had dipped dangerously low and he therefore had no choice but to return to his mother's house, and to Kobra's bed. At such times Sohrab found in Kobra an unlikely but reliable source of financial support. He knew she regularly skimmed a few *tomans* off whatever housekeeping money he gave her, and although her savings did not amount to very much, on more than one occasion it would be just enough to pay off his most pressing debts.

He was not exactly kind toward her when he took her money, but Sohrab certainly grumbled much less than usual, and when Kobra sewed herself a long, pleated dress and began sweeping through the house in it, grinning and stroking her belly with great emphasis, it was obvious to everyone that she'd more than exacted her due. Kobra strung up a moleskin hammock—a *nanoo*—from one of her bedroom walls to the other, unfurled a mattress for herself on the floor, and waited for her baby to arrive. He was born in the spring and she named him Omid, which means "hope."

For a long time Kobra believed that Omid's birth would bring Sohrab back to Avenue Moniriyeh for good. When this did not come to pass, she simply threw all her love and longing at her little baby boy. As Lili was by then twelve (and fast approaching the date of her marriage to Kazem) and Nader eleven years old, Kobra's days were taken up entirely with Omid. Never in her life had she been happier than when she was bent over his *nanoo*, cooing him into sleep. Kobra would have loved him no less if he'd been the picture of ugliness, but Omid was a perfectly beautiful baby—fair and plump, with a thick fringe of lashes around his black eyes and a sweetly dimpled chin. She dressed him in navy blue sailor suits that she sewed for him herself. Every few months she sat him down on the floor of the kitchen, placed a small bowl on his head, and then sang to him as she clipped his hair. And as Omid grew from an infant into a toddler, his capers charmed Kobra so far from her cares that for a time she did not seem to have any cares at all.

One afternoon a portly, wizened woman named Touba Khanoom came to the house to pluck Lili's eyebrows for the very first time. "She has a good hand for it," Khanoom explained, and pressed a golden coin into the lady's palm for good luck. Lili was seated on a chair, facing east, toward Mecca, and her hair was pulled back in a white kerchief. As Ma Mère and several other of Lili's in-laws-to-be waited with coins clenched between their fists, Touba Khanoom cut a length of thread with her teeth, dipped it into a bowl of rose water, and then, with a great flourish, called out, "In the name of God, the Merciful, the All-Knowing!" At the first pluck, Lili's aunts let loose the traditional wedding trills—unending waves of "Lilililililililili!" that echoed Lili's name.

"May there always be weddings in this house!" Touba exclaimed as the women pressed more gold coins into her pockets. "May she give you ten sons!"

At dawn the next day, two porters came to the house and took away the *khoncheh*, the two ceremonial wedding offerings. On one silver tray rested thousands of wild rue seeds that had been dyed and arranged into long, flowing arabesques. On the other lay foot-long sheets of saffron-spiced bread. Each of the porters lifted a tray and placed it on his head, straining visibly under the weight.

The first nuptial ceremony—the *aqd konoon*—had been scheduled to take place exactly six months before Lili's thirteenth birthday. Khanoom had insisted that it be held in the traditional fashion, with separate wedding parties for the men and women. The first night, when the *aqd* was to be performed, was only for the men, and there would be musicians and a troupe of dancers to entertain them in the garden. The second night, a much less lavish affair in all but the foods to be prepared, would be for the women of the two families. The Khorramis thought this arrangement unspeakably backward but had eventually sent their grudging consent.

Sohrab, meanwhile, had approved the marriage, but he'd informed Khanoom that he would not be attending the nuptial ceremony. It was generally thought this was on account of "that blue-eyed jinn," Simin. She had not been invited to Lili's wedding and had no doubt insisted that Sohrab not attend any event from which she'd been excluded. "Please tell him to come!" Lili had begged Khanoom and her aunts, and though they nodded and smiled, none of them dared press the point with Sohrab.

On the night of the *aqd konoon*, Lili scanned the room for her father, sure he would come after all. Then toward the end of the evening she was led to a room with a silk banquette and seated there alone before the *sofreh* (wedding spread). The mirror shone brilliantly at her feet and the scent of burning wild rue began to fill the air. She could barely make out the words of the *agha* in the next room where the men had gathered, but when at last Kazem emerged and took a seat beside her she knew the ceremony was over and that her father had not, finally, come to see it.

Though their formal marriage was still months away, after the *aqd konoon* the pair became *mahram* to each other, which meant that Lili could now appear before Kazem without a head scarf. When Kazem came to sit beside her on the banquette that evening, her gaze fell toward the mirror that had been set down in the center of the wedding spread. It was there in the mirror that she saw Kazem removing her veil, and there also that she saw him without his fedora for the very first time.

Suddenly she knew that she had been right to worry, and she fought back her tears. Though Kazem's features were pleasant enough, his head, she now saw, was nearly bald, but in the front two thin, long tufts of hair had been brought together in the middle— joined, she would only later discover, by the sticky paste of quince seed he kept in a ceramic bowl next to his bed every night.

From then on Kazem came to Khanoom's house once a week. Lili learned to predict his arrivals by what meats and herbs the servants brought back with them from the bazaar each day. Lamb almost always meant Kazem would be visiting, as he had a particularly large appetite for it.

"Kazem Khan is here!" a servant would call out, and all the women of the house would reach at once for their head scarves. Only then would Kazem enter in his suit and tie. Without fail, he would be wearing his gray felt fedora.

Lili would sit across the table from him, her eye trained on his plate, ready to offer him more rice and stew as he progressed through several generous portions. At the end of the meal she rose from the table, cleared his plate, and then served him tea and sweets.

Afterward, her grandmother led them into a sitting room upstairs where they were allowed to spend half an hour alone together. "This is the time for you to get to know each other," Khanoom had explained the first time, urging Lili into the room with a reassuring smile.

In preparation for this part of Kazem's visits, her cousin Soudabeh was routinely dispatched to recite a long list of rules: "Sit with your knees pressed together." "Don't let him take off your underwear." "He cannot reach inside your blouse to touch your breasts." These rules were coupled with another set of directions, whose sum was, "Be sweet and tender, for he is nearly your husband now."

Kazem seemed always to enter the room with an understanding of these same rules, and so he satisfied himself by straddling her and rubbing himself vigorously against her thighs while she sat with her knees pressed together in the way she had been instructed. Often at these moments she thought of a picture she'd once seen of a snake eating a rabbit, its belly engorged with its kill. Kazem, though, seemed content with the arrangement and did not, strictly speaking, challenge the limits indicated by her stiff posture. In any case, his visits occurred regularly up to the wedding day.

On one occasion, Lili visited Kazem at the compound where his grandmother, mother, and aunts lived with their families. When Lili arrived there Ma Mère greeted her with kisses, and this time it was she who was waited upon and hers the first plate to be heaped with rice, stew, *tahdig* (thick crisped rice), yogurt, and a generous handful of fresh herbs.

At the end of the meal Ma Mère turned to Kazem with a gentle smile. "Would you like to take your pretty little *aroos* to your own house?" she asked.

Kazem led Lili out into the street and back into his own quarters. Unlike the main building of the Khorrami compound, which housed all manner of ornate French furnishings and Persian carpets, the two rooms that made up Kazem's suite were practically empty. His bedroom held only a bed and a gilt-framed mirror that ran from the floor to the ceiling.

Lili found herself drawn to this mirror as if by a magnet. Up until that day she had seen herself only in Kobra's old handheld mirror, an instrument with which Lili had been able to study only a few inches of herself at a time. But here for the first time she could see herself from head to foot, and she stood, entranced, before a body she scarcely recognized as her own.

"Do you like to look at yourself?" Kazem asked her. His voice was soft and tender, and she could see him smiling at her in the mirror.

She watched as he advanced toward her with slow, even steps, and then she looked back at her own reflection and she nodded.

Kazem rested his hands on her shoulders. Their eyes met in the mirror and he smiled at her again.

Suddenly, with one swift yank, he pulled her dress over her head. For a moment she stood staring at herself in nothing more than a pair of underpants, and then she bowed her head and began to cry.

"Shhhh, be quiet!" Kazem hissed, and tossed her dress back at her before leaving the apartment.

They came for her one day with a droshky, a horse-drawn cab, to buy fabric for her wedding dress. It was late afternoon on a Thursday, the busiest shopping day of the week. All up and down Avenue Moniriyeh chador-clad housewives were bustling home from the bazaar, gripping their veils between their teeth so as to leave their arms free for their baskets, packages, and infants. Across the street from Khanoom's house a peddler had set up two handcarts, one stacked with baked beets and the other with iced cherry sherbets.

Lili settled into the seat beside Ma Mère and peered out of the curtained window. The carriage turned down one alley after another until soon Lili was looking out at parts of the city she had never seen. When they reached the newly christened Electricity Avenue, she caught her breath at the faint orange glow of the streetlights at dusk. The carriage turned another corner and proceeded farther north. On the Avenue of the Tulip Fields, where the streets were much broader and also smoothly paved, an enormous building rose before her, seeming all of light. The letters above the crimson awning read: "Cinema Lalehzar." Cinema of the Tulip Fields. Saeed, her father's driver, had once told her about a movie house he'd snuck into uptown. "Pictures that come alive!" he'd exclaimed. "People bigger than trees!" She had not believed him, but here it was after all. She would have liked to hop out just then except for the promise of what was to come.

When at last they reached the row of shops and cafés near Execution Square, Lili stepped out of the droshky and was astonished to find that there was not a single veiled woman on the street. It was only after the prohibition against the veil had been lifted that her own grandmother and aunts went out into the city at all, and on Avenue Moniriyeh even a quick trip to the bakery three doors away always called for at least a kerchief. But in this part of Tehran there were dozens of unveiled women, and like Ma Mère and Kazem's other relatives, all their heads were not only bare but also elegantly coiffed.

What's more, from time to time a pair or a small cluster of fair-haired women would pass by, the click of their heels sharp and smart against the pavement. *Foreigners.* The only foreigners Lili had ever seen were soldiers, and even grown men cowered from them. But these women were beautiful, and she could not tear her eyes from their red lips and bare calves.

Ma Mère caught her staring and smiled. "Has our little bride come out to the world?" She laughed.

In the shop they picked a fabric for Lili and let her touch it. It was not white but the palest blue, with a hint of shimmer to it. She stroked it gently and the shimmers danced under her fingers. Did she like it? "Yes," she stammered, she liked it very, very much. They took her to a back room and told her to undress. But as soon as the fabric was pulled around her torso, her hands went to her shoulders and she began shivering with fear. The dress would be sleeveless! What would Khanoom say? She had never been allowed to wear even a short-sleeved dress, or even one that left her forearms exposed, and now she was to wear a sleeveless dress to her wedding? Then all at once it seemed like ten pairs of hands were on her, pulling the fabric tighter, lifting the hem, smoothing the bodice. With the way the women were looking at her, smiling and cooing and fussing, her hands fell from her shoulders to her sides, and her worries slipped at once from her mind.

The Khorramis were well-to-do and would certainly provide for her in the years to come, but it would have shamed Khanoom to send her granddaughter into marriage without a decent *jahaz,* or trousseau. In the months leading up to the final nuptial ceremony, she gathered the best she had managed to put aside for Lili over the years and also bought a few things to round out the offerings. Khanoom filled a large leather trunk to the very top with embroidered linens, a fine silken carpet from Kāshān, a pretty china teapot, and a brand-new samovar. This trunk and a hand-carved dining set, several mattresses, and a full assortment of kitchenware purchased by Lili's father were then sent to the Khorrami compound a week in advance of the wedding.

Then, a few days before the Night of Consummation, Lili was led to the room farthest from the streets and encircled by the women of her family. First they dusted her from head to foot with precious face powder from America. Its perfume tickled her nose and she began to laugh, but they told her to lie very still. Out of the corner of the eye Lili saw one of her aunts unraveling some string and twisting it between her fingers. Lili had had her eyebrows plucked once before, before the first nuptial ceremony. The ritual would be repeated once more on this occasion, but only later. Only after.

Suddenly she understood why so many of her aunts and cousins had come to the house that day: they were needed to hold her down as every last hair on her body was plucked out with the string her aunt was now twisting and tightening between her fingers. Lili had been taken to the room farthest from the street so that the neighbors would not hear her cry out, and on the unlikely chance that she'd

break free and bolt out of the room, one of her cousins stood blocking the door.

"*Bah, bah, bah!*" the women cried, as one of them began thumping on a *tonbak*. "How lucky her husband is! What a happy bride she
will be!"

It was at this point that Lili started to scream.

Lili flinched and whimpered with each tweak, but afterward they
all kissed her and rubbed a cool paste over her smarting flesh and
Khanoom had soothed her with sugared milk and even slept beside
her that last night.

Then, on the day before the final wedding ceremony, the Khorramis rented the whole bathhouse, and it was there that her aunts
and cousins commenced to groom her from head to foot. First they
washed her body with a mixture of milk and honey, lathered her
hair with yogurt, and rinsed it clear with rose water. Then they sat
back and consumed several dozen potato and spinach pancakes, followed by quince-lemon sherbet and tea from the samovar that had
been brought especially to the *hammam* that day.

With a few deep puffs of the *qalyoon* they were ready to resume
their work. They scrubbed Lili vigorously with *kiseh*, the rough
woolen mitts that drew out every impurity from the skin. They
worked quickly, two of them tending to each part of her body, and
when they finished rinsing and toweling her off they rubbed her all
over with a mixture of Vaseline and rose essence.

After a lunch of pomegranate-and-walnut stew, they slapped their
copper bowls against the tiles to make music and danced for each
other in turn. So great was their din that some of the neighborhood
women climbed onto the roof of the *hammam* and peered through
the skylights for a glimpse of the festivities. After a final round of tea
and sweets, they perfumed Lili's hair, twisted it into tiny topknots
all around her head, and then threw a veil over her head to shield her
from jealous eyes in the streets.

At dawn the porters came to take away the final items of the trousseau. To announce the Night of Consummation, the porters would carry these offerings on their heads all the way from Khanoom's house to the Khorramis' compound. Once more her aunts and cousins groomed her. They traced *sormeh* all around her eyes and brushed her hair loose, then blotted her cheeks and her lips with rouge. Khanoom had surreptitiously affixed the thinnest gauze sleeves to her wedding dress, and now, as the dress was slipped over Lili's head, they all stood back and studied the results of this and their many other labors. "*Masha Allah!* Praise God!" Khanoom exclaimed, her eyes bright with tears, and at this one of Lili's aunts scurried to the kitchen to burn a last pot of wild rue to shield Lili from the Evil Eye.

Finally, in the hour before dusk, the two porters reappeared, this time in a gleaming white sedan.

Lili did not doubt that her grandmother and aunts and Sohrab's stepmothers would miss her, but her belief was shaken when she learned that none of them would accompany her to the Night of Consummation. Khanoom always spoke highly of the Khorrami family name, and tolerated their modern ways on this account, but the wedding itself had provoked a genuine crisis. Though the Khorramis had consented to separate parties for the *aqd*, when the time came for the final wedding party (scheduled for the eve of Lili's thirteenth birthday) they were no longer in the mood for compromise. It would be a mixed party—men and women all together on a single night—or no party at all.

"These Khorrami women, they only wish to show off their bodies to men!" Khanoom had exclaimed, shaking her head in disgust.

Talks and deliberations went on for many days, but with only a week to go until the Night of Consummation, no truce was yet in sight.

"We will not go," Khanoom declared at last.

"What do you mean, Khanoom-*joon*?"

"I mean that even though they will soon be your family, we cannot go to the wedding if they insist on a party with strange men and women pressed close together in one place. It is indecent. Some of your other relatives will be there, I'm sure, but I am sorry, *madar-joon*, your aunts and I cannot come with you to such a gathering."

When the car came for Lili that last day, Khanoom, Lili's aunts, and Sohrab's stepmothers all gathered around her by the door to hug and kiss her good-bye. Shedding copious tears, they reassured her that everything would be fine, that her marriage would be a good one, and that she would soon be very happy. On the threshold they passed the Koran over her head three times, and when she turned away they sprinkled water at her feet. Khanoom also gave her a necklace that had belonged to her own mother, and at the last minute her aunts had pulled off the heavy golden bangles from their own arms and piled them onto Lili's wrists one by one.

"May God accompany you!" Khanoom called out as the white sedan pulled out of their alley and into Avenue Pahlavi.

Though it was the immodesty of the proceedings that prevented Lili's grandmother and aunts from attending the Night of Consummation, it had never been customary for the bride's parents to attend this particular gathering—their sole task being to await the bloodied handkerchief that was proof of their daughter's chastity. Sohrab would not stay long enough to fulfill that task, though he did join the send-off on Avenue Moniriyeh. He brought her an exquisite ceramic bowl decorated with wild birds and flowering vines, which he'd had filled to the top with tangerines, grapes, and pomegranates. "It's come all the way from China for you," he told her with a wan smile. For the first time in many years he drew his arms around her and Lili smiled into his chest as he held her to him. "Good-bye, *dokhtar-joon*," he told her. He kissed her, very gently, on the top of her head, and before he turned away Lili thought she caught a tear in his eye.

But whatever the dictates of tradition, Kobra found she could not bear to send Lili to the celebration alone. At the very last minute Kobra pulled on a dress and made up her face. She dressed Nader in his one handmade suit and slicked back his hair with a comb. Then, as Khanoom called out her last blessings, Kobra passed a squalling Omid into Zaynab's arms and climbed with Nader into one of the several cars that had come to Khanoom's house.

In order to give passersby a chance to see the bride, the bridal cortege moved so slowly that sometimes it did not seem to be moving at all. The cars were followed by a half-dozen attendants walking alongside the cars and throwing fistfuls of sugared almonds and golden coins into the streets. The drivers blasted their horns in turn. "They're bringing a bride!" someone would cry out from the sidewalk every few blocks, and for the whole length of the journey people stepped out into the street for a glimpse of the bride and the bridegroom. Lili was wearing the sleeveless pale blue wedding dress, but it was hidden underneath a lace-trimmed ivory veil that Khanoom had sewn to keep her safe from the hundreds of lustful glances of men and thousand evil eyes of envious women.

She would remember little from the party apart from one fateful dance. Of course there was much she might have remembered, or remembered better: electric lights strung through the spindly branches of the orange trees outside; white lilies brought over from a village five hours to the south; huge steaming platters of orange-rind rice; richly fragrant trays of barbecued lamb; saffron pudding in crystal bowls; a many-tiered wedding cake such as she had never seen. In the garden an enormous rectangular pool had been covered with wooden planks and transformed into a dance floor complete with a European-style band. And the women's dresses alone were nothing Lili could have imagined. Chiffon, velvet, silk, each a lovelier shade than the next. Some were no more than slips, or so it seemed to Lili, and even Ma Mère's pistachio green gown exposed a generous expanse of the elderly matron's bosom. Several of the women there held glasses of liquor as casually as though they were men, and a few even smoked cigarettes encased in long, silver cigarette holders.

For much of the evening Kobra sat by herself in one corner of the parlor. Lili and her mother did not exchange a word all night, but each time their eyes met she felt grateful that her mother had come along at the last minute. From time to time Lili would catch sight of Nader in his ill-fitting hand-me-down suit, ducking between the guests, gorging himself on wedding pastries, and throwing her an impish look. But of all that she might have remembered about the Night of Consummation, it was the tango Lili would never forget.

It did not happen very often, but from time to time her aunts and stepmothers danced for each other at the house on Avenue Moniriyeh. They would form a circle on the floor in the living room and someone would start thumping a *tonbak*. Soon enough one of the women would rise, step to the center of the circle, and begin to sway her arms and hips. They clapped and laughed like girls then. The shyest, primmest ones were often the most skilled and sensual dancers, though they were also often the ones who needed the most coaxing to get started. Lili hadn't yet danced in the center of a circle like that, but when she was very little Kobra had sometimes pulled her up onto a chair and showed her how to frame her face with her hands as she moved her hips from side to side.

This, so far as she knew, was dancing, but on the Night of Consummation Kazem pulled her up from her seat, and before she could protest they were already surrounded by dozens of other elegant couples. All eyes were suddenly on her. She could not stand to look so uncultured, but how was she to begin? She could not follow the tempo, much less the movements. Kazem had taken no more than two steps when she started stepping on his feet. First the heel of her shoe planted itself squarely on his toes. He winced and drew in a sharp breath. She tottered and tripped and once she very nearly brought them both crashing to the ground and her cheeks flushed with embarrassment, but each time they stumbled he merely set his jaw, strengthened his grip around her wrists, and pulled her closer to him.

Just past midnight, when the guests had left the house at last, Kazem and Lili climbed the stairs to the attic, where they were followed by Ma Mère and the eldest women of his family. Kazem opened the door and Lili followed him inside. Their bridal suite had been decorated with tuberoses, lilies, and white tapered candles. Her eyes fell on a peach-colored brocade cloth nestled on one of the pillows of the four-poster bed. She recognized it from the weeks her grandmother had spent trimming its corners with intricate golden braids, and she knew that tonight it held within its folds a single, perfectly ironed white handkerchief.

Kazem pulled off his jacket and caught her eye from across the room. A smile played, just faintly, on his lips. Working his fingers through the knot of his bow tie, he moved as if to embrace her, but instead he turned and left the room.

As soon as she heard water streaming from the bathroom faucet, she pulled the white handkerchief from its brocade cover. Then, just as she'd been advised, she laid it on the pillow, smoothed her dress, and waited.

When Kazem returned, she saw that his face had been stripped of all expression. She worried that he was still angry with her about her poor dancing, and was about to make an apology for her clumsiness when he began to undress himself. She turned her eyes away quickly toward the wall, and all at once her arms and legs felt as stiff and as cold as marble. "It's nothing at all!" her cousins had assured her, though some of the older ones hid their smiles behind their hands and giggled, but Kazem's manner was so brusque that she was now beset with fear.

Kazem lowered himself onto her, raised her dress, and fumbled for a moment. Then he sat up abruptly. Something was not right.

"Get down on the floor," he told her.

She reached for the handkerchief. She could hear the women on the other side of the door, whispering noisily to one another. She slipped off the bed, clutching the silk handkerchief between her fingers as she went. The fibers of the rug itched terribly, but she did not dare move. Kazem lowered himself onto her again, and when the pain tore straight up through to her belly and she opened her mouth to cry he grabbed the fabric from her fingers and pressed it firmly over her mouth. Time seemed to stop then, to slacken and dissolve and recede, but she knew it was over when at last he thrust the square of fabric between her legs and rose from the floor.

His eyes ran across the blood seeping quickly through the handkerchief, and then, opening the door slightly, he passed it outside to where the women stood ready to receive it.

"May God give you many sons!" she heard one of them cry out just as their ululations broke out from behind the door.

For a few minutes she lay on the floor, uncertain what to do next. She lifted herself slightly on her elbows and looked around the room. Kazem had returned to the bed. Was she supposed to sleep there on the floor all night? How would she manage without a blanket or pillow? She'd soil the carpet with blood, and what would happen then?

His voice interrupted these thoughts. "Now come up again," he told her.

She lay awake for some time afterward, hugging her knees in her arms at the edge of the bed, her throat raw. There were no more sounds coming from behind the door. The women had all left now. Kazem had fallen asleep with his back turned toward her, and except for his breathing the room was completely quiet and still.

When Lili awoke the next morning she felt nothing but a dull ache between her legs, but when she went to the *hammam* to purify herself she found two dark purple bruises on each of her wrists from where his fingers had gripped her when they danced the tango. It was the first day of her marriage and already she had learned to face the wall and to stifle a cry when it came.

Three

The Opium Dream

"She was a jinn, that woman—a witch—but you've never seen anything as beautiful as her blue eyes." My mother paused for a moment before continuing her story. "Still, they never asked me if she was the one who gave me the opium, and I never told them, either. Even when they took the baby from me, I still didn't tell them anything."

F OR LILI, MARRIAGE HAD meant the loss of her lovely gray school uniform and the company of her girlfriends, and it was a loss she felt keenly. But because the wedding had taken place in the winter, over the school holidays, Ma Mère convinced her to simply think of the suspension as a longer vacation. And so for a while Lili looked forward to the new public school Ma Mère promised her she would attend in the spring, and, in the meantime, she set about learning the ways of her new family.

Like all the houses of the middle and upper classes in those years, the Khorramis' house was actually a sprawling compound enclosed by high stone walls. It had five levels: the kitchen, which was also its basement and storeroom; a first floor that held the guest parlor, or *mehmoon khooneh*; and two levels for the family's private quarters. Of these, the second floor was taken up by Kazem's aunt and her husband, while the third floor belonged to his own parents and Ma Mère. The uppermost level of the house was an attic, which had long served as a storage space for the entire family. After their wedding the attic was cleared of most of its contents and Lili and Kazem were given this floor for themselves. Kazem brought the bed and mirror from his old bachelor quarters, and it was here that Lili unpacked her trousseau.

During the daytime Kazem and the other members of the family were gone from the house, which left Lili alone with the servants and Ma Mère. In the first weeks following the Night of Consummation, Lili mostly stayed by herself in the attic, tidying up the room, arranging and rearranging her belongings, and watching the street from behind latticed window frames.

But one morning after breakfast Ma Mère called Lili to her.

"Follow me," she ordered, rising from the sofa to lead Lili down into the basement.

Lili had not seen the basement before this and knew it only as the place from which the servants emerged with the day's meals. When, gradually, her eyes adjusted to the darkness, she looked around and saw that here the walls and floor were all of a gray-colored mud. Newly skinned eggplants lay on a wooden table alongside chopped herbs and walnuts soaking in salt water. From the basement's one small window she could see where the garden rose up behind the walls of the kitchen, exposing a sliver of blue sky beyond.

"Listen," began Ma Mère. "It is true that we have servants, thanks be to God. But you must know that no matter how delicious their cooking, your husband will always want to eat the food you prepare for him."

Ma Mère pointed to the corner of the basement, where a charcoal brazier sat low to the ground. "That is your own stove," she explained. "You may use it for cooking all your meals." She shuffled over to a cabinet and hauled out a large sack of rice and a jug of oil. "These are also for you, but keep them upstairs in your own quarters, so they do not get mixed up with our things down here."

Lili took the items from Ma Mère's hands and nodded. "Yes,

khanoom!" she chirped, but the truth was that she had never made even a single pot of rice and could not begin to think how she would manage to prepare entire meals by herself. But no sooner had Ma Mère mounted the stairs than the servants took pity on Lili and began coaching her in the rudiments of cooking. Over the next several weeks they took turns showing her how to rinse and soak rice, dice and fry strips of onions to the point of translucence, and brown the lamb for Kazem's stews. *Khanoom kuchak*, they called her—"little missus"—and minded her progress with growing affection.

When she was not cooking, most of Lili's time in those early days of marriage was spent learning how to wash clothes, a solitary task that took up almost two full days each week. There were no washing machines in the country yet, and all the washing took place outside in the *hoz*, the rectangular pool that sat in the middle of the courtyard. It was a job most families with means delegated to their servants, but as with the cooking, Ma Mère assured Lili that it would be far more pleasing to Kazem if she herself tended to this chore.

In wintertime thick sheets of ice covered the *hoz*. To wash the week's clothes, towels, and bed linens she had to first boil a kettle of water in the basement, carry it up to the courtyard, and then pour the water into the pool to melt the ice. This procedure was repeated two, three, sometimes even four times. From one of the servants she learned to carry a knife among her bundles of laundry in order to pierce through the ice on the coldest days. Turning back toward the kitchen to fetch another kettle of hot water, she would often catch a glimpse of Ma Mère's face in the upstairs window, watching her as she worked.

She'd stand at the edge of the pool, the wind whipping the hem of her housedress as she poured water from a brass kettle into the *hoz*. Steam rose from its surface and the ice began to crackle. She'd hurry back down the steps to the basement, and even if stews had been simmering there since dawn, it was always the scent of the mud, loamy and sweet, that first greeted her down there. As she stood waiting for the water to come to a boil again, she learned every slope and sinew of those mud walls, and in time her eyes began to linger on the places where jagged lines arched from floor to ceiling in one continuous crack.

By the time she returned to the courtyard, the linens had already turned stiff at the cuffs and hems, as if in her absence the cold had bled into the fabric. For a while it startled her, this greed of the winter chill, but she learned to expect it with the same certainty with which she knew that if she turned her head toward the house, she'd always be met by those black eyes and that unmoving mouth.

One day after the washing was done, she climbed up to the attic and fell into her bed for a nap. She had just drifted to sleep when the door swung open and hit the wall with a sharp clap. Before she could open her eyes, she felt Kazem bearing down on her and felt his breath coming out hot and moist against her cheek.

"You've disgraced me in front of my grandmother!" he shouted in her ear. He began pummeling her with his fists. "*Gendeh!* Whore!"

"But why?" she finally managed to sob from underneath the sheets. "Why?"

He stopped, ran the back of his hand across his forehead, and told her what his grandmother had witnessed that morning.

Every day when he returned to the house, Kazem first went to Ma Mère's quarters, where he would kneel and kiss her hands and then have his own head kissed by her in turn. On this particular day, he'd gone to greet Ma Mère and she'd refused his kiss. Ma Mère had been watching Lili and had seen that she'd neglected to rinse the soap from her hands before beginning to rinse the clothes and so had soiled the laundry. The stupidity and ineptitude of his bride were, Ma Mère assured him, unrivaled.

Kazem cleared his throat and pulled up his sleeves. Seeing this,

Lili shrank farther into the sheets and pulled her arms over her head. The beating went on until at last a voice rose from the stairwell.

"*Baseh!* Enough!" Ma Mère called out from below. "You've disciplined her enough for now!"

At these words Kazem rose from the bed and left the room, only to return much later in the night, smelling of alcohol and something else, an odor she would later come to recognize as the sweet, sharp scent of vomit.

It was not yet spring when she first felt the sickness. Just two months had passed since the Night of Consummation when it began. It always came first thing in the morning, just as soon as she opened her eyes. It started like a tickle or a cough playing at the back of her throat, but then all of a sudden she would feel it snaking its way up from her stomach, hot and fast, and she'd race to the bathroom and thrust her head into the washbasin to relieve herself of it.

For a while she'd thought the sickness was on account of the beatings, but then one night Ma Mère caught Lili's eye over the dinner table, tipped her chin up with her thumb, and delivered a diagnosis: Lili was pregnant and there would be no going back to school that year.

"But how could you let this happen?" Kobra asked Lili when, later that week, the neighborhood midwife confirmed the pregnancy. "Did your cousins tell you nothing?"

Such intimacies were, in these years, not routinely conveyed by mothers but rather by the bride-to-be's recently married relatives, usually her closest female cousins. Lili's cousin Soudabeh, however, had conveyed little more than giggling assurances of pleasures of the conjugal bed; contraception thus eluded Lili as wholly as that promised pleasure. Indeed, such were the limits of Lili's knowledge that Kobra's question completely baffled her, and it was through tears that she begged to know what she could have done to stop a baby from coming. At this Kobra slapped her own cheeks and shook her head sadly, by which she meant that the situation was too far gone for such discussions now.

"You need to take her away," Lili next overheard Ma Mère telling Kazem. "I can't stand her swelling up like a cow, and then all the noise of a child! It will be the death of me!"

Within a week Kazem moved Lili to an alley close to the train station in South Tehran, or Tayeh Shar, the Bottom of the City. The two-room flat was part of a squat family compound long since cordoned off into half a dozen individual apartments. The larger of the rooms had no windows and no electricity and consequently became a storage space for her trousseau and most of their furniture. They took their meals and slept in the room with the sink and a makeshift stove, shared a toilet with the landlord, his family, and the other tenants, and for baths they walked seven blocks to the closest *hammam*.

On the first day of every month Kazem placed three hundred *tomans*—his entire month's wages—onto the dining table and told her it was her responsibility to manage their household expenses. Two hundred *tomans* went straightaway for the rent, and with the rest she was supposed to feed and clothe and otherwise care for the two of them. How such a meager sum could be made to accommodate not just herself and Kazem but also a child was yet another worry Lili added to her steadily mounting heap. She also found it impossible to sleep in the new apartment, and soon the misery of these early months of pregnancy was exacerbated by an unrelenting bout of insomnia and an understanding that she'd likely never return to school now that she was expecting a child.

Lili might have gone to her own mother to unburden her heart, but by that time Kobra was nursing what would be the deepest grief of her days: the death of her youngest child, Omid.

That horrible day, Kobra had been in the kitchen cooking rice pudding, which Omid always ate by the bowlful. It was a delicacy that, when left too long without stirring, quickly congealed into black clumps, and Kobra had already been stirring the pudding for some time when Omid wandered out of the kitchen to play by himself.

Lili would never know for sure what happened to him. Once she'd hear a cousin speak of the child mistaking a chunk of opium for chocolate, but it could just as well have been a spider bite. And of course autumn had brought droves of baby tarantulas to the garden. No one paid them much mind even though they were known to be poisonous, but to two-year-old Omid the tarantulas would have been new, and maybe also beautiful, and perhaps he'd caught one and let it plunge its stinger into his small fist. In any case, when Kobra finished dusting her bowls of rice pudding with cinnamon she stepped out into the garden and found him lying at the foot of the *hoz*, curled up as if in sleep, his lips and eyelids tinted blue.

Since then, Kobra's eyes had taken on a glassy cast, with black half-moons underneath that told of her own sleeplessness. When Omid died, Lili was already several months into her pregnancy, and no one would tell her much about the circumstances of her little brother's death for fear that grief would enter her blood and disturb her unborn child. But Lili could see that Kobra's grief had only deepened in the last months, and now it was Lili who could not bear to burden her mother with her own troubles, and so whenever Kobra asked about Kazem or her pregnancy, she would force herself to smile and to speak of happiness.

The first few times he cried for hours afterward. He'd drop to his knees and beg her to forgive him. Swear she was more precious to him than his own life. That he would never again raise a hand to hurt her. So desperate, so completely genuine, did Kazem seem with his pleas and promises those first few times, so apparently bewildered by his own behavior, that she smoothed his brow and hushed him as she would a child.

But soon hardly a week passed without his beating her, and every time he cried less afterward until eventually he didn't cry at all and the excuses and apologies stopped altogether.

At night she fell asleep wondering whether he would wake up angry or happy the next day. As soon as he left for work in the mornings, she would try to guess whether he would come home for lunch or stay away until dinnertime. What could she do to please him when he returned? Should she greet him with a smile, or should she avoid his eyes until he spoke to her? Should she comb her hair and put on a fresh dress for him? Would he be glad to see her looking pretty or would he accuse her of having made herself up and gone out by herself?

The worst, by far, always came at night.

When he did not return for dinner one evening, she laid a blanket on the floor, intending to rest there just until he returned. Sometime after midnight she'd worn herself out from thinking and finally fallen asleep. Near dawn he stumbled into the apartment and kicked her sides. Her hands went at once to the bump in her belly. She shut her eyes and he lowered himself onto her. She opened her eyes for an instant and saw two strands of hair hanging loose from either side of his otherwise bald head. In the first weeks of their marriage he'd been scrupulous about grooming himself before coming to her, but over time such niceties had fallen by the wayside. She shut her eyes until, gradually, inevitably, he finished.

From Thursday afternoon until late Sunday evening she was marched from relative's house to relative's house to be appraised and advised and feted until her cheeks burned with the effort of smiling through it all. It was at these gatherings that she first realized how much had been hidden from her about Kazem throughout their courtship. He flew into a rage at the smallest pretense, mocked and belittled everyone who crossed his path. Lili observed how guarded his family seemed in his presence and the care they took when addressing him. Many of them, she discovered, would not so much as meet his eyes from across the room. Of all of them, Ma Mère was the only one capable of coaxing a smile or kind word from him.

And then there was the conversation that revealed to Lili how little she herself had managed to hide about her life with Kazem.

It happened during one of her visits to the Khorramis' extended family. After lunch, she rose to fetch Ma Mère a fresh cup of tea when she heard one of the women asking Kazem's aunt, "Is that your *aroos*?"

"Yes, the poor thing."

The poor thing? Lili stole a sideways look at the two women and realized that they were talking about her. She hustled away, but then, from behind a banister, she strained to make out the rest of their talk.

"*Sadisme*," she heard Kazem's aunt saying. "You remember how he was as a child?" She paused, shook her head sadly, and continued. "His parents used to send him to the countryside for it. We'd all hoped it would help him to marry, but..." Here her voice trailed off.

Sadisme. Lili mouthed the foreign word to herself. What did it mean? From the way Kazem's aunt had said it, Lili guessed it must be something terrible, some sort of disease. She repeated the word silently to herself several more times. If she could somehow find the meaning of this word, surely she could also find its cure?

In the meantime, she made a lesser but still useful discovery: a well-seasoned herb stew with rice could sometimes soften the edges of her husband's temper. With this realization she quickly devoted herself to perfecting her cooking. Every Thursday morning she walked to the *bazaarcheh* down the street and brought back cilantro, chives, mint, and parsley by the bucketful. The freshest, most fragrant herbs always came with the stems and roots encrusted with dirt. Back at home she rinsed the herbs many times over, pulled out her biggest copper pot, and bathed them for an hour in salted water before starting on the rice.

It was when she was cleaning and rinsing the herbs one day that year that she discovered a way to make herself disappear. By focusing all her attention on a chore, she could summon a distinct sensation of cutting loose from her worries, from the room, from her own body. She practiced the trick over and over until she could sustain this peaceful state for intervals of an hour—or even longer.

Five months pregnant, her fingers and feet swollen beyond remedy, she was making herself disappear one June afternoon when she suddenly heard loud voices in the stairwell. Kazem was arguing with the landlord and his wife again. Lili shut her eyes and kept her knife moving over the pile of herbs. The voices grew louder and then stopped. Kazem flung the door open, but before he could slam it shut the landlord and his wife shouldered their way inside the apartment. Lili felt a sudden sharp pain in her temple, but it was only when she opened her eyes again and met Kazem's that she looked down and saw the blood.

Slowly and with something strangely resembling indifference, she traced the fine red rivulets now soaking through the herbs until she found the source of the bleeding. The tip of her index finger, she saw, was dangling from her hand. She blinked—once, twice, again. The knife dropped, just barely missing her foot.

"You clumsy idiot!" Kazem shouted. He lurched toward her and she screamed.

"I've told you," the landlord called out, "no more of this, no more hitting her—"

"It's nothing to do with you!" Kazem snapped, but the landlord and his wife had seen Lili's ravaged finger and her knees as they buckled under her. "That girl's got to see a doctor!" he shouted, and pulled her off the floor and into the open air.

The landlord's wife had been so kind to Lili that night, had told her to come at once if ever she had troubles again. "Troubles"—that's exactly how she'd put it, and she'd been so tactful, too, bending toward Lili and whispering so that no one in the crowded hospital ward would overhear her. Lili had nodded and promised that she would, but from that night on Kazem was always careful to hit her only in the places where no one could see the bruises, and she was both too ashamed and too frightened to tell anyone when next the "troubles" began.

Even to those closest to her, the fact that the abuse she suffered was not, strictly speaking, uncommon made it no less difficult to name. Khanoom and her aunts all guessed at her situation from the start, and yet they never spoke of it. They reasoned that any intervention on their part would only anger Kazem and therefore add to her difficulties. They said nothing at all and, in some unspoken way of her own, Lili understood that their silence was meant as kindness.

As consolation, perhaps, for their reticence, Khanoom often urged her to visit the family, but as her pregnancy advanced, Lili had less and less inclination to leave her own apartment. In part this had to do with the astonishing changes in her body. Her belly seemed to grow by the day and then by the hour. While her feet and legs swelled to gigantic proportions, her cheeks hollowed out and her face took on a yellowish pallor. She could barely make out the symptoms of pregnancy from the effects of Kazem's beatings; the two would always be irrevocably linked in her mind. Indeed, any pleasant reveries she indulged about the baby were overshadowed by her fearfulness. And the uglier and more awkward she seemed to herself, the less she troubled with her hair or her clothes and the more frequently she resorted to throwing her chador over her housedress when she went out to the market or the bathhouse.

It was in this state that Sohrab made what would be his first and only visit to her as a married woman. She'd pulled on her veil, grabbed a large tin canister, and set out to buy some kerosene from the neighborhood market. A few steps from the apartment, she spied a well-dressed gentleman approaching her from the opposite end of the alley. She strengthened her grip on the canister. With her free hand she held her veil under her chin and prepared to lower her eyes.

She looked up and realized that the gentleman approaching her was her own father.

"*Baba-joon!*" she sputtered. "You've come to visit me?"

"Yes, yes," Sohrab answered impatiently. "But what is that you're holding?"

"Holding?" It took her a moment to realize he meant the canister. "Oh, this! It's for the kerosene."

Sohrab frowned and reached his hand out to take it from her. "You go back home now," he told her.

She'd never seen her father holding anything half as common as that rusty old canister, and she now wished desperately to snatch it back from him. "But we haven't got any kerosene," she protested, "and the rooms get so cold at night."

"I said it's time to go home."

Back in the apartment, she flung off her chador and watched as his eyes took in the peeling paint on the walls, the exposed pipes above the kitchen sink, the uncurtained windows. Had her aunts spoken to him about Kazem? Her cheeks burned with shame at the thought. She hurried to the kitchen to brew him a pot of tea. She found no sweets in the cupboard and so, hands trembling, she piled chunks of sugar into a small bowl for him.

He didn't stay long enough to finish even one cup of tea, but before he left Sohrab pressed several hundred *tomans* into her hands and told her she could always come to him for more money. Then, the following morning, her aunt Zaynab came around to tell Kazem that Sohrab would soon send someone to help her with the house- work and errands. He'd already arranged a room for a servant with the landlord and would pay all of the servant's wages himself.

"Does Sohrab Khan think these are his own princely quarters in Shemiran?" Kazem chided when Zaynab approached him with the offer. "She'll do her own work, like any decent woman." No servant was sent to help her, but from then on every Friday at noon a basket full of provisions—a fresh chicken and some rice in a pot, cantaloupes and apples, two jugs of milk—showed up alongside a full canister of kerosene on her doorstep, and she never had to guess who'd sent it for her.

The weeks wore on in this way until, just a few days shy of her delivery date, Lili at last moved back to Khanoom's house for her lying-in period.

They were all sleeping around the *korsi* (a low table with a heater underneath it), their arms and limbs intertwined under piles of quilts, when she felt a surge of warm liquid pass between her legs. She kicked off the covers and cried out for Khanoom. "Shhh, shhh," her grandmother soothed. "This means it's time, *bacheh-joon*. It's time...."

Hearing this, the others untangled themselves from the blankets, threw on their veils, and together lifted Lili from the *korsi* and hauled her into a taxi.

"How young you are!" the midwife exclaimed when Lili appeared in the clinic sobbing and clutching her grandmother's hand. Very young mothers were becoming less common, at least in the capital, and the midwife seemed utterly charmed when she learned Lili was still just thirteen years old. And when, after just three-quarters of an hour, the baby emerged, to be laid on Lili's chest still slick and warm with blood, the midwife declared it another blessing of youth as well as an auspicious start to her life as a new mother.

Lili lifted her head and peered at the newborn. Here she was at last, Lili thought, her own baby! Kazem's family had chosen a name for her—Sara. Lili looked for the first time at Sara and for a moment a feeling of tenderness overtook her pain. Finding Sara whole, with all of her fingers and toes in place, Lili fell back against the pillows. A cloth soaked with chloroform was passed under her nose, and with that she sank almost immediately into a deep sleep.

"Wake up and see who has come for you!"

Lili rubbed her eyes and raised herself onto her elbows. Every part of her body, from her head to her feet, felt impossibly sore. She looked out the window and saw that the sky had turned dark. How long had she been here? Somewhere in the room a woman was moaning. From another corner there came the high-pitched squalling of a newborn.

The midwife was holding a crying baby—*her* baby, Lili realized with a start. Sara had been swaddled in a white woolen blanket. Her little face was pinched and red. She looked exhausted.

Lili reached out for her.

"She'll want her milk now," the midwife said, smiling kindly as she handed Sara over to Lili.

First the midwife showed Lili how to cradle one hand behind the infant's head and cup her breast with the other. She lowered Sara to her chest and nudged the little mouth toward her nipple, but the baby showed no interest whatever in latching on. "*Khanoom,*" Lili said, looking up at the midwife, "why won't she drink?" The midwife shushed her, patted her hand, and then told Lili to lie down on her side and positioned the baby facing toward her that way. But no matter what the midwife or Lili did that day, the tiny pair of pink lips stayed locked in a tight line.

Why, Lili puzzled, wouldn't Sara take her milk? Was it true what everyone said, that a fetus fed on its mother's emotions? Had her baby come into this world already full with her own grief? Tears spilled from Lili's cheeks as she considered this, but the midwife hushed her and told her not to worry, that there was no child yet born who would not drink from its mother's breast once it grew hungry enough.

Four days later, when Lili finally left the hospital for Khanoom's house, Sara had still not taken so much as a drop of Lili's milk. On the fifth day sweat began beading Lili's forehead at dawn and by noon it had thoroughly soaked her bed linens. Her hair clung to her scalp in wet tendrils; her breasts grew heavy and then turned hard as rocks. Her temperature rose and fell, climbed past a hundred, and settled at 102 degrees, where it would hover for the next three days.

Khanoom put her faith in timeworn methods. At regular intervals throughout the day, she pressed boiled cabbage leaves against Lili's breasts and then kneaded them with her calloused fingers. To bring down Lili's fever, Khanoom held a cold compress to Lili's temple and spoon-fed her ice water tinged with *limoo shirin*, sweet lemon. When, finally, Lili's milk let down, it was Khanoom who cried out to God in thanks and vowed she'd sacrifice two lambs for His infinite mercy. For the next few days Khanoom, her eyes full of sleep, appeared at Lili's bedside at dawn, and held out a saucer while she expelled her milk. As promised, Khanoom had two lambs slaughtered, cooked, and served up as alms to the poor.

It was not enough to stop the fever, though. Lili's whole body shook and shivered, slackened like a doll's until finally she became so delirious that she would not even answer to her own name. Engorgement had led to infection. Late one night she was rushed back to the hospital to have her milk ducts sliced open with a knife, and for days afterward bad milk seeped from her breasts.

She woke one morning feeling completely hollowed out, but her forehead had cooled considerably. She sat up and ate a full breakfast, her first meal since having left the hospital over one week earlier, and Khanoom, in her fine deep voice, sang out prayers as Lili ate.

At noon Khanoom came to Lili's room with a basket full of caramel-colored puppies, and she woke to find three identical pairs of brown eyes squinting at her.

"A gift?" she asked.

"Yes." Khanoom nodded. "A gift."

Lili sat up and clapped her hands. The three puppies scampered out of the basket and began crawling across the bed. One of them, the littlest one, began to lick her fingers, and Lili giggled.

"You can keep that one if you like," Khanoom told her, giving the puppy a pat. "But to make you feel better, *bacheh-joon*, you must first let it suckle."

"Suckle?"

"Suckle."

Lili gasped. "I won't!"

"You must!"

But after that Lili turned her face to the wall and crossed her arms over her chest and would not so much as look at the puppies. Khanoom frowned and squared her shoulders. She lifted the puppies up one by one, placed them back into the basket, and turned from the room.

She would appear again the next day with another basket. This one held a pair of six-month-old twins belonging to a distant cousin. The twins latched on expertly and, in so doing, brought immediate relief. Their mother, no doubt grateful for the respite from her own duties, sent them once in the morning and once in the evening for a week. The second week the twins came three days, the third week just twice. In this time Lili's own baby was given goat's milk served from a glass bottle affixed with a plastic yellow nipple, but after the twins cured Lili's engorgement, Sara learned to latch on with ease.

Lili's pain slowly diminished and Sara began to settle into a routine, but for days afterward Lili would still think about the three puppies Khanoom had brought to her bedside. Lili would close her eyes and imagine their velvety coats and their moist brown eyes. She thought about the littlest one, the one that had licked her fingers with its rough tongue and lifted its head to let her scratch under its chin. She wondered where Khanoom found the puppies and where they'd been taken after Lili had refused to let them nurse.

Kobra, meanwhile, could think of nothing but her own baby lying dead in the garden. She barely spoke anymore and had grown painfully thin. She spent the days huddled in her bed and the nights pacing the house with a curious vigor. She hadn't visited Lili in the hospital, not even for an hour, and when Lili returned to Avenue Moniriyeh with Sara she could not even look at the new baby without wishing desperately that she herself would die.

To temper Kobra's anguish, Khanoom and the others sequestered her in a corner of the house, far away from Lili and Sara. So successful were they in shielding Lili from Kobra's grief that Lili would always remember the weeks after the delivery as one of the happiest times of her life. She'd been gone for over a year, but she fell easily into the old rhythms and rituals of Khanoom's house. Lili listened eagerly to all the gossip and grew intimate with everyone's ailments, but most of all she let herself be tended. Everything was done for her—expertly and devotedly. There was always a pair of extra hands to hold and rock Sara, and in all that time Lili did not have to change a single diaper or even her own nightgown.

She spent entire days by the *korsi,* with heavy quilts and cushions heaped all around her. Khanoom sent her manservant to the bakery every morning and he'd return with two sheets of long, heavy flatbread, one slung over each shoulder. The bread was still warm when Khanoom dipped it into the cream for Lili and poured her glass after glass of cardamom-and-saffron-spiced milk. For lunch and dinner everyone gathered under the *korsi* and ate *ash* (soup) with noodles, ground beef, fresh chives, and thick creamy dollops of *kashk* (fermented whey), or else the enormous herb-and-chickpea meatballs that were Khanoom's other cold-weather specialty. "You must eat. You must grow strong again," Khanoom told Lili at every meal, and so she did.

"She has come! Sohrab's woman has come!"

Sometime before Sara's birth, Khanoom, fearing for Sohrab's soul, had demanded that he either formally marry Simin, his twice-divorced, blue-eyed mistress, or else put an end to the relationship. Sohrab responded by cutting off all contact from his family. The ensuing separation had lasted one year, in which time Khanoom seemed to age ten.

It was understood by all that Khanoom would not survive another such episode, but it was Simin herself who'd initiated the rapprochement with Sohrab's family. Every few weeks she invited Khanoom and Sohrab's sisters to her own house for a lavish lunch. They always returned full of praise for Simin's fava bean pilafs and her pomegranate-and-walnut stews, her well-appointed rooms and her artful entertaining, and when Simin mentioned that they should not hesitate to come to her for loans the clan grew fonder of her still.

And yet the speculations raged on. Had Sohrab officially married his woman? Performed a *siqeh*—a temporary marriage? Dispensed with all rites and formalities? When Simin appeared at Lili and Kazem's apartment to greet Lili and her new baby, the visit would add a new question to this long-running debate. Had Sohrab sent Simin as a gesture of respect or was her visit meant, rather, to establish his woman as beyond his family's reproach?

She was not pretty and she was not beautiful. Sohrab's woman, as they would always call her among themselves, was ravishing. Her glossy black hair fell long past her shoulders to the small of her back, her skin seemed completely poreless, and her eyes were an unearthly pale blue. The dress she wore—pale lavender with a row of tiny pearlescent buttons running from her throat to just above her waist—was a garment otherwise so plain that Khanoom herself might have worn it, except that it was exquisitely cut to reveal Simin's tiny waist and sumptuously rounded rear.

When Simin joined the gathering, Lili had for some time been seated on an expanse of cushions at the farthermost end of the room. She had taken more care than usual when dressing that morning, slipping on her prettiest peach-colored silk blouse, loosening her hair from its braid, and even running a bit of kohl along her eyes, but when her aunt announced Simin's arrival Lili was at once painfully self-conscious.

Lili tucked her bare feet quickly under the blanket and raised a hand to smooth the frizzy strands at her crown. When she looked up again, there, suddenly, was the blue-eyed woman who'd linked arms with Lili's father in a garden outside the city and bathed with her in the river lined with beech trees many summers ago. Lili had not seen her since that time, not even once, but now the lady had come just to visit her.

The moment seemed to call for her to rise, but she could not. Four weeks after the delivery of the baby, her stomach was still bound in the homemade girdle Khanoom had fashioned for her from long strips of muslin. Lili could scarcely breathe in this garment, and with Sara lying on her legs with her little head propped at her knees, she found it impossible to move.

"*Salaam, khanoom,*" she offered from the floor.

Simin bent down to brush her cheeks with two kisses. "*Salaam, dokhtar-joon.*"

Certainly it was fear of Sohrab that inspired the clan's ministrations toward Simin that day, but their attentiveness was just as much a surrender to the irrefutable proof of the woman's beauty, grace, and—though it was not a word they would so much as whisper or even let themselves think in connection with anyone but foreigners and prostitutes—*lavandee*. Sexiness. Simin was sexy. They felt it, they could not deny it, and it inspired them to do the one thing they knew best: to serve her.

Thick honey-soaked squares of *baqlava* were the first delicacy to be set before Sohrab's woman that afternoon. Next came the almond-stuffed dates, then the puff pastries clotted with fresh cream. They waited and watched. Simin's eyes did not so much as linger on any of it. "But *khanoom*!" they wailed, genuinely aggrieved. "You must at least try a small piece of the *baqlava*!" Simin made no answer but to smile faintly and take another sip of tea. Glasses of cherry sherbet, plates of fig compote, and bowls of saffron pudding came flying out of the kitchen in quick succession. But no matter what they set before her, Simin's lips would go nowhere but to the rim of her crystal teacup.

Having at last exhausted their offerings, the clan left Lili and Simin alone in the apartment and congregated in the courtyard to discuss their next move. What could Sohrab's woman possibly mean by her refusal to eat? Various explanations were put forth, but when someone suggested that it was only right that Simin would wish to preserve her splendid figure, all of them nodded in assent, and then even the ones who thought themselves beyond such vanities vowed to practice more restraint with respect to their own appetites—if not on this day, well, certainly the next.

"I congratulate you," Simin said to Lili as the clan's deliberations reached a close and the women began straggling back to the apartment. "You are a mother now."

Lili flinched. *A mother*—it was precisely this distinction of motherhood that had always governed her grandmother's and aunts' treatment of Kobra and Simin. However much Sohrab favored Simin, however they themselves had come to think her superior, the fact of her infertility could simply not be overcome. It was Kobra who was the mother of Sohrab's children and Simin who was not.

When, just a few short months later, Lili replayed the scene of their meeting again and again in her head, she would remember that there'd been an unmistakably cool tone to Simin's congratulations. But that Simin should resent not only Kobra's presence in Sohrab's life, however broken, but also hers and Nader's was something Lili had not considered before and would not consider that day. Indeed, at the time she had felt nothing so much as an overwhelming sense of gratitude for Simin's visit.

"*Merci*," Lili stammered. "Thank you, *khanoom-joon*."

Lili cried miserably on the day she returned with Sara to her own flat in the Bottom of the City, but her anguish would soon be overshadowed by news of Ma Mère's death and the attendant obligations of mourning. When Ma Mère died that year she was mourned for forty days and forty nights. An enormous framed photograph of her was mounted in the main parlor of the Khorrami compound and flanked by a pair of candelabra the height of trees. The photograph showed Ma Mère with a lovely smile that rendered her unrecognizable to Lili. It was an impression she chose to keep to herself throughout the mourning rites.

She'd only recently left Khanoom's house and returned to her own dingy apartment. When Lili was alone for the first time with Sara, the routines of motherhood baffled and thoroughly exhausted her. Now she was also expected daily at the Khorramis' compound to greet and attend the mourners, and there was nothing for it but to bundle her baby up and take her along for the task.

To Lili's surprise, Kazem's relatives, who'd so recently mocked her own family's fidelity to traditional wedding customs, now mourned with the sexes separated and the women veiled and grieving with all the ritualized abandon Lili had long associated with such occasions. The Khorrami women held silk fans to keep themselves from overheating, fainting, or both. Some threw themselves onto the floor, while many approached the point of collapse, only to be revived by handkerchiefs doused in valerian and rose water.

The arrival of every new visitor would inspire the others to recount in intimate detail how Ma Mère had passed into the next life. Though the lady had died suddenly of a heart attack and with little apparent suffering, the story of her death inspired the mourners to lash their chests and pull at their hair. One woman clawed her face deeply enough to leave tracks of blood along her cheeks. Through all of this, one lament was continually repeated, sometimes singly and sometimes by the whole party at once: "Why have you gone, why have you gone, why have you gone..."

Mourning in this fashion demanded constant refreshment. Dates, almonds, and halvah were thought particularly revitalizing, and in place of tea they drank the thickest, most bitter concoction of Turkish coffee. By afternoon, dozens of neighbors began drifting into the compound, accompanied by their own family members, friends, associates, and acquaintances. Night after night the servants were ordered to cook twelve pots of rice and twelve pots of stew. If this threatened to fall short of satisfying the crowd's appetite, they cooked a thirteenth pot of rice, spooned in another cup of tomato paste, and with that they fed every last person who came to mourn the matriarch.

When Lili had first returned to the apartment after Sara's birth, Kazem would begin shouting at her over some detail of housekeeping—a poorly prepared pot of rice or a dusty mantel—and when Sara began crying he'd shout at her, too. Lili didn't know how to make Sara stop crying and often she found herself crying along, too. But now, with Ma Mère's death, Kazem had fallen into a depression so deep and constant that he did not even seem to notice Lili or the baby. He spent whole days slumped in a chair in the corner of their apartment, his face in his hands, completely silent. It was to be the calmest interlude of their marriage, though it would end much differently.

That end came in summertime, on one of the many days of which it was commonly said that the sun could force open a flower bud by midday and fry its petals crisp by sunset. Lili had packed a bag with a change of clothes and towels and set off with Sara for the bathhouse. Bruises—faint now but still visible—ran along Lili's torso, arms, and legs. She knew she could try to bathe discreetly in the communal pools, winding a towel or two around herself to hide her bruises from the other bathers. Because the effort of this was great and ruined what was one of her few pleasures, she'd begun squirreling away a couple of *tomans* to hire a private stall once or twice a month. That was her plan on this particular day.

She took a number from the attendant and waited in the courtyard for her turn. Once inside the stall, she held her baby to her chest, closed her eyes, and let the warm water envelop them. She washed Sara first, all over her rounded belly and behind her ears and inside the folds of her thighs. When Sara was still a newborn, Lili had set her on a towel by her feet so that she could wash herself, but when at five months Sara began crawling she'd had to develop a new tactic for bathing. Tucking Sara under one arm, Lili lathered and scrubbed the opposite side of her body with her free hand, then switched the baby over to wash the other side. Between washing and rinsing herself like this she often caught her daughter's black eyes smiling up at her through the steam.

She'd timed her return home to coincide with sunset, the hour when the heat finally ceased to ripple off the streets and rooftops and the city came alive with the clap of thousands of shutters and grilles being thrown open. The streets, she'd always been told, were the source and stimulus for every last misery in this world, but on these walks after her weekly bath she had the simultaneous feeling of being lost and utterly at home there, and it was a feeling she'd come to love.

A few paces from the bathhouse she stopped to buy an ear of freshly grilled corn, pried the kernels loose, and fed them kernel by kernel to Sara from her hand. They pressed on, the crowds growing thicker all the time. After just a few blocks, Sara fell asleep. Lili decided to stop for a sherbet, cherry or melon flavor or both if she had the money for it. She ducked into a shady stairwell and as she sipped her treat Lili took in the crowds, the scents, and the rhythms of her city. A gramophone was playing an old folk song somewhere down the alley. She tapped her foot idly to the music, working out the tune in her head. She finished her sherbet, bought another, and then started for home.

At the entry to the house she stopped to straighten her veil. The stairs were uneven and cracked, and every few steps she held her hand to the wall to steady herself. When she reached the landing she felt around in her pocket for her key, but then she saw that the door to the apartment was wide open. She hesitated, straightened her veil again, and stepped inside.

Blood was streaming down Kazem's forehead, dripping onto his shirt and down onto the floor. He made no effort to wipe it away. *A burglar has attacked him*, was her first thought, but then she saw that he was holding a knife. He had done this to himself, she realized, had slashed his own forehead and cheeks with a kitchen knife. In her confusion and fear, her bag fell from her hands, spilling its contents at her feet. Trembling from head to foot, she bent down and scrambled to pick up the mess.

"Where have you been?" he shouted. At the sound of his voice Sara's eyes flew open and she began to cry.

"The baths," Lili stammered. "You know I go there every Friday afternoon—"

"But why have you come home so late? Where did you go afterward? Did you meet someone in the streets?"

She started to tell him that the *hammam* had been crowded, it was Friday after all, and she'd had to take a number, and then on the way back Sara had been hungry and she'd bought an ear of corn and stopped to feed it to her and then she'd been thirsty herself. With every word she spoke he only grew more agitated. His eyes flashed and he lunged toward her, but she ducked and flew down the stairs with Sara pressed against her chest.

Sara was howling now. Lili began rocking her, which only made her cry harder. A woman passed by, throwing Lili a look as if to say she should take better care of her child. Lili shifted Sara onto the other arm and realized she'd been holding her so hard that her own knuckles had turned white. She loosened her grip and gently ran two fingers along Sara's cheek to soothe her. Lili's heart was knocking against her chest. Where would she go? She'd left her pocketbook upstairs in the apartment. She'd have to walk all the way to Khanoom's house, and her legs, already weak from her long walk through the city, were now shaking with such force that she could barely stand.

She bit her lip and cursed herself for spending her money on snacks on the way back from the *hammam*, for staying out so long, for leaving her pocketbook in the apartment. He began calling her then, and his voice was so sweet, so very full of regret and longing, that for all the world he sounded like a lovelorn hero out of a fairy tale. "I'm all right now," he called from the window. "Come back," he called. "It's all right now."

That night as she ran a wet washcloth over his face and wrapped rags around the cuts, he pressed his head against her chest and for the first time in many months he had cried again. It was then, at that moment, that she understood if he was capable of hurting himself like this, neither she herself nor her own daughter would ever be safe, and more than anything that had happened so far in their marriage, it was this realization that frightened her.

*　*　*

Walking down Avenue Pahlavi on her way to the dentist that morning, she was worrying her loose tooth with a finger when a slight
breeze on her newly naked neck had brought on another of her
spells.

She'd had her hair bobbed to look just like an actress she'd seen in
a magazine at her in-laws' house. It suited her—even Khanoom had
told Lili so—but then sometimes, when Kazem was away at work
and she was alone in the apartment with Sara, she would get so lost
in her thoughts that she'd forget she'd had it cut. She'd raise a hand
to twirl her braids and, finding them gone, she'd panic. Sometimes
it was enough even to make her scream.

But this was more and more the way with her. Some of her senses
and faculties seemed to fall off completely, while others would never
be as keen. She was constantly forgetting things—silly things like
having had her hair cut, but also whether she'd fed Sara or visited to
the marketplace yet that week. She hardly heard Sara when she cried
anymore and could sit in one place for hours at a time, staring at the
wall or the floor, absent from everything around her, but then, all at
once, the faintest noise from the apartment above hers could set her
heart racing, her hands shaking.

And she had not wanted to visit the dentist. For several weeks
after Kazem had pushed her down the stairwell—landing her jaw-
first at the bottom of the stairs—she'd tried desperately to pry the
loose back tooth out with her fingers. It had not worked. The pain
had gradually become excruciating and she'd finally had no choice
but to borrow money from her aunt Zaynab to have the tooth pulled
out for her.

"We'll fix this for you straightaway, young lady," the dentist
assured her, smiling warmly from behind round-rimmed glasses.

His fresh white smock had put her immediately at ease, and she drew in a long, deep breath and closed her eyes.

He was halfway through the procedure when, suddenly, Lili remembered. *Sadisme.* She hadn't thought of it in many months, but here, finally, was her opportunity to find out what it meant.

She tugged at the hem of the dentist's smock. "Does it hurt so much?" he asked, pulling the tongs from her mouth.

Lili sat up in the chair and shook her head. "*Sadisme*, Mr. Doctor," she said, taking care to pronounce the word just as she'd heard it. "Is it a sickness?"

"Well, I suppose so, yes." He tapped a finger to his temple. "A kind of sickness here."

She considered this. "But does it go away?"

"I should say not," he answered. He narrowed his eyes at her. "But tell me, where would you have heard about something like that?"

"My husband...," she said absently. She had not meant to tell the dentist anything at all, but from the look in his eyes just then she realized he understood everything—about how her tooth had come loose and many more terrible things besides.

"Have you told your parents?" he asked quietly.

She shook her head. "No!" she cried, and sat up straight in the chair. It suddenly occurred to her that he might take it upon himself to contact Kazem—or, worse, her family. The prospect was so awful that she threw off her bib, grabbed her purse and her jacket, and scrambled out of the room.

"Your tooth!" the dentist called out after her. "Young lady, what about your tooth!"

By the time she'd made it back home, the tooth was loose enough to yank out on her own, but the pain had only increased tenfold.

"You go to a doctor and you come back like this?" Kazem chided her, pointing to her disheveled hair and her tear-swollen eyes. That time he shoved her against the wall, thrust his knee hard between her legs, and caught her throat in one hand and her wrist in the other. He began to tighten, then loosen, his grip, and she felt her legs sway and melt, her vision dissolve into a thick white haze, but suddenly and without another word, he let her go and she crumpled to the floor.

Then, in the middle of the night, he grabbed her by the shoulder and shook her awake. "I know you don't love me," he began. "Tell me you don't love me."

"Please, Kazem, just let me sleep—"

"You'll leave me," he continued. His voice was calm and nearly cheerful in the dark. "You'll marry a rich man. A handsome, very rich man." For some time Kazem was silent, but then he told her she should close her eyes and dream of her new husband because he'd kill her before she could even lay eyes on him.

In the hours that followed, Lili lay awake, thinking and crying by turn, and when dawn at last broke these were the things she knew:

She knew that Kazem was sick and that he would never be cured of his sickness. She knew that he could, and likely might, kill her—if not soon, then eventually. She did not know, but was relatively sure, that she did not want to die. She knew—with complete certainty— that she could do nothing on her own. She knew that Kobra had no means whatsoever of helping her, and that if she went to her grand- mother or her aunts they would only tell her that this was a woman's life, worse than some, yes, but not unlike many others. And, finally, Lili knew that the only person to whom she could now go for help was also the only person she feared more than her husband.

Sohrab would not help her.

"A fourteen-year-old girl with a baby wants to sit by my side?" He frowned and shook his head. "This is not possible."

Sohrab and Simin were sitting together in the garden when Lili arrived at her father's house. Earlier in the afternoon she'd managed

to leave Sara with Kazem's sister and taken a taxi to Sohrab's house
on upper Pahlavi. Twice Lili lost her nerve, setting off toward home
only to circle back and pace the sidewalk in front of his building
again. By the time she'd worked up the courage to pull off her veil
and bang the knocker, it was evening and the table set before Sohrab
and his woman on the terrace had been spread with gold-rimmed
English porcelain and goblets of red wine.

"But *pedar-joon*," Lili said, struggling to keep her voice even.
"Kazem, he..."

"He what?"

"He threw me down from the stairs. And this..." She opened her
mouth to show Sohrab the missing tooth.

Sohrab's frown deepened. "Why didn't you tell me about this
before?"

There was then a long silence in which she struggled to find her
voice and she cast her eyes down at the ground and tried, with a
desperate determination, not to cry. When she looked up again her
eyes skipped from Simin's red lips to the garnet brooch on her lapel
and then to her red fingernails. Simin raised a spoon to her mouth
and Lili's stomach gave a twist. She realized she hadn't eaten a single
thing all day.

"I can do nothing for you," Sohrab told her. His voice was not
unkind, but the words rang with unmistakable finality.

"But if you can do nothing, then..." And here she blurted out the
most terrible thing she could imagine. "Then I want to die!" She
began crying in earnest then—a messy, heaving, hiccuping cry—
and for a long time after her father left the garden and she lay crying
on the flagstones she still felt Simin's eyes on her.

Much later, when the scent of honeysuckle had grown so sweet that
the air seemed heavy with it, Lili turned her face to the house and

saw that all the windows were dark. She pulled herself up from the ground, clipped a sprig of flowers from the garden wall, and as she brushed her fingers along the still-warm stones she felt herself grow calm. She knew what she must do now. She would wait for her father to return, she would speak to him again, but this time she'd maintain her composure, she'd tell him everything, and she would convince him to help her.

She walked into the house and placed her veil in the small alcove by the door. Upstairs, she lay down on the bed in the spare room next to Sohrab's suite. She'd meant to close her eyes for only a few minutes, but she was so exhausted from all the hours pacing round Sohrab's house and then all her crying that she soon fell asleep.

Sometime after midnight the door to the room swung open and jolted her from sleep.

"I'm leaving now!" Simin called out. Lili rubbed her eyes and lifted herself onto her elbows. Simin was standing in the doorway. She'd draped her coat over her shoulders and was holding a thin leather pocketbook in front of her with both hands. Her lips, Lili saw, were freshly painted. "I'm worried about your father," Simin told her. "He hasn't come back to the house and I'm going out to find him."

Lili quickly smoothed her hair with her fingers, straightened her skirt, and followed Simin downstairs. The rooms were completely quiet and still. The servants had long since retired to their own quarters, and she and Simin were alone in Lili's father's house now.

"It's chilly at this time of night," Simin said when they'd reached the landing. It was true—the tiles felt ice-cold against Lili's bare feet. As Simin turned to leave, she nodded in the direction of Lili's veil. "You should cover yourself, you know."

Lili slid the latch and bolted the door. On her way back up the stairwell, she picked up her veil from the alcove, shook it loose, and then watched as a cigar box fell from its folds and landed with a soft thud by her feet. She bent down and examined it. It was crimson with black lettering. English, she thought, or maybe French. As a child she'd fetched boxes just like it for her father at parties, but this one felt strange in her hands.

She rubbed her eyes and felt inside for the contents. It was two large chunks of *taryak*, opium. This she recognized from her grandmother's house. Her aunts sometimes shaved a sliver from such rolls and placed it onto an aching tooth or swirled a bit into their tea to cure a headache. But these two pieces of opium were as thick as Lili's thumb, and, when she pressed them together, they were also nearly as long. How had the box found its way into her veil? Had one of the servants misplaced it before leaving the house? Puzzled, she folded her chador and returned it, and the box, to the alcove.

Half an hour later the doorbell woke her.

"I've come to check on you," Simin said brightly. "Are you feeling better now?" As she said this Simin's gaze fell toward Lili's veil. "But you haven't put on your chador to warm yourself!"

Lili shook her head. She returned to the alcove and pulled the opium from the cigar box. "Khanoom, I found this in my veil."

Simin's eyes widened. "But have you eaten any of it?"

"Eaten?" She shook her head. "But this isn't to eat."

"So you've had none of it?"

Again Lili shook her head.

"Look, I want to tell you something." Simin's voice was soft and gentle, and as she spoke she took both of Lili's hands in her own. "I want to tell you what to do so that you won't cry anymore. You see, it's just as well you found this," she said, touching a finger to the opium in Lili's palm. "It will help you sleep. When you wake, your father will be here, and he will help you. I promise."

"You'll speak to him for me?"

"Yes, of course, but you must go to sleep now. You must rest."

She brought a glass of water from the kitchen. For a moment Lili hesitated, but when she saw Simin smile and nod she placed the opium on her tongue.

"But it's so bitter!"

"Of course it's bitter. It's medicine, you silly girl!"

She swallowed the opium whole then, and to chase away the foul taste in her mouth she drained the water from the glass Simin held for her.

"Better?"

Lili nodded. "Yes, *khanoom-joon*."

She was, in the next few moments, intensely aware of Simin's closeness to her—the rise and fall of her breasts as she breathed, her lilac perfume, and under that a different, muskier smell. The pale blue of her eyes was barely visible in the darkness. A pleasant warmth swept through Lili's head and down to her chest. She smiled at Simin and moved to embrace her, but Simin drew herself up and turned to the door.

"But won't you stay, *khanoom*?"

"No, I need to find your father. You remember I've promised to talk with him for you?"

When Simin left the house for the second time that night, Lili thought this woman was nothing like the woman Kobra had cursed all these years. She was a good person, so kind and generous. The warmth in Lili's chest was already spreading down to her limbs when all at once a familiar ache shot through her breasts. She'd promised Kazem's sister she would come back for Sara. She'd be so hungry for her milk now, Lili thought as she stumbled across the hall to the telephone.

"Auntie Zaynab, I left the baby with Kazem's sister...." Her words were coming out slurred and thick and she had to hold her hand to the wall to steady herself as she spoke.

"But why do you sound like this, *bacheh*?"

"I ate opium; the lady, she said—"

"Opium?"

Before Lili could answer, the line went dead, and that was the last thing she would remember about that night.

Afterward it will seem as if she's traveled across the sea to a distant shore and then back again. She will hear Kobra shrieking and see her pulling at her hair and beating her chest with her fists. She will watch Nader staring down at her with his large, pensive eyes and Khanoom's fingers spread open and her palms raised up to the sky. Suddenly the women—two women? three?—begin slapping her face, but she doesn't understand why. They're wearing white uniforms and screaming, "Don't sleep! Don't sleep!" They slap her until her cheeks burn and flush and begin to bruise. They force milk into her mouth until she vomits. They pass a bottle of ether under her nose, hold down her arms and legs, and then they plunge a black rubber hose down her throat.

When she wakes it's so bright that she's screaming from the pain of opening her eyes to the light. "Don't sleep!" the women in the white uniforms shout, and begin slapping her again. Sometimes Sohrab is there, too, rubbing his chin, looking away from her, and she wants to tell him something, but he's slipping away again and she can't keep her eyes open.

Sleep. She wants, desperately, to sleep.

Suddenly they're slicing her skin with a thin blade whose edge catches the light like a wink. Two long plastic tubes are thrust into the veins of her left arm. Through heavy lids she sees them—two streams of red-black blood, one poisoned, one fresh. For the rest of her life, in Europe, in America, whenever she goes to the doctor for a shot or to have her blood pressure checked, the nurse's eyes will linger on the scars—two long white seams running along Lili's forearm. They will know that she once overdosed and she will turn her face away, refusing their looks and their questions.

When next she opens her eyes it is to the talk of money. A public hospital, a man is saying, very limited resources for such cases, already two thousand *tomans* for one transfusion, at least five thousand more for a second one, and still they cannot promise... And it's her mother who finally silences the doctor. "I'll get it, every last *toman* of it!" Kobra shouts as Lili descends once more into that strange sea.

They hadn't exchanged so much as a glance from across Lili's hospital bed, but Sohrab knew Kobra would come to his house for the money. That night he unlocked all the cabinets and drawers of his carved mahogany desk. When Kobra arrived at his house she found the bills and gold coins stacked in meticulous heaps for her. She stuffed the money into her pockets, her prayer shawl, even her stockings, and since it was dawn and there were no buses or taxis to drive her, she ran all the way back to the hospital with Sohrab's coins jingling in her pockets and his bills chafing against her skin.

More transfusions would be needed, Lili was weak and feverish, and progress was slow. Several weeks later, when the danger had finally passed, a nurse wheeled Lili away from the screaming and wailing of the drug ward and left her to rest outside in the shade of a flowering ash tree. It was nearly the end of summer, the last week of August. Kobra had gone back to Khanoom's house to cook Lili a proper meal, and though no one had expected it, sometime in the afternoon it began to rain.

At first it felt soothing and gentle against Lili's face and bare arms, and when a scent rose, sweet and fresh, from the grass, she drew deep breaths, filling herself as if with a blessing, as if with grace. Across town, Kobra looked out the window of her kitchen and saw the first drops of rain dotting the pavement outside. By the time she made it back to the hospital the sky was dark with clouds and the rain was falling hard and cold. After a frantic search, Kobra finally found Lili lying on a cot in the hospital's inner courtyard, soaked through to her hospital gown and shaking uncontrollably.

An orderly ran toward them, waving her hands and calling out apologies. Kobra flapped her arms like a crazy woman, screamed and cursed and wailed. Hearing this, Lili opened her eyes and smiled. Kobra unfurled her veil and spread it over the two of them like a tent and then, with her arms pressed like wings across Lili's body, they held each other under the rain and they cried.

For many days she would wake to the scent of wild rue and the sound of her father's rage.

"What am I to do with this child now?" Sohrab bellowed from the parlor of his house on upper Pahlavi.

Heavy shades were drawn against the light. Weeks of lying prostrate had weakened her limbs. Her voice, when she tried to speak, came out as a rasp. Her head ached terribly. Whenever she opened her eyes, Lili would see Kobra sitting cross-legged on the floor by her bed, rocking back and forth and working her prayer beads between her thumb and forefinger in endless rounds. Kobra would smile, just faintly, and then rise from the floor, hold a glass of water to Lili's lips, and press a cold compress to her forehead.

In the parlor, three doors down from the darkened room in which she and Kobra now spent their days, Lili's aunts and cousins and Sohrab's stepmothers were called forth one by one to account for their role in what was assumed to have been Lili's suicide attempt.

"How could you have allowed her to marry this man?"

"She wanted to marry...," one of Lili's cousins offered.

"She was so happy about the wedding...," Lili's aunt noted feebly.

"We knew nothing...," said another.

Sohrab cursed their ignorance, their piety, their cowardice, and one after another they bowed their heads, clasped his hands in their own, and begged for his forgiveness. He shook them off and cursed them anew. Between interrogations and indictments, Sohrab paced the halls, stormed through the rooms, and slammed every door in his path. "What am I to do with this child now?" he roared, and no one, not even Khanoom, dared answer him.

It's as if I've died after all, thought Lili from her bed.

Suicide, as she well knew, was the greatest conceivable sin against God. A hundred hells awaited those who took their own lives, and it was not at all uncommon for a family to disown relatives who'd attempted suicide. But Sohrab thought if he sent Lili back to Kazem she very likely would try to take her life again, and this time she might succeed.

Keeping Lili in the house posed its own quandary. As long as they were still married, Kazem could claim her back at any moment. Without any legal rights of her own, the only way Lili could divorce Kazem would be for Sohrab to petition for a divorce on her behalf. Yet if he chose this path, he would be releasing her from marriage only to condemn her to the life of a divorcée. In the minds of many, nothing distinguished a divorced woman from a prostitute. A wealthy woman in her circumstances—a woman like his own woman Simin had been—might hope to overcome such prejudices and eventually remarry, but Sohrab's finances, though much less precarious than in years past, still fell far short of what would be necessary to wash away the double taint of an attempted suicide and divorce.

While he considered what he could possibly do with Lili, Sohrab summarily realigned living arrangements. As the only member of the family who'd opposed Lili's marriage to Kazem, Kobra now became the only one to whom Sohrab entrusted her care. The result left the clan speechless. Kobra, who'd shuttled between her mother's house and her mother-in-law's for well over a decade, now moved into the home where Sohrab had until recently entertained Simin.

If not, exactly, the lady of the house, Kobra was now indisputably the mother of the house. It was a vindication of sorts, and it roused her at once from the grief that had claimed her in the year since Omid's death. She now whipped, steely-eyed, past her mother-in-law and sisters-in-law to single-handedly command Lili's sickbed. "It's the Evil Eye," Kobra intoned. "She's been struck by the Evil Eye." Kobra proceeded to burn wild rue by the hour. Nearly every time Lili opened her eyes in those weeks, she would find Kobra passing a little iron pot of cracking, smoking kernels above her head and singing,

> *Wild rue, wild rue, wild rue seeds,*
> *Hundred and thirty kernels of rue,*
> *All-knowing rue,*
> *Blind all jealous eyes.*

One day Kobra set down her pot of burning rue, sat at the edge of Lili's bed, and pulled off the amulet her own mother, Pargol, had tied around her neck when she was a baby. The black string had grown soft and frayed at the ends and there was a tiny crack the size of a pinprick on one side of the eye. It was the only piece of jewelry Kobra always wore, and certainly the most precious piece she owned, but she now slipped it over Lili's head. The little blue bead was still warm when it fell against her neck and Kobra leaned toward her and pressed her lips to Lili's cheek.

Sohrab's rages continued, but even when the scent of wild rue had suffused the sheets, the walls, and her very skin Lili would still tell no one who'd given her the opium.

When she returned from the hospital, no one, not even Sohrab, had wanted to upset her by asking her questions. Everyone assumed she'd meant to kill herself, and from then on her family treated her with that particular strain of deference reserved for the insane.

Much as she did not wish to be thought crazy, there was a usefulness in maintaining the fiction. During her convalescence Lili would find many reasons for withholding the truth from her family, the most compelling of which was that Sohrab would not have believed her. Had she named Simin, he would almost certainly have refused to help Lili at all, and if Kobra learned the truth, she would have dragged Simin through the streets by a hank of the woman's hair.

It was, therefore, to Sohrab's woman and to her own silence and secrecy that Lili owed her new life.

She was still very young, Sohrab counseled her when he'd finally found his bearings, just a little over fourteen years old. He would help her; he would petition for a divorce on her behalf. There might be talk, but she shouldn't worry about that for now, and in time those who knew might forget. She had to promise just one thing, and that was to leave her baby with the Khorramis.

For a while after Lili returned from the hospital, her aunt Zaynab had called on Kazem's mother and brought Sara to visit Lili every day or two. When she took Sara into her arms, Lili's milk would let down, forming two large, wet circles on her blouse. It seemed amazing, and strange, that her body should spring to life in this way. She was not to nurse Sara, however, as her blood was not yet free of the opium, and so Lili held a bottle to her lips instead and was relieved when Sara took it with no trouble.

Sometime during Lili's weeks in the hospital, Sara had learned to curl and squeeze her tiny fingers. Her hands were plump, with a deep indentation that ran like a bracelet all around her wrists. They'd sit together on the floor, Sara gripping Lili's finger as she played and then took her bottle and fell asleep. It was enough to make Lili sleepy, too, and she'd curl herself around Sara, drawing her close and dozing off to the scent of her hair and her skin.

But here the campaign began. Kobra, Khanoom, and every last member of the clan banded together to wage it. For Lili's own sake as well as the child's, she must leave Sara with Kazem's family. A child belongs to its father, they told Lili, and no woman who left her husband could contrive a different fate. "Do not even speak her name," they advised. "Not even to yourself." They themselves spoke of Sara now as "that child," "the girl," or some variant of these. They reminded Lili, none too gently, that she herself now had nothing apart from what her father allowed her.

"But Sara won't be safe with him!" Lili whimpered. "He'll hurt her, he'll—" They quickly shushed her. Kazem's mother, not Kazem himself, would raise Sara. Khorrami Khanoom was a good woman, kind and forbearing, and, unlike Kazem's grandmother Ma Mère, had always seemed to genuinely love "that little girl." Had Lili's own grandmother Khanoom not been more of a mother to her than Kobra? Well, then who better to care for Sara than her grandmother? And, what's more, Khorrami Khanoom ran a school of her own, and in just two years "the child" could join the children there.

It was then that a worrisome thing started to happen. Where Lili had once seen only her baby's round face and lovely black eyes, now she saw only Kazem. When Sara cried, her brow furrowed just like his, and Lili was sure her eyes were his, too.

Really, though, there was no choice, and therefore nothing to consider. One week her aunt Zaynab stopped bringing Sara to her and soon afterward Khanoom wrapped Lili's chest with long, thin strips of cotton to stop her milk, pulling them so taut that several times she caught her breath and cried out from pain. Gradually her milk dried up and the soreness in her chest began to ease, but for many weeks afterward her throat would feel so tight and raw that she could not speak for all her grief.

★　　★　　★

"Let her sit and wait until her hair turns as white as her teeth!"

When, after several weeks, Lili had still not returned to their apartment, Kazem refused to divorce her. Sohrab had consented to let him keep the bride money as well as all the items in her trousseau. He'd even hinted that Kazem could expect even more money on top of that. Still Kazem refused. "Let her sit and wait until her hair turns as white as her teeth!" was his reported reply to the divorce petition.

But Kazem's willfulness was no match for her father's, nor for Sohrab's unique resources. Over the years Sohrab had collected a wide assortment of friends and acquaintances, and among the men with whom he regularly gambled and drank were a number of the city's most prominent government figures. In the end it was no less than a top-level minister who was dispatched to procure Lili's divorce. Though this gentleman began his appeal respectfully enough, he proceeded quickly to issue threats. "You'll find yourself squatting in the middle of the Sahara," Kazem was told, "with nothing but a hollow reed to air out your misery." The exchange ended with curses on both sides, but not, finally, without Kazem's concession.

Then one day the summons arrived.

It was the first time Lili had left the house since returning from the hospital. Her hair, so smartly bobbed just weeks before, had grown scraggly and uneven. On the day the summons arrived, Khanoom trimmed it for her and combed it until it crackled and shone. Lili pulled on one of Kobra's skirt suits, slipped on a pair of her round-toed heels, and then she and one of her aunts walked to the court-house arm in arm.

It was autumn by then, the season of pomegranates and quince. There was a hint of cold in the air as Lili made her way up Avenue

Pahlavi. The leaves of the plane trees had turned golden and had begun fluttering down to the sidewalks. In the distance she could make out the brown peaks of Mount Damavand rising above the city. Soon the whole of Tehran—from the mountains to the rooftops to the streets and the alleyways—would be brushed over with snow. There was a chance Sohrab would let Lili return to school after the winter holidays, and there she might once again be just a girl among many others.

The clerk, a portly, mustachioed fellow with heavy-lidded eyes, removed his glasses, peered into her face, and asked her—repeatedly—if she was certain she understood the meaning of the petition. "Divorce," he intoned, "is a most serious matter. The most serious, in fact. Are you certain you wish to proceed, young lady?" Each time she nodded her head a firm yes, but he'd asked her again and again. Finally, though, the clerk returned his glasses to his face and, after a last deep sigh, he slid his pen to her side of the desk. With a slow and certain hand, Lili signed her name, and with that she was at last free.

Four

In Sohrab's House

"I had nothing, I was no one. A divorcée was considered no better than a prostitute back then. But he made something of me, my father, and that would be the second miracle of my life."

B Y THE MIDDLE OF the century rich *Tehroonis* had already begun their exodus to the north, toward Mount Damavand, where the air was more pure and more temperate and land was still plentiful, and from the day he first left his mother's house on Avenue Moniri-yeh, Sohrab had followed their lead. Edging farther and farther up Avenue Pahlavi, he'd sought out a series of increasingly smart living quarters for himself. The same exacting eye that had served him so well in his work appraising Persian carpets he also turned to the decoration of his own surroundings, with the result that every room he called his own boasted gold-footed banquettes, lacquered coffee tables, velvet drapes, and the very finest silk carpets piled three and four deep. Sohrab was also most particular about keeping up with the latest technical innovations to come to Iran. Each new apart-ment or house he rented boasted another set of wonders—running water, electricity, a phone line, and so on.

Yet Sohrab had divided the rooms of his grand house on Avenue Pahlavi in a manner that would have been familiar to his father, grandfathers, and great-grandfathers. One wing, which older gen-erations would have called the *andarooni*, or inside of the house, he turned over to Kobra, Lili, and Nader; the other, the onetime *birooni*, or outside, he kept for himself. Like patriarchs of old, he was the only one free to move between the two quarters, and on Ali, his wiry, aged manservant, he now conferred one additional responsibility: to keep close watch over the comings and goings in the other half of the house.

Meanwhile, in his own quarters Sohrab continued to entertain his friends and associates in the manner to which they'd long been accustomed. The men passed the evenings drinking *araq*, smoking cigars, and playing cards and backgammon. If his woman (or any other women, for that matter) came to visit Sohrab in his rooms, the other members of the house certainly never bore witness to it. And as for Kobra, the only time Sohrab suffered her presence in his private quarters was when she went there to drop off a bowl of dill-and-cucumber yogurt or the garlicky eggplant dip so popular among his guests.

But that spring Kobra ruled every last corner of Sohrab's house. In the final weeks of winter every window and door was thrown open at her command. She disassembled the *korsi*, washed all the quilts and cushions, hung them to dry in the courtyard, and then removed them to the basement. She hauled the furniture outside, gave every piece a thorough dusting, and commenced to rub them all with linseed oil. She rolled up the carpets and curtains and beat them with a broom until they yielded their last specks of dirt. She scrubbed the ceilings, then the walls, then the floors. She polished all the dishes and bowls and spoons in the house. She soaked lentils, set them in the sun, and sprinkled water over them until they sprouted green shoots. She laundered every last item of clothing the family owned, and when she strung the clothes outside to dry she knotted them together to bring everyone closer together in the coming year.

With one week to go before No Rooz, the Persian New Year, Kobra set up a huge vat in the courtyard for the *samanoo*, a dense, sugary paste made from germinated wheat, and everyone, even Sohrab and all the male relatives who passed through the house, could be counted on to give it a stir, because they knew it would bring good luck in the new year. Then, on the day before the new year, she laid the *sofreh* with the seven *seens*—the seven totems of spring—a Koran, and a bowl of plump goldfish with a tangerine bobbing above their heads. She trekked to the bazaar for the choicest chickpea cookies and the most fragrant pomegranates and oranges. She sent Nader and Lili to the baths with horsehair mitts to scrub their bodies and bowls of vinegar to rinse their hair. She dunked strips of whitefish in a batter of egg yolks and saffron and fried them up along with two gigantic platters' worth of spinach pancakes. She pinched her *dolmehs* tight and stacked them neat and even.

And only when every room of the house smelled of ammonia and hyacinth and a plate of thick, amber *samanoo* was placed on the *sofreh* alongside a lush swatch of greens did she settle down and wait for the earth to make its way round the sun so that the new year could begin.

It was then, in springtime, that the *kolis*—the Gypsy girls—came down from the mountains to the city with their arms full of branches from the mulberry trees. They had coal black eyes and hennaed hands. Silver flashed at their throats, their wrists, and their ankles. Their plaits swung out from under their bright, patterned kerchiefs and their long, flounced skirts skimmed the ground as they walked. Their feet were always bare. And though they came to sell their mulberries, there was always a sweet-tongued Gypsy among them to trade a story or a fortune-telling for a silver plate or a bolt of pretty cloth.

Every spring Lili's grandmother Khanoom went down to the street to greet the *kolis* and then carefully pick out the branches with the greatest quantity of mulberries. *Shahtoot*, they were called—king's berries. It had been Lili's job as a girl to pluck them from the branches, drop them into her grandmother's pot, and carry them to the court-yard when she was finished. Crimson with halos of pink near their stems, the *shahtoot* berries always reached up to the top of Khanoom's biggest cooking pot. She'd watch as her grandmother rinsed them under water from the fountain in the courtyard. Then together Lili and Khanoom would grab fistfuls of *shahtoot* and scatter them onto large aluminum sheets. After a day or two outside, the sun would call up all their sweetness and then, finally, they would be ready to eat.

Having missed the *kolis* the last time they came to the city, Lili was the first to greet them this year.

As he had been raised by a passel of illiterate women and bound to another by marriage, nothing aggravated Sohrab as much as an igno-rant female. However carefully he'd guarded her as a girl, on the matter of Lili's education he'd always been the most forward think-ing of fathers; the continuation of her studies had, in fact, been the sole condition he'd extended for her marriage.

And yet, after her divorce, Sohrab refused to allow Lili to return to school. With her expulsion from the School of Virtue still fresh in his mind, he thought it unlikely that a private school would take her. The city's public schools, where one teacher was often entrusted with as many as fifty students, he would not even consider. But beyond such practical considerations was another, far more press-ing worry. A divorcée, it was said, surrendered to seduction as eas-ily as a ripe peach slid down the throat. Sohrab predicted that any young man who discovered Lili's status would make advances on her—or much worse—and since she was no longer a virgin there would be no recourse for such actions. The only way to protect Lili now would be to keep her at home.

"Why trouble yourself with school?" Lili's aunts and grand-mother asked her. "You'll be wiping another bottom soon enough!"

This was the height of optimism, but even if they could manage to find her a suitor, nothing made Lili more miserable than the thought of marriage. One by one her female cousins were leaving school to marry or else help their families by working in the house. The young brides among them sidled up to her with wide grins and steadily rounding bellies. "You'll marry again," they, too, assured her, and proceeded to recommend that she take up some practical skill such as embroidery or else take a turn holding one of their newborns.

Sulking, Lili refused to take up so much as a single needle. To live in her father's house, to go only where he allowed, she would never dare question. But she was her father's daughter and she could not stand to become one of the ignorant females he scorned. It also did not help that at family gatherings her male cousins had taken to quizzing each other with obscure questions about calculus, physics, and chemistry—subjects she had never even studied. Before her marriage she had been just as clever as the boys, but now, having fallen nearly three grades behind in school, she could only listen mutely as they tried to outwit one another.

Most humbling of all, her favorite cousin, Sina, the most brilliant of all her male cousins, was now studying to become a doctor. He was only a first-year medical student, and yet everyone, even Sohrab himself, had already taken to calling him Mr. Doctor. Lavished with the respect usually reserved for family elders, Mr. Doctor was consulted on everything from the purchase of a new radio to the proper method for removing algae from the *hoz*.

Then why not, thought Lili to herself one day, put Sina to work on her behalf? After several desperate entreaties she managed to convince her cousin to take up the cause of her education. "Impossible," Sohrab replied whenever Sina broached the topic, yet Mr. Doctor's appeals—polite, logical, and undertaken with the greatest consideration of Sohrab's vanities and prejudices—would continue for many weeks.

$\star$ $\star$ $\star$

In the meantime, the world was splitting open. The whole city had poured into Avenue Pahlavi. The shah sent his soldiers marching through the streets of Tehran, pounding drums and blasting pistols into the air as they swept across the city. Gigantic posters of His Majesty Mohammad Reza Pahlavi were held aloft while hand-printed leaflets denouncing him littered the pavements. Men clambered onto the roofs of cars. "Down with the monarchy!" shouted one contingent. "Down with Mossadegh!" shot back the other. Armored tanks barreled down the streets; lampposts announced the names of those to be hanged there the following day. Children broke loose from their mothers' hands and were instantly swallowed up by the crowds. Husbands and uncles and cousins disappeared just as suddenly; unlike the children, they rarely turned up again, and the few who did resurface after many months came back haggard, silent, and hollow eyed.

By summer's end five thousand would be dead in the streets or behind prison walls.

For this latest crisis it was Sohrab's house that served as a refuge for the entire clan. During the days, the men ventured out of the house—either to work where work was still possible or else to take part in the demonstrations—while the women stayed behind to mind the children and nurse their rattled nerves with prayer. What, Lili asked, was happening in the streets? And why couldn't they go outside? Khanoom, Kobra, and Lili's aunts, one as illiterate as the next, were no help at all explaining the turmoil that had overtaken the country, and every night the men of the family, wishing to stave off the women's hysteria, retreated to their own quarters to listen to Sohrab's Philips radio and kept the details of the coup to themselves.

Had they been inclined to share the news with the female population of the house, Lili might have learned that she was living atop an ocean of oil—not the type of oil she associated with cooking and lanterns, but the kind that fueled her father's American-built automobiles. She might have learned that while Iranians had lived on this ocean of oil for thousands of years, it was the British who first plunged a pipeline into it in the early 1900s. She might also have learned that for several decades Iranians had enjoyed scant revenue from their oil reserves but that two years earlier, in 1951, Iran's democratically elected prime minister, Mohammad Mossadegh, had finally nationalized the country's oil. And, finally and most critically, she might have discovered that the chaos in the streets had been started as part of an effort to force the country's oil revenues westward again.

But what not even the men of the clan knew was that while it was on account of oil that their world was splitting open, in the summer of 1953 it was being split by a different hand. "The British," everyone sniffed, and shook their heads at the young shah who'd been reinstalled onto the Peacock Throne after Mossadegh's ouster. In fact, though details of "Operation Ajax" would remain sealed away for nearly fifty more years, the coup had been financed with American dollars and carried out by the CIA.

In any case, Lili, newly divorced and still in exile from school, was simply told that the chaos tearing through the country was nothing that concerned her, and so for her the coup of 1953 meant nothing so much as a complete retreat back into the house and to hunger and her grandmother's ingenious strategies for appeasing it with gigantic pots of *ab goosht*.

Khanoom began boiling the lamb for the soup at sunrise. After it had simmered for several hours, she checked to make sure the lamb had softened and slid from the bone and then she added an onion, a tomato, and a cup or two of beans. If anyone wandered into the kitchen before dinnertime, Khanoom handed them a slice of flatbread and a few slivers of pickled onion and warned them to steer clear of her pot.

When the curfew fell over the city and the men turned back into the house, Khanoom at last hauled her soup from the kitchen to the parlor. They commenced by drinking the broth—lemon tinged, with an inch of fat glistening at the top—and once they'd had their fill, they took long draughts of water from a communal bowl, sat back against the cushions, and began nursing their bloated stomachs. Khanoom returned to the kitchen to pound out the remaining lamb and beans into a thick paste. On her return, all hands flew straight back into the pot to scoop up the tasty concoction with sheets of stale bread. When everything had been cleared away and the men had retreated to their own quarters, Khanoom poured the tea and everyone stretched out on the floor and told stories and traded memories as a chorus of bullets, sirens, and screams pierced through all the windows of Sohrab's house.

By the time the coup ended, Lili's hair had grown long enough to braid into pigtails again. Mr. Doctor had finally succeeded in his appeals on her behalf, and these pigtails would be instrumental to the plan he and Sohrab formulated for her; they lent her the virginal look necessary for enrolling her in a new private school. The rest of the plan went like this: If he could not restore her to the status of a respectable woman, then Sohrab would make her into something else entirely, something hitherto unknown in their entire extended family, an educated woman, a professional woman. She might never again marry, but Sohrab was certain that a high school diploma, followed by some kind of occupational training, would shield her from the curses and insults that would trail a divorcée through the rest of her life.

But first he would have to bring her up to grade level. To this end, Sohrab enrolled Lili in not one but two schools, a regular day school—the School of Ambition—and also a remedial night school, both situated clear across the city, where she was unlikely to meet any-one she knew. Lili's free hours were immediately given over to being tutored and studying. No cousin, no matter how distant, was spared a role in the effort. Mohammad, Mohsein, Hamid, and even Sina—Mr. Doctor himself—were called to her side, frequently all appearing at Sohrab's house on the same day. Over the next few years they would take turns tutoring her in everything from algebra and chemistry to French and English. As a reward, the cousins were given generous allowances to fritter away as they pleased, a gesture that would endear to them the uncle they might otherwise have remembered as the one who could set their knees quivering with a single sideways glance.

It did not end there. Sohrab sent his nephews to scour the city's bookstores for every last European novel—all the French and English classics he himself had never read but that had always seemed to him an indispensable part of a truly educated person's repertoire. He ordered her to read them all. In the beginning Lili understood two words out of every ten she read, but she was so determined not to disappoint her father that she traveled everywhere with one or more tomes tucked under one arm and a gigantic dictionary under the other. Very slowly the two words out of ten grew into three and then five and then seven out of ten, and reading, once a burden and a chore, turned into a favorite pastime. She even became devoted to certain authors—Balzac and Dickens were her particular favorites—and she wept at the heroes' every tribulation and cheered at their every triumph.

Nader, though unclear on the reasons for Lili's divorce and hospital stay, was nonetheless grateful to have her back home. He quickly devised his own plan for rehabilitating her. His first project was to teach Lili how to ride a bicycle. Since she was now forbid-den from leaving the house, even to visit her aunts or grandmother, these lessons always took place in the garden. Lili spent many afternoons looping around and around the large tiled pool while

Nader trotted alongside the bike, holding the handlebars for her as she pedaled. When she made it all the way around the pool by herself the first time, Nader clapped and cheered for her. Lili looked up from the handlebars, smiled at her brother, and then sailed straight into the water. Nader dived in behind her, untangled her legs from the pedals, and brought her, gasping, then laughing, back up to the air.

The bicycling lessons were abandoned, but soon afterward Nader presented her with a notebook, a fountain pen, and three little glass vials of ink—red, blue, and black. At first the pen felt heavy and strange between her fingers—nearly two years had passed since she'd written a single line—but very quickly her hand eased back into her old penmanship. With one notebook and three vials of ink her brother had given her opportunity to let loose all the words inside her, and she filled page after page. Regular entries were recorded in either blue or black ink, and with the red ink she began writing poetry dedicated to Sara in the manner of Hāfez.

"Do you want to hear one of my compositions?" she asked Sohrab one Thursday afternoon.

"Read," he told her, and then he leaned back in his chair, laced his fingers over his chest, and closed his eyes.

"My days are dark, and deep, and full of you...," she declaimed. The poem went on in this vein for some time, and when she came to the end Sohrab opened his eyes and frowned.

Generations of Iranian poets had emulated the rhyming couplets of Hāfez's *qazal*; the crafting of desire and desperation along these lines was, in fact, nothing short of a national pastime. Lili's poem was a passable imitation of the master's, though likely the first time an aspiring poet had installed her infant in place of the Immortal Beloved.

The innovation did not please Sohrab.

"Get dressed," he told Lili, drawing himself up from his chair. "We're going out."

But when she pulled on her coat and presented herself to him, Sohrab frowned again.

"Have you nothing better?" he asked, pinching the worn collar of her cotton coat.

She shook her head. "No, *pedar-joon*."

"Lalehzar," he ordered his driver, indicating a high-end shopping district in the area.

That first Thursday Sohrab took her to a fancy dress shop where the ladies smiled sweetly at her and then flashed their pretty eyes at him, and there he bought her a sweeping mohair coat with a black velvet collar and matching velvet belt. The purchase occasioned many others—a wide-rimmed felt hat and strappy black shoes to go with the mohair coat, a dress to wear with the shoes, and seamed stockings to complete the outfit—so that by the end of the day she'd acquired a splendid ensemble she was allowed to wear only on her weekly outings in the city with her father.

From then on Thursdays meant strolls down Avenue of the Tulip Fields and Ferdowsi Square. Thursdays were the sunken garden at Café Naderi, where couples waltzed to a full band in the early-evening hours. Thursdays were *café glacé* at Yas with heaps of whipped cream and long, slender spoons. Thursdays were The Golden Rooster, where white-gloved waiters bowed and fluttered around their table proffering French champagne, fizzy lemonades that arrived in the bottle so as to show off their European provenance, and tender, bloody hunks of filet mignon for which she was shown the proper angle to hold her knife and fork. Thursdays were concerts in the Hall of Culture, where Sohrab taught her to sit with her ankles crossed under her seat and to clap her hands for elegant intervals. Thursdays were every fine habit, air, and affectation that her father had acquired and cultivated in his many years away from his family and that she now learned happily at his side.

When Sohrab finally enrolled Lili at the School of Ambition, she was on strict orders to tell no one there about her marriage or her child. Any breach, Sohrab warned her, even a single girlish confidence, and he'd send her straight back to Kazem and have nothing else to do with her. Terrified, Lili pulled on her new seventh-grade uniform—a white blouse, a pleated navy blue skirt, and a narrow silk necktie—and made a silent vow not to talk to anyone about her marriage, her child, or anything at all.

For several weeks she sat by herself in a far corner of the schoolyard during recess, watching the older girls play volleyball. They wore shorts, high-top sneakers, and lace-trimmed bobby socks. Many of the girls used their neckties to pull their hair back into ponytails, and a few even rolled up their sleeves to show off their muscles. From her first day at the School of Ambition, Lili was captivated by these older girls. Their playfulness and confidence awed her. They longed, surely, for marriage, or at least for the liberties they associated with marriage—to pluck their eyebrows, wear lipstick, dress in women's clothes, and go wherever they pleased—just as she had once longed to do. But the girls at the School of Ambition would offer Lili her first glimpse of another kind of life. She knew that if her classmates did not, in fact, marry first, the very clever ones among them would become nurses, secretaries, and teachers, though every year one or two exceptional girls might even enter medical school. Would they be called Madame Doctor? Lili was not sure, but it thrilled her to think so.

Meanwhile, in the afternoons, after a hasty lunch at home, she found herself among dozens of girls who'd been held back by tradition, financial hardship, laziness, or some other incapacity. In Lili's

remedial classes it was not uncommon to see a girl of eighteen holding up a fourth-grade reading primer, her face either screwed up in
concentration or completely slack with incomprehension, but even
here, as at the School of Ambition, Lili kept up her vow of silence.
There were no volleyball games to distract her, and so to relieve the
torture of silence she began singing to herself. She favored the soul-
ful Delkash songs that streamed from every radio in the country in
those days—tunes she could reproduce with uncanny vocal likeness
and perfectly genuine tears.

Her talents did not go unnoticed. Not so long ago, her emerald
engagement ring had drawn classmates at the School of Virtue to
her side, but now the girls at her remedial school slid beside her, one
at a time and then in pairs and eventually as a small crowd, in order
to hear her sing. They cupped their hands under their chins, closed
their eyes, and, completely absorbed in their own tribulations and
passions, listened to her sing until the bell rang. Finally, after many
days, one of them, a skinny olive-skinned girl called Mina, asked
Lili if she was sad on account of having fallen in love with a boy, and
this had seemed so preposterous to her that Lili broke into a violent
fit of giggles, shocking and silencing them all.

With Lili back in school, Kobra once again dedicated herself to
the care of Sohrab's appetites and vanities and, somewhat more discreetly, to the enlargement of her own estate.

At dawn each morning a plump, sprightly young hen was pulled
out of the chicken coop, butchered, plucked, and boiled to make
a fresh cup of broth for his breakfast. Sohrab tossed it back in one
gulp, wiped his mouth with the napkin Kobra held out for him,
and then passed the empty glass back to her. As soon as he set out
from the house, she headed straightaway for the kitchen to cook him
a fragrant stew and saffron-soaked crisped rice. Though Kobra no

longer sought out the city's back-alley spiritualists and had ceased to sprinkle love potions about the windows and doors, she still kept her pots warm late into the night, and, increasingly, she also held her tongue on the nights when Sohrab did not return to the house until morning.

And slowly, in the course of her housekeeping, Kobra became a landowner.

Sohrab had long been in the habit of kicking off his slacks and tossing his jacket onto the floor before falling into his bed. As Kobra made her rounds through his quarters in the mornings, she would come across his suits lying about in heaps. She'd pick them up, shake them gingerly to loosen the wrinkles, and then she would dig into the pockets of his trousers and jackets for change. With the clothes draped over her arm, she hustled back to the other end of the house, tucked the coins and bills into a chest of drawers, locked the chest, wrapped the key in a kerchief, then locked that key in a second chest of drawers, and proceeded, finally, to launder and iron Sohrab's suits by hand.

As soon as the bills and coins threatened to outgrow their hiding place, Kobra threw on her veil, boarded a bus, and struck out for the countryside. While real estate was once the province of the very few, the future, most wealthy Iranians now thought, pointed toward the capital. As a result, in the last few decades ancestral lands the length and breadth of the nation had been parceled out into cheap plots. These plots were where Kobra now set her sights for her own future. With the first thousand *tomans* Kobra collected from Sohrab's pockets she bought herself a scrubby single acre in Youssefabad. With the next two thousand *tomans* she bought three acres of wild yellow grass on the road to Karaj. She would eventually turn over both these parcels, followed by several others. The deeds to her lands, and the profits from her sales, she would continue to deposit into one of several hiding places within hiding places in Sohrab's house.

Kobra's real estate transactions were undertaken without counsel or intermediary of any kind. Unlettered, she simply pressed her inky thumbprint on the line allotted for her signature. She told no one of her schemes, and certainly nothing of her modest though growing fortunes, but never before had she tackled the laundry with such devotion.

Sohrab, wholly ignorant of Kobra's rapaciousness, continued to prefer her labors to any French-style dry cleaner in the city, but he was busy drawing up schemes of his own. In these years any Iranian family who could afford it, and plenty more who could not, were sending their sons away to be educated in the West. The practice had its origins in the nineteenth century, when the Qajars began sending their princes to Europe. With that dynasty long since dismantled and the current one waffling between foreign dictates, in the 1950s a young man's surest path to advancement in Iran was to acquire Western credentials. At the time, the "West" was defined almost exclusively as England, France, and Germany and the only worthy credentials were thought to be in the fields of medicine and engineering.

Having settled on his son's future profession, engineering, Sohrab considered to which of these three countries to send fourteen-year-old Nader. The English, though elegant, were dismissed as ruthless imperialists; the French, even more elegant than the English, Sohrab imagined as heirs to temptations unfitting for a teenage boy. Of the Germans Sohrab knew little apart from the two points his gambling cohorts had impressed upon him: first, that the Germans had done remarkable work toward rebuilding their country after two wars and, second, that their university fees were considerably lower than those charged by the English and the French.

Germany it would therefore be.

For several weeks Nader himself wandered through the house looking alternately stupefied and euphoric. Khanoom, Kobra, and the other female members of the clan wailed and clutched their chests and tore at their clothes, but their agony failed to dissuade Sohrab from his decision. As the date of Nader's departure approached, Sohrab brought Nader three silk carpets to sell abroad. On Nader's last day in Iran, Sohrab slid off his most prized possession, a diamond of a thousand facets that he'd had mounted for himself onto a thick gold band, and gave it to his son as a keepsake.

No one in their family had yet gone to the *farang*, that place beyond the seven rivers, the seven mountains, and the seven oceans. For her part, until this moment Lili had conceived of Europe only in terms of the cinema and certain highly prized objects, brassieres and chocolate truffles being the chief of these, and the images proffered by the *Shahreh Farang* Man, the European City Man. Every year at the Persian New Year, Lili and her cousins lined up at the bazaar to peer through the European City Man's copper nickelodeon. Big Ben, the Palace of Versailles, and the Luxembourg Gardens—there they were in their glory, and all at just a few coins a peek! The images had long since inspired a deep and nameless longing in her, yet now, as she ironed her little brother's best suit in preparation for his departure for this wondrous place, Lili found herself choked with grief. To ease her own misery, she fed Nader as if he were a man going to war. By the time he set off for Germany, his cheeks had filled out and he'd even acquired a small paunch.

As soon as he left, she and Kobra locked the door to Nader's room, lay down side by side on his bed, and cried with the fervor of two young widows.

It was all very well, Kobra thought, that Sohrab had sent Lili back to school, but she now had a program of her own, and it was guided by a single principle: everything that Sohrab now refused Lili, Kobra was determined to give her. What Kobra lacked in material resources, she made up for with a combination of innate cleverness and hard-won guile. When Lili admired a short plaid jumper in a foreign fashion magazine, Kobra hunted down what was surely the only bolt of Scottish tartan in the whole of Tehran, traded one of her golden bangles for it, ordered Lili to sketch the garment for her, and then sewed an exact replica. When Lili asked for lace-trimmed anklets just like the older girls at the School of Ambition all wore, Kobra sacrificed her best nightdress and used its lace to decorate seven pairs of plain white socks. And when Lili's new girlfriend Mina invited her to a party, Kobra packed herself and Lili each a bag, announced that they were off to visit her own mother, Pargol, and then secretly sent Lili along to Mina's house with a ten-year-old male cousin as a chaperone.

That night a dozen Iranian girls would rumba and tango together in wide skirts and curled bangs. There was a tray of little round cakes slathered with a dense, sugary paste. "Cupcakes," Mina explained, licking the pink icing and offering her one. Lili took a bite and thought she'd swoon from the pleasure. She ate three cupcakes, one after the other, and she had just reached for her fourth when Mina took her hand to give her a private tour of her bedroom.

Together they admired Mina's bed with its rose-print coverlet and matching cushions, her closetful of party dresses and pleated skirts, and her collection of three pale pink lipsticks. "My auntie's been to Paris," Mina explained of this last, and most impressive, of her treasures. On their way back to the parlor, Mina paused at a half-open door at the end of the hallway. Lili caught sight of a tall, fair-haired young man fumbling with a screwdriver and a shortwave radio. He looked from his sister to her and then gave Lili a slow, crooked smile. "My brother Farhad," Mina noted, adding, "He's going to America."

America! That, Lili thought, was *yengeh donya*, the other side of the earth—and much, much farther than even her own brother's travels.

"But are you *really* going there?" she asked.

He nodded. "I'm leaving in the fall," he said, his smile breaking wide open. "And when I get there I'm going to shave my head just like Yul Brynner."

Before he left Iran, Mina's older brother Farhad sent her a dozen letters, which Kobra made Lili read to her aloud first but had the courtesy of letting her keep afterward. In the most beautiful hand-writing she'd ever seen, Farhad promised they could marry just as soon as he returned from America. Such declarations of love were not altogether uncommon in those years, but Farhad's had been especially quick. On the pretense of chaperoning his sister home, he also began to appear by the gates of Lili's school to chat with her some afternoons. Once he'd even brought her a red-black rose, a genuine rarity that revealed itself as purple only when Kobra plucked one of its petals and held it to the light, and from then on Kobra had to bribe Sohrab's driver to keep news of the romance to himself.

For Lili, the hastiness of Farhad's proposal was completely over-shadowed by the impossibility of his plan. His parents would never accept her, a divorcée. It was not just beyond hoping; it was beyond imagining. Lili could not bear to tell him so herself, and so she'd been forced to confess to Mina that she'd been married and had a child. "Please tell him he mustn't write me any more letters," she begged Mina. "And please, please tell no one else what I've told you!"

After that Mina had not asked Lili to her house again, and she could not even meet Lili's eye in the hallways at school. But the letters still came for many months after Farhad left Iran—beautiful, strange letters about how the air in Los Angeles smelled of oranges and dust and the ocean there was so blue that it melted into the sky. For her birthday that year—her sixteenth—he sent her a Parker pen, the top half of it gold and the bottom half turquoise, along with a Polaroid of himself. He was standing outside his college dormitory in a striped sweater and he'd shaved his head just like Yul Brynner.

"He's asked for a picture of you," Kobra noted when Lili finished reading the letter to her.

"I know," she answered sadly.

It was, they both knew, a hopeless request.

Somewhere in Sohrab's private quarters there were a dozen framed pictures of him in profile and full face, standing and sitting, black hair slick and shiny and his suits always impeccably pressed. But however much it pleased him to commission portraits of himself, when it came to his women Sohrab thought the practice too costly. It would only encourage their vanities, and, most damningly, it would subject them to a photographer's groping hands and lascivious gaze.

"We'll go to Avenue Shah Reza," Kobra whispered.

She grabbed twenty *tomans* from her cache, and then she and Lili draped themselves in veils and set out for a photography studio.

The picture, which came out beautiful, was slipped between the pages of Lili's next letter to Farhad.

It was not love, exactly, that she felt toward him, but over the next several months this boy with his strange and beautiful letters became her only friend. Despite her better judgment, and her fear of Sohrab, Lili found she could not stop herself from answering Farhad. But eventually his letters thinned out and then stopped completely. When she had not heard from him in many weeks, she summoned all her courage and hauled Kobra along to pay a visit to Mina. They arrived at a house of mourning. Mina, dressed in black and her face ashen, opened the door. Farhad, she whispered through tears, had shot himself with a pistol. He was buried in America now, she sobbed, somewhere close to Hollywood.

★   ★   ★

Months after the divorce became final, Kazem continued to seek Lili out. He'd turned gaunt, with an unbecoming stubble and perpetually wrinkled suit. "I only want to speak with her for a moment, Kobra Khanoom," he begged, and much as this offended her sense of Muslim charity, Kobra dared not invite him into the house for fear of crossing Sohrab.

Finding no success with this approach, Kazem next began bribing Sohrab's manservant into disclosing Lili's school schedule. Kazem would pull the rim of the fedora over his eyes and linger in the alley until Sohrab's driver brought her back home in the afternoons for lunch. Sometimes Kazem brought her a bouquet of tuberoses or a box of prettily wrapped nougats. The gesture did nothing to assuage her fear. The sight of Kazem terrified Lili, but now, after the divorce, she was less frightened that he'd hurt her or make a scene than that her father would find them together and throw her back at him, this time forever.

When again and again Lili refused his presents, Kazem began to press photographs into her hands instead. Not photographs of himself, or the two of them together, but photographs of the baby. Of Sara. They were recent pictures, all of them lovely studio shots with scalloped white edges and the photographer's embossed signature running along one corner. "She talks now," Kazem would tell Lili. "She asks for you all the time." Sara's hair had grown out straight— there was no trace of the curls she'd had just a few months earlier— and her eyes seemed larger, more knowing.

Lili studied these pictures until her throat went dry and her temples throbbed, and then, invariably, she handed them back to Kazem. He would never take them from her, though. He stood with his hands buried deep in his pockets, and so the pictures fell, one after the other, onto the ground.

But after learning of Farhad's suicide, Lili was suddenly seized by a longing to see Sara again. At first it was an idle wish, entertained only late at night in her bed, but it soon forced all other thoughts from her mind. But how could she manage it? Even if she could somehow overcome her fear of meeting Kazem, her hours were now so closely guarded that it would be impossible to sneak away to the Khorramis' house for even an hour.

The only way to see Sara would be to somehow bring her into Sohrab's house. In this mission, she realized, she would have only one ally, her aunt Zaynab. It was Zaynab, childless and besotted with children, who had coddled Sara since the day of her birth, and Zaynab who'd continued to bring her to Lili in the period between her release from the hospital and her divorce from Kazem. Zaynab had even been keen to raise Sara herself, but Sohrab had not allowed it on the logic that a complete break from the family would be best for all.

"Nothing good will come of this," Zaynab whispered, but she was grinning all the same as she smuggled Sara in through the back door one afternoon. In an apparent effort to disguise Sara as a bundle of laundry, Zaynab had swaddled her in several sheets and quilts. When Zaynab peeled back the layers they found Sara's cheeks flushed pink and the hair at her temples damp with perspiration. Sara blinked and let out a small cry, but when she saw Lili her face lit at once into a smile. Sara still knew her! Lili, hands trembling with joy and relief, smiled back, smoothed Sara's brow, and pressed her nose against her hot, wet cheeks.

They snuck her quickly into Lili's room and then Lili and Zaynab took turns pinching Sara's cheeks and tickling her sides. She toddled along, dragging herself along furniture to support herself as she made her way around the room.

"She ought to be walking on her own by now...," Zaynab muttered.

"Why doesn't she, *ammeh*?" Lili asked anxiously. "Is there something wrong?" she asked, but Zaynab only muttered something else that Lili could not make out and slipped from the room.

Zaynab returned with a plate of raisin cookies. She squatted against the wall, several feet from where Sara was sitting in Lili's lap, and then she held out a cookie in her palm. Sara's eyes brightened. She hauled herself up and set off at once for the treat.

"Such a clever girl!" Zaynab beamed. "We'll have you walking in an hour!" Zaynab said, and then she and Lili clapped each time Sara made it across the carpet without stumbling or crawling.

They kept her in Lili's bed that night, wedged between Kobra and Lili. In sleep Sara proved a nervous, restless child. Every hour or so she'd wake up crying. They did not know if she still took a bottle, and had none in the house in any case, and so Kobra brought a chunk of rock candy wrapped in a handkerchief and pressed it to Sara's lips whenever she stirred.

In the morning Zaynab returned to the house with a wrought-iron birdcage swinging in one hand. She set it on the floor in Lili's room, unfastened the little door, and out hopped a bright yellow canary with a perfect red circle on each of her cheeks. "She's blushing!" Zaynab announced, her own cheeks rosy with pleasure. She tossed a few seeds on the carpet and they watched as the canary snapped them up in her beak. Sara squealed, and then Lili pressed some seeds into her fist and showed her how to toss them for the bird.

Lili, Sara, and Zaynab passed the morning playing with the blushing canary while Kobra stood sentry outside the entrance to the women's quarters. Toward noon Sara began to rub her eyes with her fists and yawn. Lili put her down for a nap, and then she and Zaynab slipped, still chuckling, to the kitchen for lunch. When they returned they found Sara gone. Lili, Kobra, and Zaynab tore through the house, each in one direction. Lili flew first to the courtyard. Finding the pool empty and still, she ran back into the house, poked under all the cabinets in the parlor, then scrambled down to the basement. When she reached the kitchen she found Zaynab rocking Sara in her lap and Kobra wringing her hands. Zaynab's voice trembled as she told Lili what had happened. Sara had woken up and crawled all the way down the corridor to Sohrab's quarters. Seeing her, Sohrab had called for his manservant to remove her to the kitchen.

Zaynab swaddled Sara in the blankets once more and Lili retreated to her room to await her punishment. For a long time it did not come. The blushing canary continued to chirp sweetly and rock back and forth on her little swing, but eventually the sight of the bird made Lili so miserable that she took the cage into the courtyard and left it there to find her way out. Still no word came from Sohrab. She began to wonder if it had not been her father but one of the servants who'd found Sara that day. An eerie silence reigned over the house for several weeks, to be broken at last by the announcement that Lili would soon be sent abroad.

Five

Exile

"My brother had turned himself into a pasha—a prince—in Europe!"
Lili said into the tape recorder with a laugh. "My baby brother with
his bowed legs and skinny arms, the one who'd shaken and cried when
our father so much as looked at him. Well, if he could turn himself into
a pasha, imagine what I could become in such a place!"

L ILI WOULD LEAVE THE country dressed as if for an English
garden party. White with pale green vines creeping up its three
tiers and many flounces, her dress was easily the most beautiful one
she had ever owned, and for the entire five hours of her flight from
Tehran to Frankfurt she would not even cross her legs for fear it
might wrinkle.

As sudden as her exile was in the execution, it had, in fact, been
long in the planning. As the date of her graduation from high school
approached, Sohrab had begun to take measure of her. She was no
longer a pretty girl but a beautiful young woman. She'd grown tall,
her breasts had come in, and her waist had narrowed. Her pigtails
looked awkward and would soon have to be loosened. Suitors would
come, only to leave once they learned she'd been married and had
a child. She would contrive to see Sara again, and the habit, Sohrab
felt certain, would both distract Lili from her studies and further
compromise her chances of marrying again.

For some time Simin had been taking her measure of Lili as

well—and of her own circumstances. For nearly three years Lili and Kobra had lived in Sohrab's house. For nearly three years Sohrab had entertained Simin only in his own quarters and only occasionally. So long as Lili stayed in Iran and remained unmarried, she would continue to live under Sohrab's roof, and so, too, would Kobra. And while Lili had seemingly told no one about the opium, that, too, might change now that she was no longer a child.

"Send her to her brother," Simin told Sohrab. "She will be better off with him in Europe."

The same message was relayed to Sohrab's friends and associates until he finally adopted the plan as his own.

In the weeks following Sara's furtive visit, Sohrab had sequestered Lili in the house, forbidding her to visit even her cousins or her grandmother without a chaperone. The boredom of those weeks had been awful—much worse, even, than the isolation she'd endured before her divorce. But now, Sohrab promised her, she'd begin a new life in a place where nobody knew about her past. She'd continue her studies and become an educated woman.

Lili thrilled at the thought. And while she would never dare mention it to anyone—could scarcely let herself think it to herself—perhaps someday she'd even return to Iran and make a life for herself and her daughter.

Weeping and wailing all the while, Kobra commenced to sew Lili a European wardrobe. In addition to the white dress with the creeping vines, Kobra sewed her some half-dozen others in shades of red, pink, and persimmon. Since Kobra had heard it was very cold in Germany, she also knit Lili a wool scarf and matching hat. The others devised their own means of preparing Lili for her departure. On the day before Lili was to leave Iran, Sohrab handed her an envelope full of deutsche marks and a second suitcase that held two small carpets Nader was to sell for her in Germany. "Study," Sohrab told her sternly. As for her grandmother, cousins, and aunts, on the day of her departure they wept, passed the Koran over her head, and then imparted three bits of advice: "Don't let anyone trick you," "Listen to your brother," and "Be grateful to your father."

As Lili readied herself to leave Iran for Germany, Kobra readied to leave Sohrab's house for the last time and Simin readied herself to return to it once again.

"Hello, you donkey!" Lili's brother, Nader, called out from across the airport terminal. He was holding a bouquet of deep blue irises, and when he saw her he raised his arm and began waving the flowers. Lili hustled past the other passengers, but before she could embrace him her mouth fell open at the young man standing before her. In less than a year, her shy, skinny younger brother had been trans-formed into a dandy in a three-piece suit and rakish smile.

And this was not all. Here the boy who'd once cowered at the sound of Sohrab's footsteps had taken on his lavish habits, throwing frequent parties and outings financed by the gold and carpets Sohrab regularly sent him to sell abroad. On her first night in Germany, Nader threw her a welcome party in a pub in Tübingen, the small university town that was now to be home to them both. Her eyes went wide at the sight of him perched at the bar, surrounded by sev-eral blond girls. Pretty as movie stars, she thought them. The girls were laughing into their beer bottles, free and easy as she had never before seen any woman. She caught Nader's eye and he grinned at her from across the smoky room.

During her first days in Germany Lili and Nader walked arm in arm through the streets of Tübingen, he in his colorful silk ties and tweed sport jackets and she in the half-dozen dresses Kobra had sewn her back in Tehran. She adored the church spires and the canals, the crooked cobblestone lanes that reached up to the hills, the red and pink geraniums cascading from the window boxes of the half-timbered houses along the river. Most wonderful of all was the chorus of greetings she heard in the streets. Old men doffed their hats to young mothers. *"Guten Tag!"* they called to one another. Stout matrons greeted the fishmonger; the baker greeted a young boy passing by on a bicycle; the streetcar conductor greeted a pretty passenger. *"Guten Tag, Guten Tag, Guten Tag!"*

Lili could feel eyes following her and Nader everywhere as they toured the city. They joked that the locals must take them for a pair of wealthy exotics passing through on their honeymoon, and this only made them laugh harder and link arms more tightly as they strolled down the streets and alleys together. It was, Lili thought to herself, the *Shahreh Farang* she'd glimpsed through the old nickelodeons outside the bazaar on New Year's Day, except that now she herself was in the picture.

Nader arranged a room for her in a boardinghouse in the center of Tübingen. It was a very small room, with a low ceiling and creaking floorboards, but she had her own little wrought-iron balcony and from there she could trace the Neckar River to where it thinned to the width of a ribbon and then disappeared into the green hills. Every night she sank, smiling, into a sea of eiderdown. Every morning she woke, smiling, to the chiming of church bells. And during the week, when Nader was away at school, she pulled on one of her pretty dresses, grabbed a handful of cookies from the kitchen downstairs, and then set off to explore the city on her own.

In Tehran she'd grown accustomed to walking with her eyes cast down and if anyone spoke to her in the streets she immediately quickened her step. Now she ambled around town for hours all by herself, smiling and chirping greetings as she went, and the fact that no one said much more to her than *"Guten Tag"* only increased her feeling of liberty.

At first Lili walked without any particular purpose in mind, but she found one soon enough. With her first month's allowance from

Sohrab she bought herself a tube of red lipstick, a pair of white gloves with a pearl set at each wrist, a bag of peaches, a pot of geraniums for her balcony, and a pillbox hat she liked to wear cocked to one side. What was left—about half of her allowance—that month and in all the months to come she sent back to Kobra in Tehran.

The funds would be much needed, as Kobra's circumstances had turned dire since Lili had left Iran.

After twenty years of a marriage punctuated by countless separations, two divorces, and many more near divorces, Kobra had left Sohrab's house for good. This momentous break was not attended by any formal petition or document of any kind, but Kobra did not doubt the finality of the move. With both Nader and Lili in Europe, Khanoom and Sohrab's sisters would not be hauling Kobra back to his house or to their own house on Avenue Moniriyeh, and with Sohrab still in thrall to his blue-eyed jinn, even her most heartfelt labors were inadequate to secure a corner of his house.

She spent the first few weeks at her mother's house. Long since inured to Kobra's comings and goings, Pargol still kept a spare room free for her, but this time Kobra felt herself less than welcome there. In recent years Pargol had been content to delegate most of the day-to-day affairs of her household to one of her daughters-in-law. Kobra's first few days back passed amiably enough, but when it was discovered that this time Kobra's stay was to be permanent, there was suddenly less meat in Kobra's portions at dinner—with a corresponding coolness in Kobra's own manner toward her sister-in-law. The quarrel threatened to turn violent when Kobra discovered that someone had taken a pair of scissors to one of her best dresses in the night, reducing it to shreds. Her sister-in-law swore her innocence on the graves of seven generations of her ancestors, but this did nothing to dissuade Kobra of the culprit's identity.

Kobra left the house in a huff and and found herself a flat in a derelict quarter of the city, on Zahirodolleh Alley. The landlord had not been keen to rent to her, a single woman. "Trouble," he said, shaking his head, "always trouble," but in the end he'd found himself unable to refuse the bills she pressed into his hands. To support herself, Kobra began taking in sewing here and there, mostly for women in the neighborhood but only as much as was strictly necessary. She ate just milk and flatbread, and quite often she forgot to eat at all. And so great did her losses now seem that not even the great passion of the last several years, her passion for real estate, could spur her toward greater enterprise.

Kobra would entertain just one visitor in her new home, her former son-in-law, Kazem. When news of Lili's departure from Iran reached him, Kazem wasted no time seeking Kobra out on Zahirodolleh Alley. By then there was nothing at all left of the courtesies with which he'd once approached her at Sohrab's house. The one time she refused to open the door for Kazem, he made such a scene that the landlord threatened to put her out and keep the month's rent as penalty for the disturbance. It was impossible to turn Kazem away after that.

As soon as she heard him knocking at her door—three hard, quick raps—Kobra would spring at once to her feet. Kazem would shoulder his way past her and make a quick search of the apartment's three small rooms. When he finished rifling through the drawers and cupboards and tossing the contents about the floor, he'd grab her by the wrist or the neck, grind the heel of his shoe over her bare foot, and demand that she tell him where Lili had gone, and with whom.

"I know nothing," Kobra would tell him, careful always to keep her voice low, her face impassive. "I know nothing at all."

"May her spine rot—and yours, too, you hag!"

These episodes invariably left her trembling and rushing to the stove to burn wild rue to cancel out the curse, but however unsettling, however terrifying, Kazem's visits were not mentioned in any of Kobra's missives to Lili. "I have nothing to complain of but your absence," Kobra's nieces wrote to Lili on her behalf. Of Sara, Kobra consistently reported: "She is thriving in her grandmother's care," and Lili, newly arrived in Germany, had no reason at all to doubt the honesty of Kobra's claims.

One day, after Kazem had come round for her and she felt herself growing truly desperate, Kobra raised her eyes and then her palms heavenward. She stated her case in the simplest terms. On account of the blue-eyed jinn she now had no husband and no home. One child—her littlest, her baby—was dead and now her other two had been spirited away. Of Kazem's torments she felt no need to say anything at all. "I leave the judgment to You," she said finally. Kobra lowered her gaze, folded her hands back into her lap, and then she began waiting for her answer.

Since his own arrival in Germany several months earlier, Nader had taken a room in a house of five women, a widow and her four young daughters. They were all exquisitely beautiful—with long, flaxen curls and bright blue eyes—but none more so than Margarethe, the sister with the shriveled arm. "A birth defect," Nader had whispered in Lili's ear before taking her to visit the family for the first time. "Something to do with a drug her mother took during the war."

He proceeded to explain that the three other daughters of the house left each morning at dawn for jobs in town, leaving Margarethe and her mother, Isolde, to labor in their tiny cottage kitchen. Isolde baked fruit pies she sold to restaurants and boardinghouses while Margarethe sewed tablecloths, dish towels, and aprons. When Lili first laid eyes on her, Margarethe was holding a large square of yellow-and-white-checkered fabric between her toes and working her needle and thread through it with her good arm. She was to Lili a vision of industriousness and good cheer, and through the ensuing months of their friendship Lili would rarely encounter the girl otherwise.

Margarethe was also exceedingly bright. No sooner had Lili offered her one of her cheery but poorly pronounced "*Guten Tags*" than Margarethe proposed, for a small weekly fee, to tutor her in German. From then on, three afternoons a week Lili walked from her room in town, through an enormous wheat field buzzing with insects, and into the crumbling four-room cottage for her German lessons. Margarethe's pedagogical method consisted of ordering Lili to memorize twenty words from the dictionary every night and then teasing her as she struggled to pronounce them. As the tutorial progressed, the cottage filled with the aroma of vanilla, cinnamon, plums, and apples, distracting Lili no end from her studies. On some lucky days, she and Margarethe ate the slightly burnt pies Isolde could not hope to sell in town.

Lili spent her evenings in the boardinghouse poring over her newly acquired German grammar books until all the *ders* and *dies* and *dases* threatened to make her head burst, and then she'd go sit on her balcony and watch the people in the street below. On Saturday and Sunday evenings she joined her brother in town, looked on as he held court with his many new friends, and thought about all the wonderful things to come.

There were few jobs for a foreign girl like her, but at Sohrab's word Nader had made inquiries and secured a spot for her as an orderly at a foundling hospital run by Catholic nuns. If she did well there, Nader promised her, she could eventually earn a place in medical school. She'd be a doctor! The prospect thrilled her, and so Lili wasted no time in joining the ranks of skinny, dark-skinned immigrant girls—Turks, Greeks, Yugoslavians—who'd come to Germany after World War II to be thrown together with no common language, and jobs that left them little time to wonder about one another's circumstances or even to give much thought to their own.

They would assemble at the clinic doors each day at dawn and wait there until Schwester Maria appeared with her white robes billowing behind her and her headgear rising a full two feet up and three feet across. Each girl was given a headpiece identical to the nuns'. This item was to be Lili's first true source of agony abroad. The headgear seemed to wrinkle and smudge the moment she placed it onto her head. She could not get the knack of holding her head still enough to balance it and therefore resorted to shuttling down the corridors clutching her headdress with one hand and her loads of diapers and bottles with the other. Worst of all, twice a week her headgear was disassembled, bleached, starched, pressed, and at last returned to her in individual components to be reassembled by her own hand. She ruined half a dozen fresh bundles before Schwester Maria stated flatly she would be sent away if she could not manage to pin her headgear neatly. The terror induced by this warning sharpened her mind sufficiently for her to master the skill.

The clinic was devoted to the care of abandoned infants, ranging from newborns to toddlers, who were too sickly to be housed in a regular orphanage. The infants arrived with measles and mumps, whooping cough, shingles, broken limbs, and an assortment of unclassified fevers and random gastrointestinal ailments. Some recovered within days or weeks, while others would linger in the clinic indefinitely, or, in the very worst cases, permanently.

Attachment to any particular child was discouraged by the nuns, but Lili quickly found a favorite among the three dozen or so orphans, a blond, blue-eyed boy called Franz. He'd been born with a congenital lung disease and lay tethered to a hunkering respirator. Her heart fell each time she passed his cot. When no one was looking, she cooed over him and whispered Iranian folk songs in his ears, with the result that soon enough he refused to take his bottle from any of the other orderlies and Lili took increasing pride in the motherly skills she'd someday lavish again on her own child.

Their bond would go unnoticed, as the rest of the clinic was involved in its own love affair with a seven-month-old black baby rumored to be the abandoned offspring of a local German girl and an American soldier. The baby had appeared one day at the clinic with a face and torso covered in plum-colored splotches. They called him Kenya and treated him like a visiting royal. At any hour of the day a crowd of nuns, nurses, doctors, administrators, orderlies, and janitors could be found clustered around his crib, vying with one another for a chance to hold him. Kenya spent several weeks being coddled and fussed over until finally the splotches disappeared and one of the doctors took him to live in his own house.

Lili was shown the precise methods for bathing and diapering and swaddling the infants, and she practiced until her hands seemed to fly through the various steps. Twice a day she wheeled the babies onto the balcony so that they could take their naps in the open air. The humid summer days gave way to autumn and then slowly to winter, but in all but the heaviest snowstorms she was ordered to wheel the babies onto the balcony for their naps. As she stood watch over the rows of cots, she shivered and pulled her cardigan tighter and tighter about herself. Within minutes the little faces turned bright pink and even in some cases purplish, but when she expressed her worry the nuns assured her that the change in the infants' complexions was but the thoroughly wholesome effect of the pure Black Forest air.

One afternoon in late October the housemistress slipped a letter under the door to Lili's room. She was busy dressing and did not immediately rise to fetch it. On her way out some time later, Lili bent down and picked up the envelope and discovered that it was the most recent letter she had written to her father. She turned it over and noticed a faint stamp, in Persian, on the back of the envelope. She struggled to make out the words. "No such person at this address." *Strange*, she thought idly. She checked the address again and, finding it identical to the one in her little brown notebook, she placed the letter back on her desk.

Nader appeared at the clinic for her the following morning. It was a rare occurrence, made stranger by his pale, stricken face. In place of one of his brightly colored neckties he was wearing a thin black tie.

"What's this?" she asked, lifting the tail of Nader's tie and waving it slightly.

He yanked the tie from her hand. "It's the new style, you donkey," he replied. It was his old endearment for her, but he did not smile as he said it. "Listen," he told her, clearing his voice. "I've got to go back to Iran for a while."

"Iran?"

He nodded.

"For how long?"

"Two or three months."

"Two or three months! But what about your studies?"

Nader would tell her nothing more that afternoon, but when she reached her room at the end of the day she would find a note from him under her door.

Father has died in a car accident. I must leave for Iran on Sunday.

Lili read the note three, seven, ten times. *Impossible, impossible, impossible*, she thought. *He cannot be dead.* But then her hands began to shake and a terrible cry heaved up from her chest. She gripped the metal bars of her canopied bed and began shaking it with such force that the housemistress rounded the stairs in nothing more than a robe and house slippers to see what could be the matter with the Iranian girl. Within minutes a half-dozen other lodgers had crowded around her. "*Was ist? Was ist den, Madele?* [What is it?, What is it, miss?] *Sind Sie krank?* [Are you sick?]" One of them held her shoulders, another one stroked her hair, and a third brought her a glass of water. Though their voices sounded kind, she begged them with whatever words she had to leave her alone.

She stayed in the room for three days, neither eating nor sleeping, eyes wide and unseeing, and then early the next Sunday morning she went to her brother. She had made up her mind. She would go back to Iran with him.

They would travel by car from Germany to Iran, a distance of nearly three thousand miles. The route wended along cliffs and across huge swaths of desolate countryside, and with winter fast approaching, the roads might soon be impassable. More frighteningly, they'd heard countless stories of thieves and murderers waylaying tourists along the way, but with Sohrab dead and their funds dwindling, they had no money for airfare. Besides, Nader's car would fetch a better price in Tehran.

They set off with such haste that Lili had neither the time nor presence of mind to acquire a simple black sheath dress from the shops along the river. The day of their departure she pulled on a lavender two-piece skirt suit, though the matching hat and gloves were left behind in the boardinghouse along with all her other clothes and belongings.

They traveled out of Germany to Austria, farther south to Yugoslavia, then east toward Bulgaria and southeast into Greece. For the length of the journey images of her father crowded in her head: the cut of his gray pin-striped suit, the elegance of his hands when he smoked, the squares of American chocolate he always kept in his pockets for her when she was a child.

"But why? How?" she'd ask her brother.

"I don't know," Nader would answer, shaking his head sadly. "They told me nothing." Eventually, though, he made no answer at all, just stared hard at the road before them.

They slept in the car, Nader at the wheel and Lili curled up in the backseat. Night after night winds whipped at the windows, setting the little car swaying on the roadside. They slept with all their jackets and sweaters piled on, with boots on their feet and mittens on their hands, but still the cold seeped in through the windows and kept them shivering until dawn. Soon they took to napping for a few hours during the day and driving straight through the night. When Nader's eyelids grew heavy, she'd yank his sleeve. "Wake up!" she'd shout. When he lost the way, she'd slip from the car to read the road signs. Often she found nothing more to guide them than the name of a village, written in chalk on a piece of wood in what looked to be a child's hand, the letters smudged away by the wind.

Two hundred miles outside Istanbul, Nader spotted a coffeehouse perched on the hillside. He left the car idling at the bottom of the hill with Lili inside and rushed in to take a quick swig of black coffee and buy some flatbread and cheese. When Lili shifted her position, her hip threw the gear into reverse. The wheels began to roll. Never having operated a car, Lili, in her terror, could think of nothing to do but stick her head out the window and scream. The car rolled farther down the hill, veering closer and closer to the wrong side of the road, but all at once Nader came running out of the coffeehouse and managed, just barely, to yank the brake before the car swerved off the road and plunged into a ravine.

"*Khareh!* You donkey!" he shouted, grabbing her by the shoulders and shaking her. "You could have died! You could have died just like..." He choked on the words.

"But I didn't know what to do," she whimpered. "I couldn't think...."

At last they reached the border between Turkey and Iran.

For centuries Iranians were known to linger here, at this juncture. It was said that the sky above Iran was a brighter blue, the earth a richer brown, the grasses and trees a brighter shade of green. In reverence, in joy, in greeting, Iranian travelers would kneel beside the road and press their lips to their native soil. *Home.* But Lili and Nader did not stop or even slow the car but instead pushed on toward the capital. Past Tabriz, past Zanjan, past Ghazvin. When, eleven days into the journey, Tehran, brushed over by a snow made brilliant by the winter sun, at last came into sight, Lili turned to Nader.

"To the grave first or to Avenue Moniriyeh?" she asked quietly.

"Khanoom's house," her brother answered—the first words he'd spoken in many days.

"May God kill me!" Khanoom wailed at the sight of Lili.

Not quite three months had passed since Lili had last seen her grandmother, but in that time Khanoom had turned into an old woman. The day Sohrab died, Khanoom had clutched at her heart and doubled over in grief. The posture stuck. Khanoom's spine would stay bent until the day she herself was put into the ground.

But to Khanoom, Lili, too, seemed much changed.

"May God kill me!" Khanoom wailed.

It took Lili a moment to understand. The skirt she was wearing just barely cleared her knees, and at this time of mourning the color of her suit was a kind of violence to Khanoom's eyes.

Lili hung up her lavender suit and changed into one of her aunts' simple black frocks. It would fall, loose as a sack, all the way down to her ankles for many weeks to come. She scrubbed her face, knotted her hair tightly at the nape of her neck, and covered her head with a black muslin veil, but still the women stared and whispered to each other whenever she passed, and the men studied her with something that was neither solicitude nor, even, curiosity.

Lili saw it plainly now, how carefully Sohrab had shielded her from just such looks, just such whispers. She was, to their way of thinking, damaged, and would always be so. She saw, too, that there'd be no one to protect her from now on, and so, despite the general disorientation of those days and the terrible depth of her grief, Lili lifted her chin and shrugged off the stares, and gradually, over the course of many days, she pieced together the story of her father's death.

"Let me off here," Sohrab had told his driver when they reached the main thoroughfare leading to Khanoom's house. "I'll walk the rest of the way."

He'd gone no farther than three paces from the car—his latest, a cherry red Cadillac with cream-colored leather seats—when a Town Car swerved into Avenue Moniriyeh and pitched him up into the air. He landed on his side, his head knocking against the pavement. Peeling backward out of the street, the tires of the Town Car had made such a fantastic screech that Khanoom had cried out to the manservant, "*Madaresh bemeereh!* May his mother die and be spared her grief! Who's been killed?" The servant rushed from the house and ran back, breathless, with the answer: "Sohrab Khan! It's Sohrab Khan who's been killed!"

He hadn't died then, though. Sohrab, refusing even to take the manservant's arm, had pulled himself up from the street, brushed off his slacks, and straightened his tie. He'd nearly reached his mother's house when two policemen appeared for him.

He would spend the next hours at Tehran's police headquarters. The driver who'd struck Sohrab was a foreigner, a *farangi*. The news rippled through the police station, rousing every last officer on duty that night. "We have procedures, protocols, routines for such cases," they told Sohrab. After a three-hour-long interrogation, he was finally taken, cursing, to the city's large public hospital and it was there, on one of the dozens of cots crowding the hallways, that he would die in the night of a brain hemorrhage. He was forty-two years old and when he died there was not even a bruise to tell of his injury.

In the morning the Washer of the Dead closed Sohrab's lids and performed the ablutions. Beginning first with the right side of his body, he was purified limb by limb, from head to foot, three times. Next he was laid down on the *kafan*, the white shroud perfumed with myrrh. The *kafan* was wrapped around him once, then again, and then a third time. The procedure was repeated with a second *kafan* and finally, because it was winter and a hard snow had begun to fall, he was cloaked once more, this time with a fine silken carpet.

At noon his friends came, hoisted him onto their shoulders, and carried him through the streets of Tehran to a cemetery encircled by cypress and plane trees. His body was laid alongside the open grave and the *janazeh* began. The men of the family—the cousins and uncles—marveled at the sight of these several dozen gentlemen, dressed in their cashmere coats and silk cravats and wailing like women. "*La elah ella Allah!* [Allah is the only God!]" they cried out as they lowered Sohrab into the ground. They guided his body to the right side, toward Mecca, toward the one who is the only One, and when the prayers were finished they set a stone above Sohrab's head and, weeping harder still, they began to throw fistfuls of soil into the grave.

Long past sunset the women of the family sat on the floor in a darkened room together, rocking their bodies back and forth, beating their chests, and raising open hands up to the sky. Their chanting would start low and even, like a moan or a hum, but it would rise steadily until all their despair, yearning, and rage was at last released into their dirge.

When it was over Sohrab's friends paid for every last funeral expense, from the plot in which they'd laid him to rest to the garlands of lilies and tuberoses they'd draped above his grave.

Few members of Sohrab's family had known him to be as beloved as on the day his friends buried him; indeed, to many it would seem that his friends were grieving a different man altogether. Nearly as astonishing as the funeral itself was the sight of Sohrab's two widows thrown suddenly together in the seven days of mourning that followed. Having circled each other, very carefully, for nearly twenty years, Kobra and Simin would spend every one of those seven days, from sunrise to sunset, together in his house. Many braced themselves for a vicious row, but without sharing a single word or glance Kobra and Simin managed to divide their grief in equal parts. When one entered a room, the other left it. When one stopped crying, the other began.

But even when the seven-day mourning period came to an end, the clan still did not manage to learn whether there had been a marriage, even a temporary one, between Sohrab and Simin. No one dared ask Simin outright, and Simin herself would stay as silent on the matter as Sohrab himself had been.

For all this, it was Simin whom Sohrab's family treated as his true widow, and for proof of this Kobra looked no further than a cup of chicken broth.

It was understood that those whose grief was the most profound would be unable to eat a proper meal during the mourning rites. To prevent this select contingent from passing out from hunger, a pot of saffron-spiced chicken broth was always kept simmering on the stove. Day after day, as crowds of mourners assembled at Sohrab's house, it was into Simin's hands, and not Kobra's, that a cup of this precious broth was passed, and Simin who was begged to keep up her strength by drinking it.

In any case, in the end it was not as his wife but as his creditor that Simin claimed Sohrab's estate. On the eighth day following his death, Simin appeared at Avenue Moniriyeh to present Khanoom with a thick stack of receipts. Some of the loans ranged as far back as twenty years, and their receipts were so faded that the sums were scarcely legible. All told, the debts ran into the hundreds of thousands.

Since there was nothing else to satisfy his obligations to Simin, Sohrab's house was picked clean. Silk carpets piled three and four deep in every room, fistfuls of gold coins, antique Chinese vases, marble-topped armoires—Simin sent no fewer than eight men for it in the night—and when the men left there was nothing left in Sohrab's house but a single, broken chair and a half-empty gunny-sack of rice in a kitchen cupboard.

"Unpaid debts foreclose a restful death," Khanoom murmured, citing a well-worn saying, and to this no one had anything at all to say in reply.

But the story would not achieve a proper ending until Lili and Nader returned to Iran.

No sooner had they dug a handful of soil from above Sohrab's grave and passed it like kohl along their eyelids than they were called to appear at the American embassy. The man who'd struck Sohrab had been an attaché of the American government, one of dozens then living in Iran, and had likely been spirited out of the country within days of Sohrab's death. Iranian law already granted foreigners immunity from government prosecution, but Lili and Nader had been summoned to Iran to sign a document waiving their individual rights to bring charges against the American attaché.

They were made to understand it was in their best interests to sign.

The following week an envelope bearing an embossed golden seal of the U.S. government appeared at Khanoom's house. Inside they discovered a letter, composed in English and addressed to Lili and Nader. Nader strained to translate it aloud for the family. The letter stated that out of respect for local custom seven thousand *tomans*—about a thousand American dollars—had been put aside for the accidental death of their relative. They could have used every *toman* of the paltry sum, but they would not claim it. More copies of the letter were sent from the American embassy to Avenue Moniriyeh, all of them bearing the same embossed golden stamp, and eventually Persian translations were even inserted along with their English original. Letter after letter arrived at Khanoom's house and the check went unclaimed for many weeks until finally Sohrab's blood money became Simin's, too.

Six

Zahirodolleh Alley

"Now, without a father, I really was nobody," Lili said. "And if I was nobody, what could I do for my daughter? What could she ever hope to become?" She paused. "We were all of us orphans when Sohrab died and I would have to find a way to take care of all of us."

THERE WAS NO QUESTION Nader would have to return to Europe to complete his degree, and also no question that Lili was now responsible for supporting him. Kobra and Lili bid him a tearful good-bye and then took measure of their circumstances. Nader's car had been sold off to pay for his airfare back to Germany, leaving him a few hundred marks to pay for his university tuition and next month's room and board. They calculated that they had three weeks, maybe four, until Nader's money ran out. Not only would Kobra need to step up her sewing, but Lili would also have to find a job, and immediately.

Lili moved into Kobra's three-room flat in Zahirodolleh Alley. The small, cracked *hoz* in their courtyard was clotted with leaves and cobwebs they felt little inclination to sweep away. They had no carpets and few furnishings and the partition that separated the parlor from the bedroom was so thin that in the mornings Lili could hear Kobra chewing the handful of walnuts that were her breakfast. For lunch every day they ate a bowl of watered-down yogurt into which Kobra dumped soggy diced cucumbers, raisins, and scraps of stale bread. Dinner was a soup of marble-sized meatballs bobbing alongside a single potato, a pot of plain rice seasoned with a pinch of cumin seeds, or else *yatimcheh*, the aptly named "little orphans" or skinny eggplants that Kobra fried in water, turmeric, and a few slivers of onion.

There was no refrigerator in the flat, and on the nights Lili came home too worn down from her job search to eat anything, Kobra would set a plate for her on a giant platter in the basement so that she could eat the leftovers for breakfast. To keep away the centipedes, sow bugs, beetles, and cockroaches that lurked there, Kobra filled the platter with water and set Lili's plate in the middle. This method proved effective until the day that Kobra acquired a stray cat, a long-haired ginger beauty with gray-green eyes. The shallow pool that drowned scads of insects every night proved no match for the kitten's appetite and daring. Kobra would routinely wake to find the platter upturned, the plate licked clean, and Lili clutching her stomach in hunger. Unleashing her choicest curses, Kobra would chase the cat around the apartment, place her in a gunnysack, and deposit her as far south as the train station.

Without fail, that cat would be mewing at their door in the space of a week. Every time Kobra declared her reappearance nothing short of a miracle, scooped her up with kisses, and then scavenged about her cupboards for a tasty little treat to satisfy the cat's hunger and assuage her own conscience. And so it would go until the next several plates of food were licked clean in the night and Kobra pulled out the gunnysack and the whole sequence began again.

Khanoom, infinitely generous despite her own poverty, lent Lili a hundred *tomans*, and with it she signed up for a typing course downtown. She took a bus in the mornings, and to save money she walked back in the afternoons. One day on her way to her typing class a man in a pin-striped suit and dark sunglasses approached her in Naderi

Square and asked her if she would like to be a movie star. They were shooting a new film about Kurdistan, he explained, and they needed a girl who could ride a horse. She seemed like just the type for the part, he went on, tall, slender, and dark haired, so would she take his card and telephone him at his office the next morning?

She could not believe her luck. She flew home that afternoon with the director's card pressed in her palm and an image of herself galloping across the plains in Kurdish garb, her hair flowing behind her like a banner. But Khanoom had nearly fainted at the very idea. "Do you know what they do to girls who become actresses?" She gasped. "Do you know what this man is asking of you?" She could not even bring herself to say it, but Lili understood perfectly. The next day she resumed her typing course, but she decided to keep the movie director's card as a souvenir of the adventure.

When, after weeks of inquiries and interviews, Lili learned that the best she could likely hope for was a job as a servant, she became the recipient of many entirely well-meaning and thoroughly aggravating attempts by her family to find her a husband. At nineteen she was fast approaching *torshidegi,* or the agedness of a pickle, and as she was a divorcée—a "touched" woman and one with a child, no less—her prospects for marriage could not have been worse. Yet Lili's circumstances, and Kobra's, were now so dire that Lili's aunts and cousins would not be deterred lest they themselves became responsible for the pair.

Lili's would-be suitors were often widowed men several decades her senior. Illiterate merchants, cripples, and even Christians were all put forth as potential mates for her—all to no avail.

"I wouldn't even marry the *shah* himself if he came for me!" she routinely announced to her family.

"The cheek of that girl!" the matchmakers scoffed. "And the ingratitude!" they added. They clucked their tongues and shook their heads. The more charitable ones among them merely thought her delusional. However evident to them the general hardships of married life, and the more particular disaster of Lili's marriage to Kazem, it still seemed inconceivable to them that a woman would actually choose to remain unmarried. Indeed, the longer her aunts and cousins thought on it, the more they were inclined to think Lili was still inflicted with the madness that had once driven her to attempt suicide. But they would all have thought much worse if they'd known the real reason for her refusal, namely that she was already scheming to make her way back to Europe.

Kobra, meanwhile, set up a sewing machine, a fourth-hand Singer culled from the local *bazaarcheh*, in the middle of the dining table and declared herself open for business. She'd taken in sewing since moving into the apartment some months earlier, but the scale of her endeavors now would be unprecedented. The commissions were modest at first, but she labored with such precision and speed that within months word of her skills had traveled from her own ramshackle neighborhood to the leafy enclaves of upper Pahlavi. It was said there that with nothing more than a picture torn from a magazine a woman named Kobra could copy even the most elaborate French ball gown down to the very last stitch.

Every Thursday morning Kobra paid a visit to Mr. Kohan, the cloth merchant to whom she'd been faithful through all the years of her marriage. Among the last generation born in Tehran's Jewish ghetto, Mr. Kohan had started working in the bazaar as his father's apprentice at the age of ten and had taken over the stall sometime in his early twenties—about the time Kobra began to call on him. He and Kobra had long since established a mutually pleasurable routine that began when Kobra took a seat in the back room of his shop and Mr. Kohan poured her a cup of tea and then one for himself. After they finished exchanging the latest news concerning their respective families, Mr. Kohan would rise and proceed to present Kobra with various bolts of fabric. While Mr. Kohan still made a show of haggling with Kobra, by this point in their decades-long acquaintance he knew enough of her trials to send her away with the most generous cuts of cloth, and their visits always ended with prayers for health and good fortune all around.

The corners and surfaces of Kobra and Lili's tiny apartment grew crowded with stacks of fabric and buttons and spools of thread in shades as common as black and white and as rare as aubergine and mustard. In the weeks before the Persian New Year, the busiest sewing season, Kobra hired a helper, usually a young girl from the provinces, to run her errands and serve tea to clients when they came round to be fitted. The Singer groaned and sputtered, short-circuited and overheated, but by the time she could afford a replacement Kobra had come to attribute all her success to that venerable old machine. She would not dream of being separated from it. The Singer remained, the village girls came and went, and Kobra's reputation grew. And though it would never make her wealthy, her work fed and housed both her daughter and herself, and for the time being that was miracle enough.

In part because they took her for a recent widow (a misapprehension she did not choose to complicate with the truth of her tempestuous marriage), but mostly because she saved them a fortune on their wardrobes, Kobra's clients began to offer her many lovely gifts: baskets of tangerines and pomegranates, golden bangles and silver brooches, as well as genuine French lipsticks and pots of face powder from America. Both then and in all the years to come, Kobra would prefer gratitude in the form of cash, but she'd smile warmly at every offering, sell or barter what she could, and tuck away the rest to give away as presents to her friends and relatives throughout the year.

From time to time, Kobra's clients showed their appreciation by inviting her to one of their private gatherings. Having attended numerous wakes and weddings and gained many more commissions in this fashion, she was loath to turn down such invitations, but when one of her most loyal customers, Nasrine Khanoom, offered to take her along to a party in a *baq*, a landholding outside the city, Kobra took one look at her daughter, growing thinner, paler, and more listless by the day, and decided to send Lili instead.

For this occasion Kobra "borrowed" a dress already commissioned by one of her other clients, a midnight blue marvel inspired by a faded studio shot of Veronica Lake, and sent out a silent prayer that its owner would not be attending the same party that night. To complete the look, Lili wore her hair loose about her shoulders, with a single long, deep wave in the front. When Nasrine Khanoom and her husband came around to fetch Lili for the party, Kobra told her, somewhat sternly, that she should enjoy herself at the party and then pushed Lili out the door.

Paradise, for Iranians, has always been a garden. Interlacing vines and buds of every imaginable variation had always figured prominently on the country's illustrious carpets, and though the paradisial garden had roots in the country's pre-Islamic past, after the Arab conquest of Iran in the seventh century images of the garden continued to bloom across the walls of Iran's shrines, mosques, and temples and along the margins and bindings of its assorted holy books— Muslim but also Christian, Jewish, Baha'i, and Zoroastrian.

By the mid-twentieth century, when much of the country seemed bent on stamping out every last vestige of tradition, the paradisial garden would once again survive in people's minds. Old *Tehrooni* families still cultivated holdings called *baqs* outside the city and would journey there en masse to escape the crushing heat of Tehran's summers. The *baq* to which Lili traveled that night lay in the foothills of the Alborz Mountains, more than an hour's drive from Tehran and farther north from the city than she had ever been in her life. She was greeted there by the exquisite fragrance of blossoms from nearby pistachio and orange groves. That night the moon was yellow as an egg yolk and just as round. Nothing, she was surprised to discover, set the garden apart from the wilds that surrounded it. There wasn't a wall or fence in sight.

The *baq* was indisputably lovely, and almost despite herself Lili felt her spirits rising. But even here she was dogged by the same questions that tormented her back in the city: "Have you come with your family?" "Are you married?" "How old are you?" The curiosity she encountered was anything but idle. It was enough for a young woman to appear unattached and from a decent family, but if she was also pretty she'd soon find herself in the unyielding clutch of matchmakers. That night in the *baq*, mothers approached Lili on behalf of their sons, elder sisters for their brothers, neighbors for their neighbors' sons. How to deflect their questions without seeming rude? How to demur without arousing suspicion?

She escaped the crush, stealing away to a corner of the garden where she stood for some time listening to the small troupe of musicians. They were playing the old-style Iranian instrumental music, with the *tonbak, tar,* and *santour,* and the women were taking turns dancing one by one in an open field while the men clapped and watched from the peripheries of a wide circle.

Eventually, a woman approached her. Dancing, the woman beckoned with a smile and a playful tilt of her head. Lili begged off, but the lady would not be refused. Lili drew in a deep breath, cast her eyes down, and began to dance. Within seconds the voices of the partygoers dissolved and their faces receded and she heard nothing but the music, plaintive and wild, filling up the warm night air all around her. Here, finally, no one could ask her questions; no one could guess at her past. From one end of the garden to the other and back again she danced, and as she danced a word drifted through her mind: *ragass.* It meant "dancer" but also a "loose woman." But she would not have stopped dancing then, not even if someone had grabbed her by the arm and tried to pull her away. She closed her eyes, threw back her head, and danced through the garden without shame.

Before Lili could contrive a way to see her, Sara herself contrived a way to see Lili again. She woke at dawn when Kazem and her stepmother were still asleep on the rooftop with the new baby swinging in a hammock close by. Sara was just six years old, but she dressed herself and slipped out of the house and into the streets. In one hand she held a square of flatbread, in the other a few walnuts, and in her head she was singing "Farhang and Pahlavi, Zahirodolleh Alley, Farhang and Pahlavi, Zahirodolleh Alley," words she'd overheard her father speak the previous night. She walked on and on toward the city center, tugging at ladies' skirts and veils, reciting the address until they pointed the way for her.

Seven hours later a policeman found her sitting by a fountain, dragging a hand through the brackish water and crying. "Farhang and Pahlavi, Zahirodolleh Alley," was all she would tell him. Not her own name, not her father's name, nothing but the words she believed would lead her back to her mother.

Kobra, alone in the apartment, thought a client had come calling. She tucked in her blouse, fluffed her hair, and, smiling, opened the door. And there she was. Sara. Her hair had been clipped into a page-boy style. She was wearing a pink cotton jumper, white sandals, and one sock.

"Do you know this girl?" the officer asked Kobra.

Three years had passed since grandmother and granddaughter had last seen each other and three lifetimes could not undo what was settled between them in that instant. "Do you know this girl?" the officer had asked Kobra, but what she heard was, "Do you choose this girl's life over your own daughter's?"

"She belongs to her father," said Kobra at length.

Sara turned her face to the policeman. Her chin was set and she would not budge. "No," she told him.

They all stood there like that for a long time, Sara planted at the entry and Kobra blocking the way, until the police officer guessed that only familial bonds could engender such animosity between two people and left them to each other.

"You must take her back to her father's house," Kobra told Lili as soon as she returned home that evening, but Lili's heart had lurched at the sight of Sara, and she'd been incapable of letting her go. "Just a few days," Lili begged, and Kobra, lips pursed and cursing, at last agreed to pay a visit to Kazem's aunt and plead Lili's case.

Sara would spend the next week on Zahirodolleh Alley. Her flight and Kobra's entreaties had convinced Kazem's family of the need for Sara to visit Lili, at least occasionally, and that first stay would establish the pattern for a handful of other visits over the next year. Every month or so, one of Kazem's aunts, cousins, or in-laws would deposit Sara at Kobra and Lili's flat with a little brown leather suitcase. Once there, Sara devoted herself completely to the study of her mother. Sara could sit for hours on Lili's lap, tracing her eyes, her nose, her lips, with her fingertips. "She's after something, that child," Kobra declared, and Lili could see it, too. It wasn't just that Sara missed her mother—though that, certainly, was part of it. It was that Sara was so clearly struggling to square what she'd heard about Lili—that she was a bad woman, that she'd abandoned her—with the pretty young lady she'd managed to find on Zahirodolleh Alley.

The task was tremendous and it tired them all out, but nobody suffered from Sara's arrivals as much as Kobra. In the evenings, when Lili was home, Sara was sweet, quiet, and utterly docile. After Lili left in the mornings, Sara kicked Kobra in the shins, tormented the cat, and swore at Kobra and her clients. They spent the days staring each other down, Kobra from behind her sewing machine, Sara from behind her bangs, until Lili appeared at nighttime with her arms full of presents—rag dolls, pennywhistles, and piggy banks wrapped in brightly colored cellophane—always too much and never, ever enough.

During these months Lili did not pay much attention to the women she encountered on her way in and out of the flat each day; in their middle age and their vanity, Kobra's clients seemed more or less indistinguishable to her. But over time Lili could not help notice that Nasrine Khanoom, the lady who'd taken her to the *baq* outside the city, was turning up more and more frequently and that Kobra always received her with particular warmth. Kobra kept a box of good cookies in her cupboard especially for Nasrine Khanoom, and she always seemed to be wearing a pretty dress or blouse when that lady called. When Lili returned from her typing class at the end of each day, Kobra and Nasrine Khanoom were often sipping tea together, oblivious to the pile of fabrics between them, and every time Nasrine Khanoom greeted Lili, her eyes seemed to linger just a little longer on her face and her figure.

The meaning of all this did not escape Lili, and when Kobra at last confessed that Nasrine Khanoom had found an excellent suitor for her she shrugged the news off just as she'd shrugged off similar news from her aunts and cousins over the last few months since returning to Iran. With that she thought the matter settled, but one afternoon she returned home from her typing class and discovered a large basket of orange gladiolus and an unwrapped box of Swiss chocolates set out on the table in place of the old Singer. The faces of her mother and Nasrine Khanoom were fixed on her with identical grins. A *khastegari*, or courtship, was under way—there was simply no missing it.

"Come sit with us, *azizam*!" Nasrine Khanoom called out to her, using the familiar endearment "dear one" and patting the empty seat beside her on the sofa.

Kobra poured Lili a cup of tea and passed her one of the special cookies. After they'd exhausted the customary greetings and pleasantries, Nasrine Khanoom turned to Lili, cleared her throat, and announced, "The more I see you, Lili-*joon*, the better I understand why Mr. Fereydoon has been so taken with you since we took you to the party that evening."

Lili could not remember this Mr. Fereydoon, but she smiled politely, took another biscuit, and continued drinking her tea.

"Mr. Fereydoon is a very good man," Nasrine Khanoom went on. She leaned toward Lili and lowered her voice slightly. "Quite capable in every last respect," she said, and then held Lili's gaze for a moment before continuing. "Between the two of us, I cannot imagine a better husband for you than Mr. Fereydoon."

"Excuse me, *khanoom*," Lili asked between sips of tea. "Is this Mr. Fereydoon your relative or an acquaintance of your family's?"

"Actually, *azizam*, Mr. Fereydoon is my husband."

At this Lili's mouth fell open and her teacup came down on the table with a loud clatter. Polygamy, though slightly less common than in years past, might be thought a divorcee's best hope—this she knew very well—but that a wife would go so far as to propose on her husband's behalf was too much for Lili to believe. A dim memory of this stout middle-aged man with the beginnings of a stoop flashed through her mind. *She's courting me on his behalf and thinks she's found a servant for herself in the bargain*, Lili thought, but before she could say a word Nasrine Khanoom pressed on with her proposal.

"I understand that you have been married before—Kobra Khanoom has told me some of your unfortunate...history. To be perfectly frank, others would not look favorably on your circumstances, but we are very open-minded people. And of course I must mention,

too, that since Kobra Khanoom"—here she threw Kobra a smile—
"has become so dear to me in these last months I feel no hesitation
whatsoever in accepting you into our family."

"That's very generous of you, *khanoom*, but—"

"There's no need to answer just yet," Nasrine Khanoom interrupted. "I'll understand if you want a few days to talk the matter
over with your dear mother, but please know that I fully expect you
to make us happy by becoming our bride."

What followed Nasrine Khanoom's departure that afternoon was
one of the longest, loudest, bitterest rows that would ever take place
between Lili and Kobra. How many more weeks, Kobra begged to
know, could Lili continue to drag herself around the city looking for
work? "A lifetime longer than I will live as someone's second wife!"
Lili shot back, adding, "I'm nothing like you, suffering that blue-
eyed jinn for two decades!"

At this Kobra buried her face in her hands and began to cry. "But
how can I possibly tell Nasrine Khanoom no?" Kobra whimpered.
"She and her husband have been so generous to both of us...."

Lili replied that Kobra needn't trouble herself as she would give
Nasrine Khanoom the news when that lady next called. This only
made Kobra cry harder and beg Lili to hold her tongue until she herself
found the most judicious words with which to refuse the proposal.

That night, after they'd finished swearing they would never again
speak to each other, Lili pulled a sheet and a pillow out of the cupboard and went to sleep on the floor in the parlor. When she woke
up the next morning, she saw that sometime in the night Kobra had
pulled the quilt off their bed and thrown it over her. The gesture
softened Lili's anger slightly, but she still refused to speak to Kobra
that day. When Kobra brought her a cup of tea and one of her special
cookies the following morning, Lili stretched out her hand to take it
and then muttered a terse and barely audible "thanks." The following day, the day when she had no choice but to convey Lili's refusal

to Nasrine Khanoom, Kobra offered Lili no tea at breakfast. They nursed their respective grudges for a week or so, and then, without ceremony or further discussion, they eased back into a mostly peaceful cohabitation that depended on the indefinite deferral of the marriage question.

As galling as Nasrine Khanoom's proposal had been to her, and as horrible as the prospect of marriage was overall, if it were not for her brother Nader's sake Lili might never have found the courage to take a job.

She'd sometimes glimpse women on their way to work in the city. It was true that there were not many of them, but with their pocketbooks, shift dresses, and high heels they seemed a smart and beguiling set. But no woman in her own family had ever worked outside the house, and to judge from the reaction of her aunts she might as well have been setting out to sell herself on the streets. "They only work because they have no choice," her aunts noted darkly. They redoubled their matchmaking efforts and begged her to stay at Kobra's side until a husband could be found for her.

But the thought of marriage was still abhorrent to her. What's more, she'd never had much of a talent or fondness for sewing, and she also felt sure that by working in the city she could earn a better wage with which to support her brother's studies, an expense that Kobra's earnings alone could never support. On a cousin's advice, therefore, Lili finally took a job as a cashier in a sundry shop near Tehran's central police station, a sprawling concrete compound that also housed various divisions of the shah's army. So far as she could make out, she was the only woman within miles of the site. Perched for eight- and ten-hour shifts behind the wooden slats of her booth, she sat counting out change and scribbling receipts. In the dead hours she busied herself with calculating her modest earnings, most of which she sent away to Nader in tissue paper–thin airmail envelopes.

For weeks she secretly admired the young uniformed officers who dropped by the shop. At the end of the day there was no shortage of policemen, soldiers, and lieutenants eager to escort her home. Some of them were so earnest in the appeals, made such heartfelt mention of their own unmarried sisters back at home and their duties to her as honorable men, that she was quite often tempted to accept their offers. She'd always chosen to go home by bus, however and more than once she'd found herself wishing for a veil to deflect the more aggressive offers she attracted on her way to and from work each day.

Then one day she met the General.

"This isn't a good place for a woman to stand by herself."

His eyes were green. Lili blinked, straightened herself, and cleared her throat.

"Excuse me?" she asked.

"A young lady, especially one so lovely as you, shouldn't stand by herself on a busy street like this." He nodded toward a limousine parked across the street. "I will accompany you home in my car."

She'd never before been propositioned by an officer of this rank, and when her eyes fell to the row of beribboned medals on his breast and he took her hand and told her to get into the car she knew there was no use protesting.

"And where do you live, young lady?" he asked once they'd settled in the back of the car.

"Lower Farhang, Zahirodolleh Alley, number forty-four."

The driver pulled out into traffic and she turned to the General and offered him a slight smile. He nodded. She caught the scent of liquor on his breath. Was he drunk? She couldn't be sure. Out of the corner of her eye, she saw him run his hands along the length of a thickly muscled thigh. She turned her face quickly back to the street and cursed herself for accepting his offer of a ride.

"Excuse me, *agha*," she said when she realized that the driver had turned in an opposite direction from her home. "But this is not the way. I live on lower Farhang, Zahirodolleh Alley—"

"Not to worry, not to worry," the General assured her. "My driver knows this city better than anyone. He will take you home just as soon as I get your advice for a building project of mine."

"But I know nothing of building projects!"

He would say nothing more, and so Lili gripped the armrest and began scanning the streets for some landmark to guide her. Were they driving north? West? Her hands were shaking now. Where was he taking her? Just when she was sure they were headed toward the countryside, the car pulled into a private street, wound its way past a long row of cypress trees, and then came to an abrupt stop. The General leaned toward his driver and whispered something she could not make out.

When they'd stepped out from the car and the driver disappeared down the hill, the General took Lili's arm and led her into the construction site. His "building project" looked to be the beginnings of a many-pillared villa with a view onto the whole city.

It was already late in the afternoon—from where she stood in the driveway Lili saw that the sun had tinted the rooftops pink—and all the workers had left the property. Inside, wooden beams lay stacked on top of each other and heaps of refuse and bags of concrete had been piled up in every corner. The marble for the foyer, the General informed her as they picked their way through the half-finished foundations, had been brought over from Italy and would surely be to her taste.

"My taste?" she stammered.

"But of course," he replied briskly. "It will be to your taste or I will not proceed with the project at all." He removed his pistol from its holster and set it on a banister, but then, as if on second thought, he picked it up, passed it from one hand to the other, and began to circle its mouth with his forefinger. "Yes. You see, *dokhtar-joon,* I've decided I want to marry you."

She understood at once the sort of marriage the General had in mind—a *siqeh,* or temporary marriage, to sanctify sexual intercourse.

It was then that everything she had been holding back, had told no one, had kept a secret for so long, came out as one breathless whole. Her marriage to Kazem, their divorce and the baby they took from her, the foundling hospital in Tübingen, Sohrab's death and the American attaché, her brother in Germany, her mother and her fourth-hand Singer, her job in the city. She could not look at him as she spoke, but she went on and on until still she had managed to tell him every last part of her story.

When she finished, the General laid his gun down and studied her. It had worked, she thought to herself. He would pity her; she would be safe now. She drew a deep breath and felt her pulse slacken. But all at once, he rose, slipped his belt free from his waist, and began working his fingers through the buttons of his shirt.

Lili looked quickly about her. There was no way out but past him.

When the General stepped toward her, she shoved him so hard with her two fists that she herself stumbled and nearly fell. "Who do you think you are that you won't let me touch you?" he taunted, catching her by the shoulder with one hand and yanking the front of her dress with the other so that it gave a loud rip and then flapped open from collar to waist. She staggered, steadied herself, and shoved him again with her fists.

He began lashing the ground with his belt then. Each time it came down he took a step closer toward her, so that soon the belt was whipping at her feet. She backed away and they began to circle the room. Again and again the belt sliced at the unfinished floorboards—*thwack, thwack, thwack!*—and the General's eyes never left her as it fell.

She spun around and broke into a run. Halfway down the driveway she bent down to kick off her shoes and heard a gunshot blast somewhere behind her. She hurled herself, barefoot, down to the end of the driveway to the main thoroughfare. There wasn't a single car or person in the street, and so she kept running with the echo of the gunshot and her own blood beating against her ears.

After some minutes she finally managed to flag down a car. It was a married couple on their way back to the city after a holiday in the mountains. "Did your husband do this to you?" the wife kept asking, the color rising in her cheeks. "You know, there are laws against this sort of thing now. You mustn't let him do this to you, you understand; you mustn't!"

"You mustn't let him"—that's what the lady kept saying over and over, and Lili nodded her head. *No*, khanoom, she swore. *I won't, I won't, I won't.*

That afternoon Kobra was waiting for Lili in the alley, as had become her habit. She'd been standing at the corner, clenching the edge of her veil between her teeth, wringing her hands, and counting the buses as they went by. She counted seven buses, then eight, then nine. When the fifteenth bus rumbled past, Kobra felt a trickle of sweat roll down her spine. She began to pray. When at last she spied Lili slipping out of a stranger's car with her chin buried in her chest, clutching at her torn dress with both hands, Kobra gripped her veil and rushed toward the car and then her screams ripped and echoed through the alley until, to Lili's unending shame, she managed to draw every last pair of eyes to them.

"Do you see what they've done?" she wailed. "Do you see what they've done to my child?"

When, after some days, she had regained her wits and calmed her mother, Lili retrieved the movie director's card, swiped on some red lipstick, and set off for his studio in Naderi Square. After the episode with the General, she could not return to her job as a cashier, and she did not have a single other prospect. Unfortunately, the director didn't seem to recognize her. She pulled out the card he'd given her just a few weeks before. "You asked if I wanted to play a Kurdish girl, remember? A girl on a horse?"

"Ah, yes, of course," he said with a quick lick of his lips, "but unfortunately that part's already been given to someone else—"

"Actually, *agha*," she interrupted, "I was thinking about a secretarial job. Surely you need secretaries here? I took a course, you see. I can type. I even have the certificate with me."

She began fumbling with her purse, but the director straightened his tie, cleared his throat, and told her there would be no need of that. A vision of Khanoom's face, contorted in pain, rose up in Lili's mind's eye but gradually faded as he put forth his proposition. Besides shooting films, he explained, the studio also employed girls for voice-over parts for foreign films. In fact, he said, it was her good fortune that they were holding auditions for voice-over jobs that very day.

The director took her by the arm and led her to a room where more than two dozen young women sat waiting their turns. She drew a breath of relief. He'd been telling the truth; he had decent work for her after all.

The audition consisted of reading a page torn from a recent, though far from current, edition of a London newspaper. She read sufficiently well to be called back the following day.

While the movies were all American, Westerns were particularly well represented. Her job was to speak for the women. Thanks to her once-fervent reading of Dickens she could still read English, but by this time her actual comprehension of the language had been winnowed down considerably. What's more, the American accents and cowboy slang totally befuddled her. When she made this confession to a studio technician, Lili was told not to worry, that creativity was the greatest of assets to a girl in this line of work.

Alone in her tiny sound booth, Lili watched the heroines drape themselves in doorways, cling to the sleeves of their gun-slinging heroes, peel off their petticoats, and strip down to lacy silk negligees. She would sit in this booth for many months to come, grateful for the seclusion and anonymity she found there, eventually earning her passage back to Europe. Longing, humiliation, terror, love— the same themes flickered before her in seemingly endless cinematic variation. She pulled on her headphones, struck up her recording machine, and it was not long before she discovered that her job was not nearly as hard as she'd first imagined.

It took her a little less than a year to save up enough money. Now she applied herself to the truly difficult part of her scheme.

"I am going to Germany," she told Sara.

It was a balmy afternoon in late August and they were sitting on a bench in Niavaran Park sipping cherry-flavored iced sherbets. They saw each other once or twice a month, mostly on outings in the city where Lili felt free of Kobra's disapproving gaze and Sara could do as she pleased. Earlier Lili had bought Sara a red kite from a street vendor. "Your big sister is very kind to buy you this kite," the old man had said as he tied it to Sara's wrist, and Sara had thought his mistake very funny and giggled.

But now, with Lili's announcement, Sara gave the kite a hard, quick tug and it began to bob up and down awkwardly. She turned her face to Lili and fixed her with an angry look. "How long will you stay there?"

"Four years—maybe three."

"Why?"

"So that I can study."

"Why?"

"So that I can come back here and buy a little house for us."

This seemed to please Sara and her expression softened. She took another taste of her sherbet and began swinging her legs under the bench. A breeze picked up and the red kite began to sway gently above their heads.

"But why don't you study here?" Sara asked suddenly.

Lili hadn't expected this question. "It's very expensive to study in Iran," she said. This was true enough. Medical school would be prohibitively expensive, and so she'd decided to study midwifery. Long practiced in informal networks, in recent years it had become a branch of study at a large, modern nursing institute in Tehran, but Lili knew it would be easier to pay her way through school in Germany and also that a foreign diploma would be worth much more in Iran than an Iranian one.

That she was fed up with her family's attempts to marry her off, that she could not stand to live in Iran so long as she was just a poor, half-educated divorcée, that her father had been right to send her away the first time—these were all points Lili judged beyond the child's comprehension.

"It's too expensive here," Lili repeated.

Sara started crying and her sherbet tipped over into her lap and spilled all over her skirt. Lili fell to her knees and began to dab at the sticky mess with the sleeves of her own dress. It was hopeless. The stain would not come out, and dabbing at it did nothing to quiet Sara's crying, nor could it stop Lili from starting to cry herself.

Seven

Damad Farangi
(Foreign Groom)

"A damad farangi? A European groom?" My mother laughed. "No one in my family had ever heard of such a thing! But that is exactly what I found when I went away for the second time. And they still can't believe it. Even after all these years, they wonder how it happened!"

O N HER RETURN TRIP to Germany, Lili found an empty cabin and stretched out on the seats. In her purse she had one hundred deutsche marks and a letter of acceptance to a *Frauenklinik*, a school for midwives in Hamburg. She pulled the letter out, read it, and tucked it carefully back into the bottom of her purse. She smiled to herself. She'd done it; she'd finally left Iran. She'd supported her brother to the end of his studies and was free now to resume her own. But if she had any hope of carrying out the rest of her plans, she'd need to keep her wits about her. She'd also have to be very careful with her money.

To avoid the cost of a night's lodgings, she'd taken a midnight train directly from Frankfurt to Hamburg. Drawing her coat over her for a blanket and laying her purse on the armrest for a pillow, she closed her eyes and fell into an uneasy sleep. Sometime before dawn she woke to the sound of a woman's laughter. Not a foot from where Lili was lying, a woman had thrown a leg around a man's waist. The man whispered something against her throat and the woman giggled. The train bumped along the tracks and wound its way through a tunnel, illuminating for some moments the metal clasp of the woman's garters, the man's hands on her neck, his exposed buttocks, and the trousers bunched at his feet.

Lili held her breath and then, after what seemed like an eternity, the man at last let out a long, deep-throated moan and the pair disentangled.

The next morning on her way to the lavatory, Lili came across the selfsame gentleman sitting in the dining car with one leg crossed smartly over the other, completely absorbed in the morning paper. A gold wedding band flashed from his finger and his companion of the previous evening was nowhere in sight. Terrified that he'd recognize her, Lili bowed her head and hustled off.

At one station a family of five had entered her cabin, considered her briefly, and then wedged themselves side by side on the three seats facing her. With a great crinkling flourish of butcher paper they assembled, and proceeded to consume, an elaborate breakfast of paper-thin slices of ham and cheese, buttered rolls, a tin of what looked to be cherry jam, a large metallic flask of coffee, and a second, smaller flask filled with cream. The family did not offer her so much as a single roll.

In Iran, she reflected, a person would have to be on the brink of starvation before such rudeness could be excused. She turned her face to look at the countryside, a wash of gray and black now in wintertime. Her stomach grumbled and she considered leaving the cabin and buying herself a pastry from the dining car, but on second thought she decided she was better off saving her money. She pulled her coat tighter about her, pressed her forehead to the cold windowpane, and consoled herself with the thought that at least she could count on maintaining her figure in this country.

Some hours later, when she reached her dormitory room, Lili discovered a girl sitting cross-legged on one of the cots with her head bent over a book. Her hair was long and dark and she had a pretty, heart-shaped face. Lili greeted her new roommate, only to be rewarded with an unintelligible mumble. She dropped her suitcase, looked quickly about the cell-like quarters, and, lacking any other diversion, sat down on the edge of one of two empty cots and began to study her roommate more closely. When she saw the Persian script stamped along the spine of the girl's book, Lili thought she'd die of happiness. She fell onto the girl's bed, clasped the girl to her breast, and kissed her on both cheeks. "Do you miss your family? Is that why you don't talk? You can talk to me now, you know. You can talk to me all you like!"

After several days of prattling on in this manner she succeeded in learning the girl's name (it was Shireen, which meant "sweet") and drawing out one- and two-word answers from her. After a few days Lili met a second Iranian student, a pudgy, giggly girl named Farideh who claimed the third and last of the room's three cots. Lili liked her less than she liked Shireen, but still it cheered her considerably to befriend another Iranian so far from home.

More than loneliness, it was hunger that sealed the girls' friendship. Every evening the instructors of the *Frauenklinik* and their German students filed into the clinic's main dining hall. Lili, Shireen, Farideh, and the half-dozen other foreign girls waited outside on a long wooden bench. The only German student among them was a heavy-set girl with a stutter and a limp. When the first group finished its dinner, the second group was called in to forage a meal from the leftovers: undercooked bits of herring, a few charred baked potatoes, strips of beef floating in fat-flecked gravy, pasty dumplings, and seemingly endless variations of pork. Suffice it to say, Lili, Shireen, and Farideh often returned from the dining hall as hungry as when they entered it.

In her desperation Shireen began collecting potatoes in her bag and frying them up in the dormitory after hours. When her mother, a widowed schoolteacher, sent Shireen a pouch of saffron stamens by post from Tehran along with a mortar and pestle, she ground the stamens round and round until she'd reduced them to a deep orange dust. After midnight, when all the other girls in the dormitory had gone to sleep, Shireen plugged in her hot plate, greased it with a pat of butter also poached from the canteen, sprinkled a bit of her treasured saffron on top, and stirred the potatoes until they crisped at the edges. Then she, Lili, and Farideh sat cross-legged on their cots and ate until they felt their stomachs would burst.

Lili's days now began in the middle of the night. At three o'clock her alarm clock jolted her from sleep and she'd jerk herself out of bed. She pulled on all her stockings, all four pairs of them, grabbed her coat, and stumbled out of the dormitory. The cold was astonishing. The streets were slick with ice and snow, and though the clinic was no more than a few hundred yards from her dormitory, she'd falter, trip, and haul herself back up several times before reaching the *Frauenklinik*. Within weeks the frozen cobblestones would grind down the kitten heels that were her only pair of shoes.

When she finally arrived at the clinic, she stripped off two of her pairs of stockings (the hospital corridors were so cold that she kept on the other two pairs), pulled on her uniform, smock, and, finally, her headdress. It made her smile to remember the dozens of headdresses she'd ruined on her first stay in Germany, back when she'd been an orderly at the foundling hospital. There'd be no fumbling about this time round. A minute, to judge from the attitude of the nurses at the *Frauenklinik*, was worth one hundred years in Germany, and tardiness was among the most severely punished of offenses. Lili pinned her headgear tight, smoothed the pleats of her smock, and set off at a clip down the dark corridors.

She'd have at least three dozen babies to clean and diaper and hand over to their mothers for the six o'clock morning feedings. After that she stripped the sheets, often still damp with blood from the previous night's deliveries, loaded them onto wheeled baskets, and delivered them to the laundry to be bleached and steamed and ironed before the day was out. At eleven o'clock she sat in the lecture hall with her clipboard propped between her legs, dividing the page into one column for the parts of the lecture she understood and another for the words she would have to look up later, first from German to English, then from English to Persian.

She earned her lunch by scouring and polishing the enormous brass pots in the kitchen. Unfortunately, most days this meant some manifestation of pork, which she simply could not bring herself to eat. To supplement her late-night potato binges, she took to scraping the burnt porridge from the pots and spooning it quickly into her mouth when no one was looking. Fortunately, the porridge tasted somewhat like rice pudding, especially when she managed to sneak a sprinkle of sugar onto it before eating it.

Like other unpleasant aspects of her new life, the details of her hunger were not disclosed in the letters Lili now scribbled to her family between shifts at the *Frauenklinik*.

The difficulty with which these letters were received made her all the less willing to write them in the first place. Khanoom and Kobra could not read or write and therefore depended on male relatives, or one of the younger girls of the family, to read Lili's letters aloud to them and to then dictate their replies.

It was a slow and laborious process, but reaching one another by telephone proved far more troublesome. With no phone of their own, her mother and grandmother would have to make a trip to Tehran's main post office and wait, sometimes hours, for their turn in a booth—all for the unlikely chance that Lili would be in her room and could be called up to the dormitory phone. The result was that they rarely called her, and for the most part Lili did not regret this, as her voice always managed to betray her misery when she spoke to them by telephone.

"We have nothing to complain of but your absence" was once again the claim put down in her family's letters to her. The same line was written in her own letters to them. On both sides, the remark only managed to underscore the hardship of their respective circumstances, but just how much these words obscured from her Lili would not discover for a long time yet.

What Lili did not know, and would not know for several more years, was that shortly after she'd left Iran, Kazem's mother had died, leaving Sara fully in Kazem and her stepmother's care. Kobra found out through Zaynab, the only member of the family who'd continued to visit Sara after Lili left Iran. Neither Zaynab nor Kobra could bear to tell Lili the news for fear it would distract her from her studies and prolong her stay in Germany or—even worse—bring her prematurely back to Iran a second time.

For some months Kobra had neither word nor sight of Kazem, and for this she had no end of thanking both God and the mercies that came only with time's passing. Her peace, however, was to be short-lived. After Lili left for Germany, Sara continued to show up on Kobra's doorstep on Zahirodolleh Alley. As in the past, Sara always came alone, but now she appeared without her little brown suitcase. Many of the same curses Kobra had suffered from Kazem fell now from Sara's lips. "May your spine rot!" was accompanied by words made doubly indecent to Kobra by the fact that they were spoken by a young girl and triply so by the fact that they were spoken by a young girl about her mother.

"She's a prostitute! They told me she's a prostitute!"

At this Kobra would cup both hands over her ears and begin chanting to herself. It was always the same words, the same prayer: "May God kill me; may God kill me...."

"She's a prostitute and you want to hide it! That's why you won't tell me where she is!"

Pacing the room, clawing her cheeks, Kobra continued her chanting. "May God kill me; may God kill me...."

It was in the spirit of such exchanges that Kobra grew familiar with the stories Sara had been told about Lili by Kazem and his family.

The Khorramis, according to this version of events, had had their doubts about Lili from the very beginning of the marriage. Apart from the obvious differences of class and education, there'd been the defects in Lili's character. However Kazem had tried to rein in her vanities and temper her restlessness, Lili had taken no heed. When she'd left Sara behind one afternoon and come home in a shameless state, with wild hair and disheveled clothes, it was immediately obvious what had happened. Lili had fallen in love with a man and "given" herself to him. After that she'd wanted nothing more of either her husband or her child. What's more, Lili's studies were nothing but a ruse devised to cover her shame. She'd likely never even left Tehran and was hiding out somewhere in the city.

"May God kill me; may God kill me; may God kill me...."

Kobra would chant these same words so loudly, for so long, and with such concentration that eventually Sara would grow tired and leave her alone. A month, two months would pass. One blessed year six months went by without a visit from Sara. But Sara always came back. And while Kobra continued to pray and burn her little pots of wild rue, for such curses as she would hear from her granddaughter over the next years she judged there would be neither cure nor any need to tell Lili.

Before graduating, Lili would have to attend exactly one thousand deliveries, the first several hundred of which she would observe until she was judged capable of proceeding on her own.

The students were each assigned a midwife and traveled in packs through the hospital and ordered to study the instructor's every move. The midwife routinely began by placing her hands on the woman's belly to determine the direction of the baby's head. Once she'd ascertained the width of the patient's pelvis, the midwife touched two fingers to the woman's wrist to check her pulse and then proceeded to measure her dilation and time her contractions. Lili and her cohorts were shown how to cut open and sew up a woman's wounds. They even learned how to sever an umbilical cord without scissors, though, they were pointedly assured, it was unlikely that most of them would resort to such primitive measures in their future careers. They grew familiar with the various tools of the trade—metal trays, surgical needles, iodine, alcohol, and chloroform—and eventually Lili and the others were trusted to prop up the patients' legs into stirrups and to wash, shave, and prep them for the deliveries. "*Drücken, drücken, drücken!*" they learned to shout when the babies' heads crowned. Push, push, push!

She was shocked to discover that most of the patients were women well into their forties, an age at which she thought most women had long since been retired from their conjugal duties. Gray-haired, with shrunken breasts and bellies distorted through five and six pregnancies, they lay hollering and heaving, cussing and praying, and easily outnumbering the young mothers in the wards. They were not told, nor did they ask, the names of the foreign girls who held their hands and stroked their foreheads and reached out to catch the children they pushed into the world.

Schwester Annelise, the midwife to whom Lili had been assigned for her training, was a jowly, big-bosomed woman from the southern part of the country. "*So ist das Leben mit Fremde Leute,*" she muttered in a thick Swabian accent whenever Lili failed to understand orders. So this is life among strangers—as though the meaning of this, too, would escape Lili's comprehension.

Schwester Annelise was well-known among the midwives and students for her method of quieting women in the throes of labor. When their cries turned too whiny or too rowdy, she yanked a bed pillow from under their heads and smothered their faces with it. Month after month Lili stood by Schwester Annelise's side, herself breathless with fear that the poor women would suffocate before they managed to deliver their babies, but Schwester Annelise always knew just how long to hold the pillow over a woman's face before lifting it again.

To all this Lili submitted herself.

Work was making a new person out of her, efficient, assured, and even a little removed from the agonies and cruelties surrounding her. Better still, it had no equal in its power to chase thoughts from her head. To fill her few spare hours, she decided to take a job outside the hospital. Apart from her growing appreciation for the oblivion induced by hard labor, there were two immediate reasons for this. First, if she hoped to make it through the winter without breaking all her arms and limbs in steady succession, she would need a pair of proper boots. Second, she could not afford to pay for her textbooks and she suspected she would soon wear out Shireen's patience by borrowing hers.

One afternoon Lili took a streetcar to the center of the city to visit the Iranian embassy, and there she sat waiting with her knees tightly pressed together, her small brown handbag on her lap, fighting the urge to flee. When the consular officer appeared, she braced herself for a tawdry proposition. None was forthcoming. She relaxed her grip on her purse handles, cleared her throat, and related her need for books and shoes. The consular officer's expression went from one of polite inquiry to one of genuine concern. In a matter of minutes, he produced a list of a half-dozen names and urged her to return if none of these contacts proved useful.

From then on she spent her Sundays with an elderly Iranian couple, the Pakravans, in their well-appointed flat near the Hotel Vier

Jahreszeiten. Her job was to watch over their granddaughter, Setareh, a curly-haired, pink-cheeked girl of five. Lili could not help but wonder how the Pakravans had landed in this corner of Germany and where the girl's parents could possibly be, but she refrained from asking such questions for fear it should inspire the Pakravans to ask more about her own circumstances. She took Setareh on long treks through the city's botanical gardens, and as they walked Lili searched her memory for all the best stories that Khanoom used to tell her when she was a child. "*Yeki bood; yeki nabood*," she always began, the traditional Iranian invocation of a story. "One was all; all was one." She spun stories of princes, princesses, and beasts, of quests and perils and prizes. As the little girl's eyes went wide and her lips fell open in wonder, Lili found she was as happy to tell these stories as Setareh was to hear them.

When they returned from their outings, Lili shared a supper of rice and stew with the family, easily tucking away as many as three helpings. Setareh always claimed the seat beside hers at the table and begged for more stories. At the end of the night, when Lili pulled on her coat and turned to leave, Setareh would throw her arms around Lili's legs, bury her head in Lili's stomach, and refuse to let her go. Clinic rules forbade her from staying overnight at the Pakravans' apartment—or any other place—during the week. She patted the girl's head and then pulled herself free. "I'll be back next week!" she'd say with as much cheer as she could muster.

The memory of Setareh's crying followed Lili into the week, and she would think, miserably, of Sara. How much longer could she count on Sara to remember her? Or had she already forgotten her? Lili, absorbed in thoughts of her own daughter, patted the little girl's head and wrestled herself free and made her way back into the streets of Hamburg. Eventually, though, she would welcome the longing she felt between these visits to the Pakravans. If motherly feelings still stirred in her, Lili reasoned, when she returned to Iran she might be a mother yet.

Her other charge in this period was a young Iranian man named

Payam. He'd contracted polio as a child and could move about only by crawling and dragging himself along the floor. By the time his family had sold off their lands and properties in Iran and sent him to Germany for a series of experimental operations, there was not enough money left for any of them to accompany him on his journey. Lili was one of a number of student nurses his family hired to keep him company a few hours each week between his surgeries. The job did not pay very well, but she found herself incapable of turning it down.

Twenty-five years old with a high forehead and beautiful limpid eyes, Payam played classical violin and could talk for hours about Rumi and Iran's mystical poetic tradition. Payam had a small library by his bedside and begged Lili to ask anyone going to Iran to bring him back volumes of poetry. He told her about the metal bands that he'd soon have on his legs, how he'd be able to walk as well as anyone after his operation. He always spoke of returning to Iran, of marrying a girl he loved there.

At night the German girls, lipsticked, perfumed, and high heeled, disappeared into the hospital basement to listen to jazz records with the male doctors. No invitations were extended to the Iranian girls, but even if they had been, none would have been accepted. Convinced that word of the slightest indiscretion would somehow make it back to their families in Tehran, Lili and her Iranian friends spent their first dozen nights off duty eating their saffron-spiced fried potatoes and trading news of home.

One evening, however, she and Farideh would hazard a visit to the Reeperbahn, the mile-long red-light district near the harbor. "You haven't seen Hamburg until you've seen the Reeperbahn!" one of the German students had insisted. "People come from all over the world to see it!" That the world's oldest profession had outposts in their own homeland was something Lili and Farideh vaguely understood, but this did nothing to quell their curiosity about how, exactly, prostitution was practiced in the West. Lili made discreet inquiries and discovered that the city's prostitutes were easily accessible by foot.

It was a warm evening in early autumn, but the mission somehow roused in Lili and Farideh a native instinct for modesty. When they set out, they pulled on their heaviest winter coats and covered their heads in silk scarves. Meanwhile, on Hamburg's famed Reeperbahn, the prostitutes were displaying their wares from behind faintly illuminated windowpanes. Holding hands and sweating profusely under their coats, Lili and Farideh discovered that European prostitutes came in an astonishing range of ages and shapes. The states of undress were strikingly diverse as well. Most of the women wore lacy slips with garters, but at the sight of the first naked prostitute, a thoroughly bored-looking redhead with enormous breasts, Farideh shut her eyes and refused, simply refused, to open them. Lili laughed and joked that a future midwife had better get over such squeamishness, but when one of the prostitutes winked and gestured to her from behind a window she almost fainted herself.

"*Schmutzige Ausländer!*" a man suddenly shouted from across the street. Dirty foreigners! He was waving his arms wildly at them, and the other men on the street all turned to look at her and Farideh. Their shame in that moment would have been more than enough to convert all the prostitutes they'd seen into nuns. They locked eyes for an instant and then broke into a run. Within minutes the pair arrived, panting and trembling, back in the safety of their dormitory room.

There were certain temptations, to be sure. Not in the city, where the males in the cafés seemed not much older than fourteen years and failed to rouse the faintest longing in Lili, but in the hospital corridors where she spent ten or twelve hours of every day. For Lili the doctors in their impeccable white smocks were easily the most appealing men in Germany, not least of all because they made her feel she was a character plucked from the pages of *The Thousand and One Nights*. Several of them were wont to pull her aside in the hallways to discuss the love poems of Hāfez and the architectural wonders of Persepolis. They were in many cases more learned about her country's history and literary traditions than she herself, and she listened eagerly to their speeches and secretly spun fantasies of her own.

When one of them, a handsome, towering surgeon, returned from a weekend in San Moritz to tell her that he'd seen the young shah and his new bride on the slopes, trailed by two dozen skiing paparazzi, Lili gasped. "Did you see how beautiful our Queen Soraya is?" she asked him. "Did you see her green eyes?" The surgeon answered that the young queen was indeed beautiful but assured Lili that black eyes and dark hair like hers were far more fetching—"more *Oriental-isch*," he added, throwing her a wink.

She delivered her thousandth baby (a howling, bright pink twelve-and-a-half-pound boy) and prepared herself for the last part of her training: the theoretical examinations. She had by this time acquired a stack of notebooks filled with several hundred German words she'd meant to look up but never had. Between her days at the *Frauenklinik* attending the deliveries of the Germans and her weekends tending to her fellow Iranian exiles in the city proper, she had not had as much time to study as she would have liked, but as the examination date neared she reminded herself that there were dozens of lazy students with far less hope of gaining their certificates. Surely she would pass.

According to *Frauenklinik* tradition, on the day of the students' final exams one of the instructors always handed out bright silver pfennigs for good luck. That year it was Schwester Annelise who handed out the coins. When Lili's turn came she smiled very slightly, and then let the pfennig fall. "Pity to have come so far only to lose your luck," Schwester Annelise said, shaking her head. "Such a pity you'll have to go back now!"

Lili did not flinch. She stepped neatly over the pfennig, sat down at her desk, and smoothed her examination book. But the pages were crawling with words she couldn't make out, and her mind would not quite settle down. Three hours later, when she and the other students filed out of the room to await their results, her hands were still shaking and her throat had gone dry. One by one the girls were called back in until Lili was the only one left sitting outside. She would not get her certificate and would not be able to return to Iran that year.

She spent five hours tramping through Hamburg, in which time she rounded the Binnenalster no fewer than fourteen times. Only when she'd lost all sensation in her fingers and toes did she turn back to the clinic. Shireen found her facedown on her cot several hours later, alternating between fits of crying and uncontrollable laughter. She hauled Lili out of the dormitory and dragged her into the psychiatry ward. There she was given a dose of morphine so massive that it put her out for two days. Hysteria, it was believed, was not uncommon with these foreign types, and in their case drugs were administered more freely and in more than the usual quantity.

Having passed her exams, Farideh returned to Iran; Shireen left for England for a round of advanced training, bequeathing Lili her little cache of saffron and enjoining her to write often; and Lili was left behind in Germany with her failure and her rage.

The episode would, however, only strengthen Lili's determination to succeed. She found a new school, this one in the town of Göttingen, and set herself to the task of repeating the academic portion of her degree requirements. One night, Francesca, the frizzy-haired German girl occupying the cot opposite hers, offered to take Lili along to a dance in a nearby village. Lili accepted the rare treat of a night out. Over blaring polka music, she spent the evening demanding of a succession of young men, "Persian, I am Persian. Do you not know the poet Hāfez? Do you not know the master, Rumi?" Wealthy Iranian families had been sending their sons abroad for several decades, but in those years Iranian women rarely left the country except as the wives of very rich men. To most Germans back then "Iran" meant either a land steeped in the splendors of Persian antiquity or else a country suspended in medieval squalor. For her part, by this time Lili had learned to read in people's expressions which of these two visions they had of her country. She herself did not discriminate between the people she met but simply confronted everyone with the imperiousness that had become native to her.

A young railway engineer in a herringbone jacket and crooked bow tie, Johann had come alone to the village dance by himself that night, but he'd been courting a German girl for some months. All his life he would be a man who was shy even of children, but because he had read mystical Persian poetry and had lived for three months on a Greek island, in Lili he would have glimpsed the almond-eyed beauties of the Persian miniatures and he would have held her gaze longer than most of the German men there that night.

How, he began, did people live in Iran? What were their customs, hardships, and ambitions? Lili smiled and answered him as well as she could. With each draught of beer his attentions grew keener. He ordered a round for their table and another for the entire polka band. Before leaving the dance he asked if he could call on her the following day. She needed, she felt, the permission of a putative father, and so she turned to the only viable candidate at the table, Francesca's inebriated father. The gentleman slurred his assent.

Lili was still sleeping when Johann appeared at noon wearing the previous night's bow tie paired with a freshly pressed suit and vest.

Francesca shook her awake, and she piled her hair on top of her head and then descended the stairs in a flowered robe. She and Johann took coffee in the parlor and he left an hour later, having promised to visit her soon in Göttingen. Grinning, he skipped out of the house and waved to her from the window of his little orange Audi.

From then on the phone rang for her daily in the dormitory, and every Friday evening he would drive out to visit her. That they did not share a common native language or culture, that she knew little of his past and that he knew even less of hers—all these gaps and fissures only put Lili at ease with her gentleman caller. They'd go to dinner at one of the city's finest restaurants and afterward they always took a turn around the town's main thoroughfare together. Sometimes he exhausted her with his questions, but he was, she thought, exceedingly well mannered and, though he was more than ten years older than her, still sweetly boyish. And when, after dinner one evening, she at last told him about her marriage and her child back in Iran, he'd listened with a tenderness that she would not soon forget.

On Christmas Eve they paid a visit to his family in Hessisch-Lichtenau, a small village outside Frankfurt. It was snowing hard when they set out from Göttingen and did not stop the entire way there. Arriving hours later than they'd planned, they found the rooms dark and quiet. Johann showed Lili to the guest room and slipped away to some other corner of the cottage. She awoke the next morning to discover she'd spent the night under the figure of Christ—or, rather, a gigantic wooden statue of Jesus impaled on a cross above the bed. It was no longer snowing, and from the window she could make out a one-lane road and a few black roofs in the far distance. More sobering than all of this, however, were the starched white bed linens and the ironed doilies of that room. Though she was by now no stranger to the German passion for order, these linens and doilies intimidated her sufficiently to pull on the cream two-piece suit she'd intended to wear to dinner that night and also to twist her curls into an officious bun.

They were all waiting for her in the breakfast nook downstairs. Mutti, Johann's mother, was a portly woman with bright blue eyes and flushed cheeks and she wore a cornflower blue housedress, a white apron, orangey-beige stockings, and a pair of thick-heeled black leather shoes. Lili shook her hand and was next introduced to Johann's two sisters. The tall one with the glasses was called Maria, and she lived with Mutti in Hessisch-Lichtenau and worked as an accountant in town. Elsa was the shorter, prettier sister with the sharp eyes. She'd moved to Frankfurt to work for a large company that traded gold, silver, and other hard currencies. Taking her place at the table, Lili could not help but notice that though it was still very early in the morning, the threesome already smelled strongly of cigarettes and peppermints.

While to Lili they seemed the picture of a German family, Johann and his family had, in fact, come to the country from a village near Danzig and were actually Kashubians, ethnic Slavs who had lived for hundreds of years in a colony of thatched cottages near the Baltic Sea. When the Nazis descended on Poland in the 1930s, the Kashubians were hauled out of their villages and appraised alongside cripples, degenerates, and Gypsies. The result was that the six members of the family were split three ways. The eldest sibling, Jakob, a strapping sixteen-year-old, was sent to the front to fight for the Reich; Johann, the youngest, and his father were sent to the work camps in Russia; Johann's two sisters and their *Mutti* were shipped to a village outside Frankfurt to wait out the fate of their men.

Jakob never returned. "He's lost," Mutti took to murmuring as she stared out the window. "He's lost somewhere out there and he can't find us." Elsa and Maria indulged the delusion for fear that without it their mother would truly lose her mind. By the time Papa and Johann turned up in Hessisch-Lichtenau, boys as young as fourteen were being sent to the front. Mutti and the sisters swept up their *Bübchen*, their little boy. If not quite so handsome as his dead brother, Jakob, with his blue eyes and blond curls Johann was still the prettiest of them all. They installed him in the basement for the duration of World War II. To pass the time, Johann taught himself Greek.

When the war ended, he emerged from the basement, sat out two years of high school as the only boy in his class, and in that time learned to speak German as if he'd lived all his life in Hessisch-Lichtenau. Papa died shortly afterward of cancer. Having looked about the village and between them found not one eligible man under fifty, the two daughters of the family went to work. Johann finished high school, won a scholarship to study civil engineering, and then joined a team of engineers who traveled the country rebuilding its railways, tunnels, and bridges.

He had a gentleness that set him apart and a taste for beer that did not. Wherever he went for his work, he rented a room for four nights of the week, Monday through Thursday, and he spent the weekends and every holiday with his mother and sisters. Late at night when he stumbled home drunk from the beer halls, Maria and Elsa peeled the clothes from his body and took turns scrubbing his face and chest with warm washcloths so that their mother would not know the worst of his drinking habit. He was thirty-four years old the year he showed up at his family's house with Lili, and though his blond curls had turned dark and wrinkles fanned out under his blue eyes, he was their *Bübchen* still, and they would not, as Lili observed after just ten minutes at their table, surrender him easily.

And yet within a week of that visit he had discarded the ring he'd bought for his German girlfriend. Lili's affection for Johann fell short of his infatuation with her, but she had reason to hasten a formal commitment: many of her relatives thought it inevitable that she would lose her morals in Europe, which only made her more determined to hold fast to them. One Sunday afternoon Lili asked Johann to drive her out to the countryside in his orange Audi. When they crossed a small trestle bridge, she told him to pull over and stop the engine. She pointed her finger in the direction of the river. Johann understood at once. He slipped out of his seat, took a few long strides away from the car, and then tossed the gold ring into the water.

Emboldened by the gesture, Johann next demanded a private interview with the head bishop of Frankfurt. In the course of explaining his intentions to marry a Muslim girl, he spoke of Lili's marriage, her child, and her divorce. When he finished speaking, the bishop retreated into the recesses of the church. Whether this was to confer with his fellow priests or to consult some ancient religious tome Johann would never know, but when the bishop returned he assured Johann that given Lili's age at the time of her first marriage an argument could be made that the union had lacked consent. It was not the definitive answer he had hoped for, but it eased Johann's Catholic conscience somewhat, or at least enough for him to proceed with his proposal.

He declared himself with a string of pearls. As he reached over to close the clasp, a tear slid down his cheek, and with that tear Lili crossed instantly from indecision to certainty. She'd known him less than two months, but such depth of feeling, coupled as it so obviously was with adoration, seemed to her a very fine qualification in a husband. She would marry him, she said, but on the condition that he would put the proposal into writing for her family.

But to whom should he write? Since Khanoom and Kobra were totally illiterate, writing to them was out of the question, and, anyway, Lili felt certain that a male relative should be called forth to speak on her behalf. In the end Johann composed a formal letter to her brother in Stuttgart, to which Nader replied by stating: "My sister is free to choose her own husband. I wish you well in any case."

Having settled this account, Johann set out for Hessisch-Lichtenau for what would prove a much more difficult task: announcing the engagement to his own family. Mutti, Maria, and Elsa looked at him and then at one another. The Iranian girl, they suddenly realized, had not been a guest but a thief. He was careful to make no mention of Lili's first marriage, and certainly not of her child, as either of these would have been sufficient to kill Mutti outright, but even so it was not long before Mutti gave him to understand that in the absence of a Kashubian bride, any Catholic girl would do, but a Muslim was beyond consideration—his as well as theirs.

Johann left the house feeling bitter and dejected but not without his best suit draped carefully over his arm. He and Lili pooled their money and bought each other a pair of matching engagement rings (the thinnest slivers of ten-karat gold—their budgets allowed for no better). Then they decided they would need something else to commemorate the occasion. They spent the better part of a January afternoon ducking into the city's finest boutiques, considering trinkets and tokens they could not possibly afford. When they tired of that game, they found an antique shop and settled on a silver candlestick and matching silver vase and three stems of nearly fresh orchids from an open-air market.

Johann booked two rooms in a hotel for their "engagement party," and since hers was the better one of the two, it was there that they slipped their engagement rings onto each other's fingers and made their promises. At midnight they kissed, said their good nights, and then Johann retired to his own hotel room. Between her past and his Catholic upbringing, there was no need for a chaperone that evening.

While his enthusiasm for the East was certainly attractive, there were certain practical conditions for Johann to meet before they could marry.

"What conditions?" he asked, confident that by defying his family he'd already surmounted the most difficult challenge Lili could set for him.

"I don't want you to drink. Well, not so much, anyway."

"Then I won't," he answered quickly. "I won't drink at all."

Lili nodded. "Good," she said. "But there's something else." She cleared her throat and, blushing slightly, put the matter forth in a single word: "Circumcision."

Johann blushed back, bowed his head, and proceeded to ask her what, exactly, that entailed. Rousing all the professionalism she'd acquired over the foregoing three years, she explained the details of the procedure, employing all the proper medical terms and even drawing him a textbook-worthy sketch. "I see," he noted when she finished, his voice even despite the fact that his face had been drained of all color.

When he left that night she was not at all certain he would return, but another hour found him knocking at her door. He had more questions for her—not about circumcision this time, but about Islam proper. The next few hours progressed with him asking her questions of increasing theological subtlety. Her German was, by then, quite passable, but she found her vocabulary limited in matters of faith. She answered as best she could. Johann spent an hour in his car only to return with more questions. There was an interlude before dawn when they slept, she in her room and he down in the street in his car.

"Call the hospital and make an appointment," he told her when light cracked over the horizon at six o'clock the next morning.

Circumcisions were far from routine even among infants at the clinic, but the procedure had certainly never before been attempted on a man in his thirties. No precautions were spared. Johann was counseled as if for brain surgery, advised to proceed only under general anesthesia, and required to spend two nights in the hospital. After he'd been wheeled out of sight, Lili sat by herself in the waiting room, studying the black-and-white tiles at her feet and biting her nails down to bloody nubs. As the hours stretched on, she began to consider what she could possibly say to his family if he wound up dying on the operating table.

Johann finally emerged after three hours, heavily drugged and smiling goofily, his cheeks the brightest shade of red she had seen in her life. Infection had set in and his condition was critical. A massive dose of antibiotics was administered, and Lili's worry now turned into hysteria. She paced the halls and appealed to God with every last prayer she remembered, and many more that she made up that day.

When Johann's fever reached 104 degrees, he turned his eyes slowly to her. "Telegraph Mutti," he whispered between labored breaths. "Tell her to come, but don't tell her anything...." Within hours, Mutti and Maria descended on the hospital in their trench coats, trailing their peppermint and cigarette perfume through the corridors. They brushed past Lili without a hello and made their way straight to Johann's sickbed. But why had he been brought to the hospital in the first place? Had he been ill? What kind of surgery had he undergone? Mutti and Maria pleaded and begged and even, in their desperation, began to suggest bribes—only to be frustrated at every turn. Elsa, arriving some time later from Frankfurt, noted the lack of visible bandages and guessed straightaway what had transpired. But was it really possible he had let this *thing* be done to him, Mutti cried, and when Johann, whose fever had finally begun to ebb, nodded weakly from the hospital bed the women's cries rose up and echoed through the halls. The Iranian girl had come straight from hell, they wailed, and she'd bury them all in time.

Against all such predictions, Johann, at least, recovered. Within a week of his operation, he returned to work and resumed his weekly dates with Lili. He visited both the beer halls and his family with less and less frequency, and in his spare hours he took to perusing volumes on Iranian literature, history, and architecture. Then, as soon as Lili sat for her final exam and extracted her diploma from the University of Göttingen, Johann handed in his resignation. He sold off his Audi and all but his most cherished books. With the money from these, his savings, and Lili's small contribution, he bought a black Mercedes sedan that he and Lili would drive to Iran.

It was 1962. For three weeks they would subsist on a diet of bread, coffee, and the occasional fruit plucked from a roadside tree. Their only luxuries were a tour of the gambling casino in Monaco and the purchase of a pair of suede pumps Lili spied in a Viennese boutique. At the Austro-Yugoslav border they were searched and questioned in a windowless room that smelled heavily of garlic and sweat. When they were well into Turkey, Lili discovered one of her suede pumps was missing. Johann turned the car back toward Yugoslavia, freed the missing shoe from the clutch of a surly and poorly shaven customs officer, and with that the couple headed back toward Iran to be married.

Eight

Peacock Throne

"I can still remember her dress," Lili said as she began to speak of the last years in Iran. "Blue velvet, cut open at the shoulders. She wore it to serve me tea. Can you imagine such a thing? To give a girl a dress like that and then call her mother kharab, *broken? And that's what she called me, too. Kharab. A prostitute."*

IRANIANS HAD WELCOMED A succession of three queens over the preceding decades: the Egyptian princess Fawzia, the green-eyed Soraya, the formidable Farah Diba. This parade of royal brides posed a riddle as complex as any of the changes to occur during the reign of Mohammad Reza Pahlavi. In generations past, infertile and otherwise undesirable wives would most likely have been kept alongside new ones, but as heir to his father's modernization campaign as well as Reza Shah's strategic, often uneasy alliances with the West, the second Pahlavi monarch had embraced the custom of taking a single wife. Whatever cost this extracted privately, in practice it meant that again and again the country would be treated to a new queen and a wedding celebration made ever more majestic by the country's oil and the shah's ambitions for Iran.

When Lili returned from Europe to become a bride in the early sixties, she did so by force of her own considerable ambitions, brandishing a foreign diploma that compelled everyone to call her Madame Doctor—the first of the family and the first for many years yet. To the even greater astonishment of her cousins, aunts, and stepmothers, she also brought with her a handsome, well-mannered, blue-eyed *farangi* eager to live in the country and also to convert to Islam in order to marry her.

"She's got herself Richard Burton!" her cousins marveled, hiding their smiles behind their hands.

"Yes, her bread's been drenched in oil, that one," her aunts and stepmothers concurred, "but just how did she pull it off?"

Day after day members of the clan appeared at Nader's apartment in a newly built concrete housing development in West Tehran. Kobra had been living in the apartment since Nader's return from Germany earlier that year, and until they managed to find work it would be Lili and Johann's home as well. As the clan filed into the apartment to greet the new couple, Lili, linking her arm in Johann's, watched mouth after mouth fall agape, flashed a brilliant smile, and proceeded to savor the clan's collective stupor.

But when, finally, the last of the introductions had been made and she was free to venture out into the streets, Lili would find cause for astonishment even greater than her relatives'. In her absence Tehran had seemingly shrugged off the last of its eighteenth-century foundations and transformed itself into a twentieth-century metropolis. Cranes and high-rise buildings had shot up in every direction. The streets were now clotted with traffic, the city skyline wreathed in perpetual smog. Scores of young Iranians had left for Europe and, increasingly, for America, but here in the streets of Tehran Lili was suddenly witness to a reverse exodus. Thousands of foreigners had come to live and work in the country (by the seventies there would be nearly a million), and to accommodate them the once-modest Mehrabad Airport, the portal through which they all passed, was swallowing whole farms as it fanned out into the countryside.

Nowhere, though, did the changes seem more striking to her than among the female population of Tehran. With their short shift dresses, pocketbooks, and bouffants, most *Tehrooni* women were now as indistinguishable from the foreign women in the streets as they were indifferent to the veiled women who walked beside them. Most shocking of all, wherever she looked in the capital everyone, from the pious old *chadoris* to the soigné young ladies, now had cigarettes pressed between their lips.

But where, Johann mused, were the rose gardens of which the poet Sa'adi had so rapturously written? What had become of the bejeweled thrones? The fabled monuments? Lili began to worry that Johann's penchant for Persian antiquity had played too great a part in his decision to marry her. She resolved, therefore, to leave this bewildering new Tehran behind for the moment and devote her fiancé's first weeks in Iran to searching for the most blighted regions of her native land.

It was to be their Tour of Destitution. She borrowed a few hundred *tomans* from Khanoom and then, beginning with some of the poorest districts of the capital and ending with the most forlorn of its neighboring villages, Lili and Johann bumped and jerked along in rusted buses for three weeks, resting at what she made sure were the most humble lodgings along the way. Johann observed everything with great care and took notes in a small leather-bound notebook purchased for that very purpose. When Lili saw that the dereliction of Tehran's southerly neighborhoods—largely unchanged despite the transformations that had taken place elsewhere in the capital—failed to rattle him, she became curious about how intimately he'd known poverty himself. Back in Germany he'd once talked of the war, of the work camps and trekking from Russia to Germany with his father, but the story had been related with scant detail.

In any event, when she saw that the Tour of Destitution did not diminish Johann's enthusiasm for Iran, or for her, she rewarded him with another tour, the Tour of Many Splendors. As part of this journey, they peeked through the gates of the shah's palace in Niavaran, surveyed the lush valleys and snowy peaks of Mount Damavand, and then headed south for an extended ramble through the architectural jewels of Isfahan, Shiraz, and Persepolis, most of which Lili would be seeing for the first time in her life.

Here there was plenty to delight Johann. His notebook was soon full of sketches and scribbles and he resorted to documenting the Tour of Many Splendors in the margins of pages chronicling the earlier Tour of Destitution. He walked the length of Isfahan's central square in a daze, traced a reverential finger along the calligraphy adorning Hāfez's tomb in Shiraz. In Persepolis, Johann fell speechless at the colossal tombs hewn of ochre rock.

But the greatest surprise came on the road back from Persepolis when a wiry, dark-skinned villager greeted Johann in English, bowed his head, and proceeded to kiss his hands. Thorough as it had been, Johann's study of Iranian history had not prepared him for such a welcome.

Lili did her best to explain. A long succession of invasions (Greek, Arab, Mongol, Turkish, English) had been wedded to the Iranian gift for hospitality and a more elemental instinct for survival. Over the centuries, the union had managed to produce a widespread strain of obsequiousness toward foreigners. That such deference came laced, at least occasionally, with suspicion and resentment was something Lili kept to herself for the time being. Johann, shaking himself free of the would-be supplicant, pronounced the episode the most incredible of their journey so far.

On the way back to Tehran, Lili chanced to read a sign for the village of Sārī and decided to dedicate the last leg of the Tour of Many Splendors to a search for her long-lost aunt Zahra.

As a young girl Zahra, with her full lips and lovely almond-shaped eyes, had been considered among the prettiest of her sisters. At fourteen, just a few years before Kobra's marriage to Sohrab, Zahra had been married off to a wealthy but ill-tempered widower. The union had not suited her at all, and so she'd badgered and tormented her husband until he at last consented to divorce her. Had she taken up widow's weeds, Zahra might have eventually been forgiven this disgrace. Instead, Zahra eloped with a second husband to the town of Sārī, and thereafter her family acted as though she had died, or else had never been born. Zahra had not been seen in Tehran for many years, though her mother, Pargol, and later Kobra had been known to send her letters in Sārī through a scribe.

Lili and Johann found Zahra sitting on the front steps of a honey-colored cottage, peeling an orange and looking resplendent in her exile. Though she was well into her forties by then, Zahra's plump lips, sweeping eyebrows, full breasts, and deep-throated laugh made her a woman of striking beauty. She clearly cared nothing for Western fashions and wore her veils in the old style, rather like an Indian sari, cut of beautiful crepe de chine and tailored to perfection. Yet Zahra's allure rested, really, on a less definable quality: saltiness. "*Zahra namak dareh*," it was said of her. "Zahra has salt," meaning that her charms were exquisitely seasoned. In the town of Sārī it was a well-known fact that with just one glance from her kohl-lined eyes and a quick toss of her veil Zahra could make old men and teenage boys alike blush. Lili found her salty, indeed, and adored her for it.

Zahra was just as taken with her niece. "*Bah, bah, bah!*" she exclaimed as she appraised both Lili and Johann. "You've done well for yourself, Lili-*jan*!" Zahra brought armloads of oranges, nearly as big as honeydews, from her basement and as she peeled them the juice sprang from under her long, painted fingernails and scented the whole room. "Second marriages are certainly the best," Zahra purred as she handed Lili slice after slice of her luscious oranges. "Don't you agree, Lili-*jan*?"

To Lili there was little about Zahra's skinny, balding second husband, Mahmoud, that suggested the amorous skills at which she more than hinted to Lili around the *korsi* every night. In fact, during the course of Lili and Johann's three-day stay in Sārī, Mahmoud loved nothing so much as to pass the evenings with Johann and his transistor radio, scanning the dial for European stations. He claimed to be especially interested in the news from Germany. "Your countrymen are the cleverest people in all the world!" Mahmoud exclaimed. Not for the last time, Johann struggled, and failed, to explain his family's origins. "I love the sound of the German language!" Mahmoud beamed, his admiration for Johann, and the Germans, undimmed by Johann's protests. "So very smart!" Mahmoud pressed his transistor radio and earplugs into Johann's hands, begging him to translate, and so great was Mahmoud's pleasure that more than once he rose to his feet and clapped his hands.

By the time Lili and Johann returned to the capital, the clan's stupor had given way to suspicion, rumor, and outright censure. "May I die!" one of Lili's aunts declared. "Sohrab Khan's daughter has been traipsing about the country in every conceivable direction."

"With a foreigner!" a cousin cried out.

"Unchaperoned and unveiled!" added another.

"And what proof is there," said the aunt, "that this man will really marry her?"

Lili's cousins, the ones who'd traveled abroad and adopted a modern outlook, did their best to appease Khanoom and the more pious family elders. A European man, they were quick to note, did not want for women, and therefore sex, in his own country. Surely, then, this one had traveled to Iran with noble intentions? And anyway, Lili's cousins continued, what exactly was there left for Lili to lose and for them to protect? It wasn't as if a young girl's chastity were at stake. This last line of argument proved the most persuasive, though her cousins were always careful not to use it within earshot of Lili herself.

Lili's and Johann's attentions, meanwhile, had turned to appeasing the demands of the Iranian government. When a Muslim man married a foreigner in Iran, his bride was instantly converted to Islam through the ordinary Muslim marriage rites, a provision that would prove handy for the Iranian men who'd begun returning from their travels with European and American girlfriends and fiancées. But when a non–Muslim sought to marry a Muslim woman in Iran, he was thrown to the mercies of Iranian bureaucracy. Johann and Lili endured a three-hour-long interview at a government ministry only to be waved away with a sixteen-point list of requirements to be fulfilled before they could even apply for a marriage certificate.

Owing to Lili's foresight, the first qualification, circumcision, had already been met. Declarations of support were made and notarized, male relatives deposed, immunizations administered, and so on until finally Lili pulled on Khanoom's longest, thickest, blackest veil and took Johann by the hand to tackle the last of the sixteen requirements: Johann's formal conversion to Islam.

The ceremony was officiated by Ayatollah Behbahani, a graceful, soft-spoken holy man with a black turban identifying him as a descendant of the Prophet. Johann sat cross-legged before the ayatollah, offered him a mangled, "*Salaam-aleykoom* [may peace be with you]," to which the ayatollah replied with a forgiving and heartfelt, "*Aleykoom-al-salaam* [and also with you]." Ayatollah Behbahani then commenced to whisper the requisite verses of the Koran into Johann's ear. From her vantage point in the back corner of the mosque, Lili could make out little of the proceedings, but when the ayatollah intoned a final, "*Bismillah rahmaneh rahim* [in the name of God, the most gracious and compassionate]," and she saw Johann shape his mouth into the words, nod his final assent, and kiss Ayatollah Behbahani's hands, Lili smiled broadly from behind her veil. Johann was now a Muslim. He even had a Muslim name, Amir. It meant "prince."

After that nobody from the highest-level government minister to her most observant relatives could doubt Johann's intentions, but no one would ever love him more than Lili's grandmother Khanoom. "Tell him to come and sit by me," she'd command her grandchildren and grandnieces whenever he appeared for a family dinner. She'd pull a chair in front of Johann, plant herself there, and tell them to translate for her in whatever European tongue they happened to have acquired in school. "Tell him we are proud he will soon be our son-in-law!" she ordered. "Tell him we are happy he is a Muslim now! Tell him how much we love him!" she exclaimed, and she always waited to make sure he understood every last word she had said to him.

In addition to such periodic declarations of love, Khanoom saved the best of everything she cooked for Johann and also kept a hawkish eye on his health. When he and Lili returned from a weekend of sunbathing in Ramsar, a town on the Caspian Sea, Khanoom took one look at Johann's skin, now burnt neon pink to his very scalp, and went wild with rage. "What have you done to him?" she demanded of her granddaughter. Khanoom flew into the kitchen to whip up a soothing concoction of rose essence and rice powder. "You make sure he puts on a thick layer," she told Lili, and then waved her away with a cutting look.

Lili and Johann's wedding became the stuff of family lore, and it would be remembered, if for no other reason than because for the occasion she cast off yet another wedding dress and instead dressed herself in curtains.

"Why do you insist on wearing white?" her aunts and stepmothers had asked her with varying degrees of approbation. "It isn't done for a second marriage; you will only call attention to yourself by wearing a white dress...."

As these were the very relatives who'd hastened her marriage to Kazem, Lili suppressed the urge to scream, curse, and strike. She did, however, go so far as to remind them that her first wedding dress, the one Kazem's relatives had chosen for her, had not even been white but pale blue. Besides, Lili told them, the marriage was Johann's first, and on his account she would consider nothing but white.

Determined as Lili was to wear a white wedding gown, with a budget of just three hundred *tomans* to cover all the wedding expenses, even the cheapest Western-style wedding dress in Tehran lay far outside her grasp. In any case, a perfectly lovely dress of beige-colored silk, sewn for her by Kobra, was already hanging in a closet when Lili settled onto her cousin's sofa one day, looked out toward the garden, and found her view framed by some handsome ivory curtains. Then, just as she'd tucked a sugar cube inside her cheek and was taking her first sip of tea, she had a vision of a glorious wedding dress fashioned from the twin folds of duchesse satin that her cousin would later claim had hailed directly from France.

Such was Lili's charm, or some later said cunning, that the curtains were taken down on the spot and the dress of mottled raw silk was left to molder and wilt in Kobra's closet until it was finally pitched into the dustbin some years later. And by evening of the same day Kobra stood in bare feet to cut the cloth against Lili's body. With her mouth full of pins, Kobra cautioned Lili against so flagrant a show of immodesty, but Lili only frowned and pulled the satin tighter and tighter across her breasts, her hips, her thighs.

"No, it must be like this," Lili directed, "like this, you see."

With the sixteen qualifications of marriage complete and the attendant documents in hand, Lili sent notice to her family of her impending wedding. The ceremony would take place just three days hence in Nader's apartment. There was not a minute to waste. Together Lili and Kobra dragged the furniture to the peripheries of the living room. They proceeded to throw open the windows, haul the carpets onto the balcony and beat them with brooms, and drop to their knees and scour every corner with ammonia and bleach.

Now Kobra began preparing the feast. For weeks anyone who'd come to visit, cousins and clients alike, had been given oranges to eat so that Kobra could collect and clip the peels for the wedding feast's jeweled rice. At dawn on the morning of the wedding, Lili's aunts, stepmothers, and cousins appeared at the apartment with their largest pots, pans, and platters tucked under their arms. They soaked the rice, mixed the tiny strips of orange peel with slivered almonds, sugared, spiced, and sautéed the mixture, and finally layered it into the rice. They fried spinach pancakes, rolled the *dohlmes*, stirred the puddings, and to steel themselves against the heady scents and the day's gathering heat they split open a watermelon and tossed back cup after cup of *dooq*, a fizzy, minty yogurt drink. At noon Lili poked her nose into the kitchen to survey their progress, drank a cup of *dooq* someone passed into her hands, and then struck out for the city with the three hundred *tomans* she and Johann had budgeted for their wedding.

Her first stop of the day was Tehran's best florist, a favorite among the wealthy foreign set. When asked the occasion, she replied coolly, "Nothing special, just a small family gathering." Had she confessed the true nature of the event, she would have been charged twice or three times the going rate, but by omitting this detail she managed to walk out with an armful of tuberoses and a second armful of white gladiolus and 250 *tomans* still left in her purse. The ruse was repeated at a pastry shop on Avenue Naderi, where she purchased three pink, beribboned boxes of pistachio-studded nougats and chickpea cookies. Finally, before turning back home, Lili stopped by a photography studio on Avenue Shah Reza and put down her remaining money—about two hundred *tomans*—on the counter along with a piece of paper on which she'd scribbled Nader's address.

In the hour before the guests arrived, Lili bent her torso over the dining table and spread her hair against a white cotton tablecloth. Kobra, still weary from three steady days and nights of cleaning and cooking and sewing, ran a hot iron back and forth over Lili's curls until they were transformed into straight, gleaming panels. Lili then sat before a mirror and watched as Kobra wound these panels around metal curlers and set each section with a slender clip. When Kobra finished arranging Lili's hair, she raised her arms to place a rhinestone tiara (her wedding gift from Zaynab) onto her own head.

"Pretty as an *aroos farangi!*" Zaynab declared through moist eyes. Pretty as a foreign bride, by which she meant "much prettier than an Iranian bride." From the kitchen Lili's aunts and Sohrab's stepmothers clucked their tongues and began whispering to one another with renewed vigor. "Yes, just as pretty as a foreign bride," Zaynab continued in a louder voice, "and all the more lovely for the newly converted *damad farangi* [European groom] waiting for her in the next room!"

Just before sunset the *agha*, the holy man, arrived and the women retreated to Kobra's bedroom as the men encircled Johann in the living room. Lili sat perched on the edge of the bed in her dress made of curtains while Zaynab and Kobra fussed with her veil and smoothed her train. The *agha*'s voice finally rang out, the men sent out their cheers, and Johann entered the room, red faced and eyes crinkling in a mixture of amusement and shyness. He took a seat beside Lili and gently lifted her veil. When the white satin canopy was at last unfurled, when two cones of sugar were rubbed above their heads and the canopy's edge stitched with silver thread (to close the mother-in-law's tongue, it was said), there would be no guests from Johann's family and more than a hundred from Lili's.

The elders pronounced the jeweled rice the best in collective memory and the saffron pudding fit for the shah and his queen, while Lili's cousins declared her tiny waist a marvel to rival a Hollywood starlet's. At midnight the dinner spread was finally cleared away and

Lili's teenage cousin Nima pulled out his *tar*, an old-fashioned Iranian string instrument. When the neighbors came to complain about the noise, they were simply invited to join the festivities. The photographer captured image after image and Nima played song after song, and since there was scarcely any room to stand, Lili was the only one of the wedding party to dance.

She rose to her feet. Nothing remained of the thirteen-year-old bride she'd been, nothing of the confusion and terror she had felt when Kazem gripped her wrists and pulled him to her on their wedding night. This was an Iranian dance, an Iranian tune, and when she began to dance her groom was smiling shyly at her from across the room. She lifted her arms, tilted her head, and swayed her hips. She kicked off her shoes and let her hem down. Her hair slipped loose from its pins and she did not raise her hand to tidy it but let it fall about her bare shoulders. One song rose and slipped into the next, and on this night Lili danced only for her groom and lifted her eyes only for him.

The next day at noon Kobra knocked gently on the door. In a much-abbreviated nod to tradition, she, Zaynab, and Khanoom and some others had passed the night on the floor of the living room, and Kobra woke in the early morning to cook Lili and Johann their first meal as a married couple. Pancakes with thick clots of fresh cream, strawberries the size of plums, almond-stuffed dates, and a little vase of nasturtium trailing its vines along the delicacies—Kobra passed the offerings into Mr. Engineer's hands and then, before taking her leave, she lowered her eyes and flashed him the shy smile with which she'd greet him in all the years to come.

By the time of Lili and Johann's wedding, Kobra's mother, Pargol, had lost her mind. It started several years earlier, when she lost her house. For over twenty years Kobra's brother Ali-Ahmad had approached their mother, Pargol, with every sweet connivance gleaned from half a lifetime of loafing and swindling. "I'll serve you for the rest of your days," he'd sworn, clutching his heart and kneeling at her feet for extra effect. He would, he continued, make enough money to buy her a new house on the smartest boulevard in the city, where he'd hire no fewer than ten servants to tend to her. He'd go around dressed in tweeds fit for an Englishman. He'd buy her a French fur so long she'd sweep the streets of Tehran with its hem, and when she grew tired of it he would buy her three more to take its place.

Year after year Pargol merely laughed her deep-throated laugh, tousled Ali-Ahmad's steadily thinning hair, and assured him that only death could part her from those rooms. But then, sometime after her seventieth year, Pargol began conversing with doorknobs and lightbulbs and staring at her hands for hours at a time—behaviors that, some decades hence, would posthumously be diagnosed as symptoms of Alzheimer's disease.

Ali-Ahmad followed her demise with care. When he at last managed to extract the deed to her beloved house, Pargol's condition, and his own circumstances, would deteriorate with astonishing speed. In short order Ali-Ahmad invested and lost every last *toman* from the sale of Pargol's house, installed Pargol in a tiny room in his elder brother's home, and began drinking himself to a premature death. In even shorter order, Pargol acquired the troubling habit of wandering into the street by herself and disappearing for days on end. They'd find her perched on a park bench or on the pavement of some far-flung alley, combing her long white hair with her fingers and mumbling to herself in a language completely of her own invention.

The only choice then was to keep Pargol locked in a room until death released her from her agony. In the meantime, Kobra did her best to shield her mother from its worst effect: loneliness. Kobra paid near-daily visits to wash and braid Pargol's hair, spoon porridge and yogurt into her toothless mouth, and listen to her warbling until

Kobra felt she herself might go mad. It was also Kobra who arranged for Pargol's care on those occasions that demanded her exclusion from the family. Lili's wedding had been one of these occasions. Pargol had spent that night eating snap peas in a basement with a servant, and though Pargol herself had seemed perfectly content with the arrangement, Kobra urged Lili and her new husband to visit Pargol just as soon as they returned from their honeymoon.

"Look here; look here!" Kobra called out brightly, straightening Pargol's flower-print kerchief and taking her by the arm to greet the newlyweds. "Here is Lili and your new *damad farangi*!" If Pargol recognized her granddaughter, there was no outward sign of it whatsoever, but after several weeks of visits from the first and last foreigner she was to see in her life, Pargol at last took Johann's hands in her own, looked deep into his eyes, and declared that she missed the purple summertime skies of the village she had left more than seventy years before.

Her marriage formalized and feted, Lili now attended to the unfinished business. "Telephone Kazem's mother for me," Lili told Kobra one morning soon after the wedding festivities had ended. Lili was sitting before the mirror, combing out her curls. "Tell her I want to see Sara."

Kobra cast her eyes down to the floor and cleared her throat. "I can't."

"And why can't you?"

"Because," Kobra answered quietly, "Kazem's mother is dead."

Lili turned from the mirror. "But where is Sara then?"

"They say she's gone to her aunt's house—"

"They say? Who says? And how long—"

But Kobra had already retreated to the next room. Lili followed her. Kobra took up her prayer shawl, turned her palms upward, and began her midmorning *namaz*. With no choice but to wait for Kobra to finish her prayers, Lili pressed her forehead to the wall and began teasing out the implications of Kobra's revelation.

Kobra's *namaz* went on much longer than usual that morning, but some thirty minutes later she found Lili outside the bedroom door, tapping her foot and holding out the phone.

"Call them and tell them I want to see Sara," Lili told her. "Tell them we are coming to see her and that my husband will accompany us. Call them *now*."

Kobra prepared herself to defend her new son-in-law against insults by her former son-in-law and his family, but two days later, when Lili rang the Khorramis' bell and the door to the villa swung open, it was immediately clear that Lili had correctly gauged the effect of Johann's presence on Kazem and his family. Although Johann spoke no Persian at all and would not have understood any insult yielded at him, he was a tall, blond, blue-eyed European, and his presence at Lili's side assured that the meeting with the Khorramis would proceed with an abundance of Persian pleasantries.

"*Salaam, salaam!*" Kazem called out to them as Lili, Kobra, and Johann crossed from the house into the terrace. Kazem wore a light gray double-breasted suit and silk tie, all much finer than the clothes he'd worn in the past, and an updated version of his old gray felt fedora. His arms were extended in warm welcome.

Silk carpets had been spread over the terrace of the Khorrami compound. Lili's eye fell at once to the lovely array of sweets, melons, and iced sherbets assembled for the visit. Kazem's aunt, Sogra Khanoom, a heavyset woman in a sleeveless shift, rose and offered her hand, and the five or six assorted relatives followed suit. Addressing Johann in halting English and with the title "Mr. Engineer," one after another the Khorramis bid Johann welcome to Iran, and then, by extension, they also bid Lili and Kobra welcome to their home. Even Kazem, when he spoke to Lili and Kobra, used the formal address *shoma* rather than the more familiar *toh*.

Lili took in the show with satisfaction, but where, she wondered, was Sara? Just as Lili began to doubt that Sara was in the house at all, there came the sound of high heels clattering against the flagstones.

"Such a good girl!" Sogra Khanoom suddenly exclaimed.

"So good with the children," added a cousin.

"And a first-rate cook," noted yet another cousin.

The heels clattered louder and louder until a girl paused just short of the terrace. She had straight black hair and olive skin and she wore a blue dress, a little too long in the arms, tight around the hips, and cut wide and deep in the front. A cocktail dress, in short. In her hands she was holding a tray, and she kept her eyes lowered as she approached the party.

"Come now," Sogra Khanoom called out. Sara began passing the tea among the guests. When she came to Lili, she flicked her eyes up, just briefly. She did not smile.

"*Salaam, dokhtaram,*" Lili said, rising from her seat to kiss her on each cheek. Hello, my daughter.

Sara looked up toward her aunt and then back down at the tray. "*Salaam,*" she said.

Lili winced. Not *salaam, madaram* (hello, Mother), as was the customary sign of respect and affection, but only "hello."

Lili struggled to maintain her composure and the pleasantries resumed around her. Sara finished serving the tea, took a cup for her herself, and then sat beside her aunt. When Sara raised the cup to her mouth, the collar of her dress slipped, exposing one of her shoulders. Sara tugged it back into place, but very casually, very carelessly.

They have not taught her shame, Lili thought to herself. *They have not taught her modesty.* It suddenly seemed very important not to look, really, at Sara in her cast-off dress, not to see this absence of shame and modesty, not to understand it as neglect.

"You're in seventh grade now, yes?" Lili asked her.

"I don't go to school anymore," Sara answered.

Lili turned to Kazem. "But why," she asked, her voice suddenly shrill, "did you stop sending her to school?"

At this, smiles faded and eyes were averted. "I have three other children," Kazem said. He turned to Johann, addressing the rest of his words to him in English. "Mr. Engineer, it is difficult to provide for all of them, and she and my wife do not get on so well—"

Before Johann could attempt an answer, Sogra Khanoom cleared her throat and began to speak. "Actually, Lili-*jan*, Sara completed her sixth-grade year, but the truth of the matter is that she didn't care much for school, and so we brought her to live with us here. The children—my daughter's children—are very fond of her, you know, and she's been a great help to me since my daughter and her husband left for America."

"I see," Lili said at length. "And when will your daughter and her husband return to Iran?"

"Ah...," said Sogra Khanoom with a sigh and a glance up to the heavens. "It's so very difficult to know. Maybe this year, maybe the next...." She sighed again and took a long draught of tea. "Surely you can understand these things after having left us yourself for so long."

"Surely," Lili answered, "you understand I had no choice."

"But Lili-*jan*!" said Sogra Khanoom with an air of pure exasperation. "What choice have we, any of us, in this life?"

No sooner had they reached the car than Lili planted herself in the backseat, next to Kobra, and let loose a string of recriminations. "Why didn't you tell me her grandmother died? Why didn't you tell me they sent her to her aunt's house?"

"What use was there?" Kobra shot back. "What could you have done for her? What could I have done for her?"

"But you let them make a servant out of her! They couldn't make me their servant, so they've made a servant out of her!"

"I knew we shouldn't have come here," Kobra whimpered. "Your father's soul is uneasy. I know; I can feel it here...." She made a fist and began pounding her heart with it. "He always said no good would come from seeing that child."

"A servant, a servant...," Lili railed.

"What are you saying to each other?" Johann asked from the front seat. He'd pulled to the side of the road and turned off the engine. "What has happened?"

"*Idioten, idioten, idioten!*" Lili shouted in German by way of answer. Idiots, idiots, idiots! Strangely, the outburst had a calming effect on her. She wiped her tears with the back of her hand. "We must bring her to our house," she told Kobra in Persian.

"Our house!" Kobra cried. "We don't have a house! Have you forgotten that we don't have a house? You don't have a house and I don't have a house. And he," she said with a nod toward Johann, "certainly has no house."

"What is she saying now?" Johann asked again. He'd turned around to face them and was looking anxiously from Kobra to Lili. "Why won't you tell me what has happened?"

Lili began to answer him in German, but Kobra caught her arm and gave it a squeeze. "Don't you upset him!" she hissed. "He's only just set foot in this country and already you want to burden him with that child!" She shook her head. "She is Kazem's daughter," Kobra said with emphasis. "They have all of them made sure of that, so let them care for her."

"But she can't stay there with them! They've turned her against me; they've made a servant out of her!"

"And do you really believe," Kobra answered evenly, "that you can do anything about it now?"

★　　★　　★

Lili made no answer to her mother that day, but she would, as Kobra had put it, do something for Sara.

The reunion had unsettled her, but it had also disabused Lili of certain foolish hopes. Sara was no longer the little girl who'd sought her out on Zahirodolleh Alley. Lili knew better than to think she could claim back Sara's affections; she had promised too much and come too late for that. Yet she was now only more determined to make something of herself. She would submit her résumé to the best clinics and hospitals in Tehran and find work for Johann as well. She'd find them a house of their own and then she'd set about making something of Sara, too. If nothing else, she would send her daughter back to school.

The campaign began by teaching Johann Persian. On the first page of a fresh notebook Lili wrote down the letters of the alphabet for him. "Copy them," she told him. He took the task up with enthusiasm. Next she bought a first-grade reading primer. He tore through it in less than a week's time. By the third week of his studies, Johann had advanced through the second- and third-grade books. "Easier than Greek!" he cheerfully announced. When he finished the fourth-grade primer, Lili began buying him a newspaper from the kiosk across the street. She'd wake up early every morning, walk to the kiosk for the paper, and then, over breakfast, he'd read every page, advertising included, aloud to her with steadily growing fluency.

Her next task was to find Johann a job. Through one of her cousins she learned that Etco, a large Iranian construction firm, was looking to increase the number of its foreign engineers. Presenting herself as Johann's secretary, Lili called the firm and scheduled an interview for him with the company's president. Johann was hired at a salary of eight thousand *tomans*, an astonishing sum and far more money than even Lili had expected. With such a salary, she mused, a home of their own would not be far off.

The work suited him perfectly. It was, however, not the projects themselves that interested Johann—the bridges and tunnels were, after all, built in modern, Western style—but the fact that his job with Etco took him far outside the capital, often for several days and even weeks at a time. He'd set off in the mornings in a freshly pressed suit only to stagger home with his hair and shoes matted with dust, his jacket and slacks crumpled, and circles of sweat under each arm. The real Iran, he called the provinces, and always returned to Lili with stories of the ruins he'd seen, the nomads and the villagers he'd encountered.

But although Johann enjoyed his work and seemed destined to rise in Etco's ranks, his guilelessness caused so many problems that for a time remedying them became Lili's full-time job. Once, in these early months of marriage, he bought her a bouquet of pale pink tulips, and when he came home he kissed her cheek and then drew the flowers from behind his back like a magician.

Lili thanked him. "But how much did these flowers cost?" she asked as she pulled them from the sheet of cellophane in which they'd been wrapped.

His face fell. "Is it so important?"

Lili nodded. "Very."

"Ninety *tomans*."

"Ninety *tomans*!" She threw her hands into the air. "He asked you for ninety *tomans* and you didn't even ask him for a better price?"

Johann shook his head. Lili let out a long sigh, bundled the flowers back into the sheet of cellophane, and headed straight to the florist.

"*Agha*," she said, waving the tulips before him. "How much will you pay me for these flowers?"

"Begging your pardon, *khanoom*," he replied, "but I sell flowers; I don't buy them."

"Then how much," she pressed on, "would you sell these flowers to me for?"

"Twenty *tomans, khanoom-jan*."

"Then why did you sell them to my husband for ninety?"

The florist frowned and began rubbing his chin. "Your husband?"

"Yes," she returned. "He was here not an hour ago." She held the florist's gaze. "The foreigner," she added. "Surely you remember?"

His frown deepened.

"I know," said Lili, "that you are in the habit of tricking foreigners, *agha*, but you're mistaken if you think you can trick this one." She took a step closer to him and narrowed her eyes. "My husband spends his days traveling to the most godforsaken parts of this country," she said, pausing to give an expansive wave of her arm. "He comes home too tired to stand or to eat and you, *agha*, are trying to steal not just his money but mine." She plunked the flowers on the counter. "I won't have it."

"*Masha Allah, khanoom!*" the florist replied with genuine pleasure. "Lucky the husband who has you to watch over his money! So tell me, lady, how can we make you happy?"

"I'll take back the difference between what these flowers are worth and what my husband paid for them, or else I will leave them here and take back the full ninety *tomans*."

The florist slapped his knee and chuckled. "Here's your ninety *tomans, khanoom*," he said, reaching into his cash register and tossing a small pile of bills onto the counter. "Take these flowers as a gift from me and may God keep you for your husband and give you ten children to increase your happiness!"

"No more flowers," Lili told Johann when she returned home that day, and from then on Johann placed all his wages in her hands, less twenty *tomans* for a week's worth of the bitter, grainy Turkish coffee he'd come to love so.

With a ban on flowers and a slew of other economies, their savings steadily accumulated until they had enough to put down the money for their first home, a one-bedroom condominium in the same subdivision where Kobra and Nader lived. Setting herself a budget of just one thousand *tomans* to furnish the three rooms, Lili purchased a bed and a set of wrought-iron patio furniture she judged just as good as the expensive modernist furniture she glimpsed in the city's chic new furniture boutiques. The chairs had the unfortunate habit of tipping over and sending their guests crashing to the ground. "If I were you," Kobra told her, "I'd get rid of this junk." She begged to know why Lili didn't buy herself some proper French antiques and Persian carpets now that she had not only her own reputation, *aberoo*, to mind, but also Mr. Engineer's.

"Leave her be; leave her be," Khanoom urged Kobra. "She's watching out for his money, as she very well should."

Khanoom visited Lili and Johann often in their new home, and when she came she always brought along huge pots of Johann's favorite stews and soups. To avoid the flimsy wrought-iron chairs, Khanoom took to sitting cross-legged on the floor. She would sit in the center of the carpet with her face propped up on her knees, staring adoringly at her *damad farangi*, her foreign son-in-law, and beseeching Lili and Kobra to leave off their squabbling.

One August morning in the first year of Lili and Johann's marriage, Khanoom surrendered her soul to God. As on many summer nights, the heat had driven the family to the rooftop with their pillows and mattresses. Khanoom woke at dawn, long before the others, and slipped down to the courtyard to perform her ablutions and say her prayers. When she finished, she pulled on a fresh housedress, returned to the roof, and closed her eyes. Some hours later, Zaynab woke to find Khanoom with her prayer beads in one hand, arms folded over her chest, her body already turned toward God. No one in Lili's family had loved Johann as much as Khanoom, and dear as she was to everyone in the family, when she died few would miss her quite as much as Lili and her *damad farangi*.

Mutti, Elsa, and Maria had refused to acknowledge Johann and Lili's engagement, much less attend their wedding, yet within months of Johann's departure from Germany their love for their *Bübchen* would draw them all the way to Iran.

Mutti was the first of the three to appear, and she came armed with the strategy with which she would approach her daughter-in-law for the rest of her life: to simply pretend Lili did not exist. But a few days into her first two-month-long visit, Mutti broke her hip, and the injury would compromise the strategy considerably. Lili committed herself to tending to Mutti with a surfeit of daughterly attentions. In the mornings, Lili would alight with a tray laden with warm flatbread, feta cheese, butter, jam, and a carafe of freshly squeezed fruit juice. In the evenings, Lili undressed Mutti, guided her into the bathtub, and commenced to scrub her with a *leef,* a horsehair mitt. "Am I so dirty?" Mutti asked, her face stricken at the sight of the thick, grayish impurities that Lili drew from her skin. She began slapping at herself to flick away the *Schmutz*, the filth. "More, more," she begged, and Lili obliged by scrubbing her positively raw.

With Johann away at work, Lili had no choice but to take Mutti to the hospital with her. On the first day, she borrowed a wheelchair, pushed Mutti down the corridors, and introduced her to the head of the gynecology department. "She is my eyes," the doctor told Mutti in German. The phrase, meant to indicate Lili's inestimable value to the hospital, did not seem to translate well, as Mutti did not smile or offer any reply. But then, as soon as Lili wheeled her into the delivery room and pulled a smock over her shoulders, Mutti began trembling with excitement. "Will she live?" Mutti asked again and again as she took in the bloody spectacle unfolding before her. "Will she possibly survive it?"

Lili feared that the stimulation Mutti experienced in the delivery room was compromising her own recovery and therefore decided to move Kobra to the apartment to keep an eye on Mutti instead. Mutti did not hide her disappointment at this change in plans but seemed content enough to have Kobra flutter around her with even more devotion than Lili herself. Does Mutti-*joon* want an extra pillow? Kobra cooed. A second cream cake? Would Mutti-*joon* like her feet massaged? Her shoulders rubbed? Mutti very much did.

"But why does she call me Mutti-*joon*?" she asked Johann one evening.

"It means you are like her life, like her soul."

"I am her life?" Mutti asked doubtfully. "Her soul?"

"Iranians say this whenever they love someone," Johann explained.

"She loves me? But how can she love me?"

They'd never share more than ten words of each other's languages, but in this time a certain affection did, in fact, grow between Kobra and Mutti. Alone together in the apartment, Mutti would begin wringing her hands and uttering curses in her native Kashubian. Kobra couldn't make out one word, but between Mutti's tone and the frequent references to Lili's name she could discern the gist of Mutti's remarks. Kobra listened quietly until the outbursts passed and then she patted Mutti's hand and pointed to the sky, by which she meant to indicate heaven—the only place, surely, where consolation was to be found.

Elsa was the next of Johann's family to visit Iran. Lili booked the flight herself (first class, nonstop from Frankfurt) and enlisted the most dashing of her brother's friends, a swarthy, square-jawed professional boxer, to retrieve Elsa from Mehrabad Airport. On the evening of her arrival, a party far more lavish than Lili and Johann's wedding was thrown in her honor. Kobra and Zaynab cooked up no fewer than five different stews and three different kinds of rice, and Lili made sure that her most educated cousins were present to converse with her sister-in-law.

All night Elsa sat perched on the edge of a silk settee with her ankles neatly crossed, occasionally smoothing the skirt of her beige suit and observing everyone with her pale green eyes. That night the dashing boxer would ask her, repeatedly, to dance. Each time she declined with a slight shake of her head. But when the prettiest young girls were dispatched to lay before her the best of the evening's feast—succulent kabobs, jeweled rice, saffron pudding—she ate it all with relish, with genuine pleasure.

Elsa's appreciation for Iranian cuisine would, however, be insufficient to distract her from her mission. By the next morning her appeals had already begun.

"You should not have come here," she told Johann. "Mutti is weak; her heart is weak. She will die if you do not come back home."

Johann hung his head. "But I'm married now—"

"To an atheist!"

"But they believe in God here, too—"

"The devil they do!"

When Lili returned from work, a hush would fall between Johann and his sister. Elsa switched from German to Polish or Kashubian and resumed her appeals. Lili did not understand either language, but the meaning of the two words "atheist" and "barbarian" failed to elude her. She'd clear her throat to signal her comprehension, and Johann would throw her an apologetic look. This she was inclined to indulge, but she could not stand to see him drunk. When he next reached for a bottle of beer, she pulled it from his hands.

"Enough now," she'd tell him in Persian.

"Yes," he murmured. "You're right. Enough."

"And why are you taking that?" Elsa demanded to know. "Can't you see that my brother is still thirsty?"

Lili brought a glass of water from the kitchen and set it down on the table. "He can drink this if he's thirsty."

"*Halt deine Schnautze!* Shut your muzzle!" came Elsa's reply.

"A barbaric country," Elsa would write of Iran when she returned home to Hessisch-Lichtenau. "The atheist will send you back to Germany in bare feet," she predicted, and so certain was Elsa of this that from then on she would put aside a hefty chunk of her salary into a bank account she opened in Johann's name.

Just as she'd predicted, Lili's foreign diploma granted her entry into Tehran's very best clinics. She soon found herself fielding several handsome offers, and from these she chose the newly built King's Serenity. A project of the shah's twin sister, King's Serenity had been built to the exact specifications of the most advanced American hospitals. Everything from the metallic clipboards to the nurses' uniforms and doctors' smocks, the medical equipment to the intercom system, had been imported from the States. The physicians, nurses, and midwives were drawn mostly from the ranks of Iranians who'd studied abroad, and all written communication between the members of the staff was, as a matter of hospital policy, conducted exclusively in English.

Lili was promptly installed as the head of one of Serenity's midwifery divisions, with her own smartly appointed examination room, a short white shirtdress, and a headdress whose compact dimensions she found both more manageable and becoming than the monstrosities of her student days. Her monthly salary of two thousand *tomans*, though generous by the standards of her profession, was less than adequate for her schemes, and so she began to supplement her income by taking additional night shifts at a less prestigious downtown clinic and snatching meals and sleep between shifts.

Among the few pleasures she now allowed herself, the most enduring would be the friendship she established with Mariam, a fellow midwife at the hospital. A stout woman of forty-five, Mariam had a fiery temper and quick tongue that endeared her at once to Lili. The two chatted and took tea between deliveries, and as neither was much in the habit of disclosing her hardships, they soon found they were natural confidantes for each other.

The daughter of wealthy provincial landowners, Mariam had been raised on a ranch in the countryside outside Tehran, breaking wild horses and riding bareback alongside her two older brothers. At sixteen she'd barreled past her father, set out alone for the capital, and apprenticed herself to a traditional midwife. While paid labor was still generally regarded as the fate of only the most unattractive or destitute of women, by the mid-sixties in some quarters of Tehran upper-class families had taken to boasting of their daughters' educational and professional achievements, shipping them off to university with parties as elaborate as weddings. Mariam had enjoyed no such support when embarking on her own career. As she was already handicapped by her own willfulness, or so her family judged her, they predicted that a professional life would seal her fate as a lifelong spinster.

Yet Mariam had married. Her tall, handsome, broad-shouldered husband, Behrooz, was considerably less educated than she, but he'd been willing to take on a professional woman as a wife, and this Mariam's parents regarded not simply as a blessing but as a genuine miracle. As Mariam's career advanced, however, Behrooz felt less and less inclination to hold down a job himself. His chief occupation became the study of Mariam's defects, particularly her lack of house-wifely skills. A scoured pot, a dusty mantel, a languishing pile of laundry—all were put forth as evidence of his wife's incompetence.

"*Boro beeshoor!*" Mariam spat out at each indictment. "Get lost, you ignoramus!"

Lili rarely failed to visit the couple's home without witnessing a heated exchange between Mariam and Behrooz. She was also present on the day that Mariam at last rounded up her three children and settled them into an apartment of her own. In years past, Behrooz could have quickly claimed back both mother and children, but the shah's White Revolution had upended Iranian family law and so it was now Behrooz who turned up at Mariam's door, swearing he would reform himself and begging her to return. She would not. And when Mariam's father, a country gentleman named Shahryar Khan, took one of the family's servants, a pudgy, green-eyed country girl of seventeen, as his second wife, Mariam swiftly hauled her mother out of the countryside and brought her to the new apartment in Tehran too.

Like most professional women of her generation, Mariam did not choose to wear a veil. Off-duty she favored tight, brightly patterned tunics with wide-legged trousers or else short skirts paired with calf-length leather boots. She was also never without a slash of bright red lipstick on her lips. But while there was little in either her appearance or her manner that suggested piety, Mariam was, in her way, perfectly observant. She kept a Koran and a prayer mat with her at the hospital, and whenever her duties conflicted with her devotions she performed the abbreviated version of the *namaz* that she considered one of the great practical innovations of Islam.

She was also a passionate advocate for the poor. When King's Serenity threatened to turn away those who could not pay its fees, Mariam squared her shoulders and headed straight for the administration offices. "Are we not Muslims?" she begged to know. "Have we lost our compassion in this country? Do we care nothing about the less fortunate here?" Hands on her hips, eyes narrowed, Mariam eventually wore down even the most hardened administrators. And to those who refused her appeals Mariam delivered her most chilling prediction. "Blood brings blood," she told them. "Blood *always* brings blood."

However much she admired her friend's outspokenness, King's Serenity would afford Lili a thorough education in holding her own tongue.

The admission of an in-law of the shah's to the hospital would provide the first of many such lessons. In preparation for her arrival, an entire wing of the birthing clinic was relieved of its standard furnishings. Silk carpets were thrown over the linoleum tiles, a proper bed assembled and encircled by gilt-trimmed French armchairs, and cut-crystal vases arrayed for the masses of tuberoses and gladiolus that would appear in advance of the royal patient's arrival.

The mother-to-be, a Frenchwoman whom the staff was ordered to call Madame, came turned out one day in an impeccable powder blue skirt suit and white gloves. She was quite pretty and, even in an advanced state of pregnancy, carried herself with consummate grace.

Madame's cesarean section proceeded without complications, but the infant, a boy, weighed barely three pounds at birth. As the sole member of the staff who'd completed a special course on the care of premature infants, Lili was quickly assigned to the tiny royal's care. A cot was installed for her beside his incubator, and she was given to understand that all her other duties were suspended so she could give full attention to Madame's baby. Lili fed her royal charge with a medicine dropper, checked his vital signs by the hour, and monitored his weight gram by gram.

The hospital director quickly cordoned off a private route for the royal visitors. A special cleaning crew worked double and triple shifts to scour and polish every tile that lined the royal path. The women came in their heels and furs, the men with rosebuds tucked into the lapels of their double-breasted jackets, and holding up the rear were a large number of royal consorts and bodyguards. As the royals swept through the hospital corridors, everyone from the janitors to the heads of surgery stopped in their tracks to bow to the procession. When the royal family then filed in to inspect the tiny infant's progress, it was Lili who entertained their questions and Lili who, out of professional pride, stifled the instinct to curtsy before them.

Every morning Madame appeared at the clinic with her dark blond hair pulled back with a black silk headband, her blue eyes bright with worry. It was unclear whether Madame had been in Iran ten days or ten years. In either case, she did not seem to speak a word of Persian. Luckily, Lili found that just two words of French sufficed for these exchanges.

"*Il fait bien avec le petit?*" Madame would ask Lili in a trembling voice. Is the little one all right?

"*Oui, Madame.*"

"*Il peut quitter l'hôpital bientôt?* [Will he be able to leave the hospital soon?]"

"*Oui, Madame.*"

One day shortly after the infant's release, a royal courier arrived at King's Serenity to present Lili with a gift. "From Madame to Madame Doctor," he said before turning on a gleaming heel. Nestled in a mass of golden tissue paper was an enormous bottle of Chanel No. 5. She gasped. The liter of perfume cost thousands of *tomans*—easily two months of her wages.

It would assume a place of pride on her dresser. Lili began each day by dabbing a tiny drop of perfume on each wrist and two more tiny drops behind her ears. She most likely would have continued enjoying Madame's gift for the next decade if not for the clumsiness of her cleaning woman, Fat'meh Khanoom. One day Lili returned from work to find Fat'meh Khanoom slumped over a chair and the whole apartment awash in the scent of Chanel No. 5.

"I beg your soul's pardon!" Fat'meh Khanoom wailed. "I plead for your forgiveness."

"But what happened, Fat'meh Khanoom?" Lili asked. "What happened?"

Eyes downcast, tears streaming down her cheeks, Fat'meh Khanoom explained. She'd been dusting in the bedroom when the bottle of perfume had fallen from the dresser and spilled, in one swoop, onto the floor. She'd dropped to her knees and wiped at the puddle with her skirt, which only succeeded in rubbing the perfume in more thoroughly and dousing her in the fragrance, too.

"Please forgive me," Fat'meh Khanoom pleaded. "Please, *khanoom-jan...*"

Fat'meh Khanoom was quickly pardoned, but for months the smell of the spilled perfume was so strong that Lili and Johann could not pass a night in the bedroom without falling prey to headaches and nausea. They dragged their mattress to the living room, but even so for one sweltering summer they sweated the perfume nightly from their pores. Very slowly the scent died down, though a year later when Lili and Johann finally moved to a larger condominium on Avenue Pahlavi they would leave behind the faint but still unmistakable scent of Chanel No. 5 for all future residents of those rooms.

In addition to high-profile visits from the shah's family and other Iranian luminaries, King's Serenity paid host to another class of highly sensitive appointments. These, too, were not recorded on any schedule, and Lili caught word of them just minutes before they were to commence. She'd be walking down a hallway or checking in on one of her patients when Dr. Nikpour, the chief of plastic surgery, would suddenly tap her on the shoulder.

"We've got an embroidery today," he'd whisper in her ear.

With the sexes mingling much more freely than in years past, "embroideries," the quaint euphemism for surgical reconstruction of the hymen, had become, if not commonplace, common enough to have acquired their own protocol at King's Serenity. Disguised, as often as not, in long, black veils, the embroidery patients were whisked into a private room in a remote corner of the hospital. Dr. Nikpour always greeted these young women as casually as if he were preparing to remove a pair of enflamed tonsils or an errant gallstone, but just as soon as the anesthesia took effect his cool bedside manner gave way to playfulness and a distinct, if curious, feminist streak. Working a length of thin surgical thread between a patient's legs with an artistry usually reserved for face-lifts and rhinoplasty, Dr. Nikpour held an imaginary conversation with her future groom. "Just as you ordered her, my dear fellow! Just so!" Then, with a final tweak and clip, he'd declare of his own handiwork, "More virginal than even a virgin!"

For every young woman with the means to be embroidered, there were many more who hazarded marriage without their virginity intact. Of these, the most memorable for Lili would always be the bride of her third cousin, Ali. Lili had fond memories of playing with Ali as a child and was pleased to discover that in the years she'd been abroad her cousin had matured into a genial, sweet-tempered young man. One glance at Ali on his wedding night and it was clear to Lili that he was besotted with his bride, and that, she thought, boded well for his marriage.

At the end of the night, when most of the guests had left the house, the women of the clan gathered by the couple's wedding chamber. The mood was festive, with much giggling, whispering, and teasing among the women. It was not for Lili to spoil their customs, but neither was she keen to participate. She slipped down to the parlor by herself. After some minutes, Ali poked his head out the door. He was not smiling.

"Is Lili here?" he asked in a feeble voice.

Inside the bridal chamber, Lili discovered Ali's bride hunched over at the foot of the bed, sobbing behind tangles of black hair. There'd been no blood, Ali confided, and in his innocence he thought it a matter of his technique.

Lili led her cousin to a far corner of the room, as far from the door as possible, and then she whispered that maybe, just maybe the blood he presented to the family needn't be his bride's. She held his eyes until she was sure he followed her meaning, and Ali was already scouring the room for sharp objects when she slipped back into the hallway.

"Whatever was the matter in there?" one of the older women of the party demanded.

"Kids!" Lili answered with feigned impatience. "They don't always know what they're doing the first time!"

Fifteen minutes later, a commotion broke out outside the wedding chamber. Lili hurried to the landing, her heart suddenly in her throat. Had her cousin experienced a change of heart? Had one of the women seen through the ruse? When she reached the landing, Lili saw that one of her aunts was brandishing a bloodstained handkerchief. "What pretty blood!" one of the women shouted out as the handkerchief was passed from hand to hand. "As fresh and rosy as a blossom!" cried another, and though it was not exactly an embroidery, through the ensuing ululations, titters, and cheers Lili did not suppress the smile that came to her lips.

With Lili gone much of the day and many nights as well, Johann began to seek his own diversions in Tehran. At work he met and befriended Otto, a portly, red-faced, fifty-year-old German bachelor anxious to make his fortune in Iran and retire to the Mediterranean island of Majorca. Night after night the pair would retire to the flat with two cases of Armenian-brewed Shams beer and several packets of cigarettes. Johann and Otto's conversations traversed the full annals of learning, not just of European and Middle Eastern subjects but of all centuries and all continents. A representative evening would find them cracking open their first bottles of Shams over a discussion of *Das Kapital* and draining their eighth bottles three hours later on the theme of modern Urdu poetry. And the next night they would pick up exactly where they'd left off.

Lili, returning home at the end of a shift, would throw her work bag onto the floor and call out a greeting in German. Johann and his friend Otto scarcely looked up from their beers. Exhausted as she was, she felt little inclination to be ignored. What's more, Johann's drinking troubled her.

She'd gesture for Johann to follow her into the kitchen. "You must tell him to go home," she whispered in Persian. "*Now.*"

"Home?"

"Home."

"But he has no family here," Johann would tell her. "He knows no one. I am his only friend."

For months Johann had submitted himself to her family's gatherings. He assumed his place alongside her relatives, took tea with the women, and drank just one or two glasses of *araq* with the men, but his voice, in these moments, suggested nothing so much as the extent of his own loneliness. He missed his countrymen, Lili reflected; he missed speaking in his own language. Hadn't she suffered the same loneliness when she'd been sent out of her country? It was, she reasoned, perfectly natural that he should seek out a German friend.

She left Johann and his friend to their beers and their talk, climbed up onto the rooftop with a cup of tea, drew a chair to the ledge, and peered over the roof and onto the city. At dusk there came the muezzin's last call to prayer, distant but still exquisite, still stirring. Eventually the crowds thinned, the streets grew quiet, and one by one the windowpanes lit up. Lili closed her eyes and listened until the muezzin's song trailed into silence, until the sky passed from blue to navy to black.

Lonesome as she felt on such nights, it was there, on the rooftop, that Lili began to put together a plan for Sara. At thirteen Lili had had little sense of how to manage an infant. Now, at twenty-five, she had little sense of how to manage a teenager. But what she knew, beyond any doubt, was that she must get Sara out of her aunt's house and back into school.

But how? It was unlikely that Kazem would release Sara into Lili's custody, and legal recourse would be both costly and slow. Besides, her working hours were too long and too erratic for her to watch over Sara herself. Kobra would be no help to Lili, and Johann, however devoted and well-meaning, was clearly incapable of the task.

Yet she was determined to get Sara back into school. The problem absorbed her for many weeks, but then, through one of her patients at King's Serenity, she learned that a girls' boarding school had recently opened in the northern suburb of Shemiran, just steps away from Sa'ad Abad, the shah's summer palace. The institution, she was told, was led by a Western-educated psychiatrist known as Mr. Dr. Headmaster.

Dressed in her best skirt suit, faux fur stole, and suede Viennese pumps, Lili spent an afternoon touring the school on Mr. Dr. Headmaster's own arm. An erstwhile Qajar mansion, the school sat on a slope between a grove of aged cypresses and aspens and the lofty peaks of the Alborz Mountains. Apart from a few tasteful innovations, the mansion's nineteenth-century fixtures—the mirror-work walls and engraved stucco tiles—had been exquisitely preserved. Daughters of princes and cabinet ministers and wealthy expatriates, the students seemed to her without exception a band of beautiful, healthy, confident, cheerful girls. By the time she'd reached the large interior courtyard, Lili longed to curl up at the base of the *beed*, the majestic old willow tree, and go to sleep.

In such a place, she felt sure, Sara would be safe and she would be happy.

"Call Kazem," Lili told Kobra once again.

In the ensuing negotiations, Kazem proved only too eager to take up Lili's offer to enroll Sara in boarding school—provided that Lili paid her tuition and covered all her other expenses. It would take many nights of scheming on the rooftop before Lili could work out how, exactly, she'd manage such an enormous expense, but with just a few more sacrifices, just a few more economies, she told herself she might find a way to enter Sara there by the beginning of the new term.

"Study," Lili told Sara.

It was an exceptionally fine September morning when Lili dropped Sara off at the boarding school near Sa'ad Abad. Sara was wearing her new uniform—a pleated jumper, white tights, and brown loafers—and her long black hair was pulled into a braid. "Lovely," Lili called her, but Sara had been surly in the taxi, turning her face away so that Lili could not meet her eyes.

But then, as they passed through the boarding school's gates, Sara pressed her palms to the window, threw a look over her shoulder at Lili, and grinned.

"I'm going to live here?" she asked excitedly. "In this mansion?"

"Yes," Lili answered, "but you must promise me you will study and that you will make something of yourself here."

Sara nodded. "I will; I will; I will!" she sang out.

Lili smiled and kissed her on both cheeks. She'd done well by her daughter. Sara would be safe here and she would be happy.

But within the space of a week the strange fits and worrying episodes and telephone calls commenced.

Mr. Dr. Headmaster's secretary would put through a call to King's Serenity. As Lili stood with her hands poised between a woman's legs or else gripping an infant's slippery flesh, an orderly or secretary would burst into the delivery room, begging her pardon but there was trouble with some person by the name of Sara up in Sa'ad Abad. Lili would pull off her mask, peel off her surgical gloves, and take the phone. It was Mr. Dr. Headmaster himself on the line, calling to tell her Sara had just thrown herself from the stairs, she was refusing to eat, she had not spoken for a week. And Lili must come straightaway.

Mr. Dr. Headmaster was a thoughtful man, educated at a famous French institute and conversant in all the latest psychoanalytic theories. Mr. Dr. Headmaster studied the mother, he studied the daughter, and then he wasted no time in delivering his diagnosis: All of Sara's strange moods and disruptive behaviors could be traced back to a lack of motherly love. *Her* lack of motherly love. To this there was no possible reply, or any Lili would permit herself to make to so genteel, thoughtful, and educated a man as Mr. Dr. Headmaster. Every time Sara made a scene at school, Lili was called into his office. She could never do anything but bow her head, press her lips together, and nod. And then, as she sat stricken with the force of Mr. Dr. Headmaster's assessment and the weight of her own unspoken words, there came Sara herself, her hair invariably disheveled and her eyes swollen from crying, making her way forward with all the confusion and rage of the child she still very much was in those years.

On Mr. Dr. Headmaster's suggestion, Sara and Lili began to spend Saturday afternoons together. "It will calm her," he assured Lili. "It will bring you closer to each other."

Saturday after Saturday, Sara pouted and grimaced, shot her dark looks or refused to look at Lili at all, but when they went shopping together she suddenly became as breathless, cheery, and spirited as a little girl. She spent hours trying on clothes—dresses, slacks, ankle boots, and jackets—all nearly as smart and expensive as the clothes the Sa'ad Abad girls brought back from their European holidays.

"Tell me, do I look like you?" Sara would ask her in the dressing room, eyes darting from her own reflection to Lili's in the dressing room mirror. "Do you think I will be as beautiful as you someday? Are my eyes like yours?"

What Lili saw, in these moments, was a strange double exposure: Sara at two, at six, then at twelve, but also all those broken intervals, the separations and the absences between all the other Saras she'd known. "Of course," Lili would say. "Very, very much."

One Saturday in summertime they visited the new amusement park in North Tehran. Lili bought them ice creams, thick dollops of rose-infused, pistachio-studded cream pressed between two wafers, and together they made their way through the grounds. At dusk young girls appeared in kitten heels and shift dresses, linking arms as they walked with their beaus. Sara's eyes always lingered on the prettiest ones. When they reached the large artificial lake at the center of the park, Lili rented a paddleboat—a red one; Sara had been most particular about its color—and then she and Lili took turns steering it around the lake with a pair of plastic oars and from there they watched the Ferris wheel, the women's skirts billowing up as it rose and fell, rose and fell, and the smears of colored lights as the machine spun faster and faster against the sky.

Lili would be a mother yet. The more unruly Sara became and the more desperate she herself felt—about Sara but also about her in-laws and about Johann's drinking—the more determined she was to have another child. This, however, was an ambition with which her body refused to cooperate, and so one by one she found her way to the examination room of every last fertility doctor in Tehran. She enrolled herself in treatments she and Johann could ill afford; endured injections and examinations and surgeries that left her dizzy, sore, bloated, and exhausted; submitted herself to Kobra's unctions, tinctures, and compresses; trekked to mosques and martyrs' shrines; gave alms to the poor; and sought her fortune in tea leaves, coffee grains, and the verses of Hāfez.

At all this, Johann looked on, dumbfounded. He was forty years old and fatherhood, when he considered it at all, seemed a vaguely appealing but hardly essential prospect.

"Muss das sein?" he asked her again and again. Must it be?

"Yes," she answered, for every failure only increased her desire for a child.

Then one year she flew to Israel by herself, spent a week making the rounds of Tel Aviv's top fertility specialists, and returned to Iran with her blood flush with hormones. She would not let herself hope for it, not quite, but she'd conceived the very first month. She began to walk with her hips thrust forward and one hand cradling her imperceptible bump. She sailed through shops, marketplaces, and department stores, bought herself a crib, bed linens, a stroller, and a rocking chair. By the second month, she had assembled a fully functioning nursery—bottles and diapers and all—and she passed all her spare hours daydreaming there in her new rocking chair. She scarcely noticed the bottles of Shams beer and the overflowing ashtrays. She smiled, brilliantly and often.

On a morning in the third month of her pregnancy, Lili threw back the sheets, swung her legs over the side of the bed, and found herself sitting in a large, wet circle of blood. She fainted as soon as her toes touched the floor.

When she came to, she found herself in a bed at King's Serenity. She jerked up and ripped off her oxygen mask. The contractions that came then were so faint and quick that she scarcely recognized them as labor pains, and it was only when she lifted her head to check the sheets for blood that she saw him. Her baby, her son.

She caught him herself.

Very gently, she wiped his face clean with the edge of her gown and pressed him to her chest. He had no pulse, no color, and was so small, no more than five inches long, that she could hold him in the palm of her hand.

For a quarter of an hour she held him to her, and she would have held him much longer but for the vein she imagined beating to life in his temple. When screams ripped loose from her throat, when her cries filled the corridors, nurses filed into the room and plunged a shot of morphine into her arm. One by one the nurses and order-lies took turns attempting to ease the stillborn from her hands. Her mouth fell slack, her lids grew heavy, but still she would not ease her grip. A doctor appeared, clipped the umbilical cord, ordered a sec-ond shot of morphine. The placenta would not come, the bleeding would not stop, her pulse grew slack, and through it all Lili kept her eyes peeled on her tiny baby, willing the vein to beat once more in his temple until suddenly there was nothing but darkness.

"Do you want the hospital to bury him?" came a far-off voice.

Lili opened her eyes. Mariam was sitting at the foot of the bed, and in her arms she held a small white bundle.

Lili shuddered. If they buried him at all, they'd pitch him into some horrid communal grave outside the city. "No!" she shouted. She reached out her arms for him, pressed him to her chest, and then together she and Mariam waited in silence until Kobra came.

Kobra did not bury the stillborn. That day she paced the street out-side the morgue for nearly an hour, willing herself to enter and have done with it, but in the end she could not bring herself to bury Lili's baby. Instead, Kobra put him in a large glass jar filled with rubbing alcohol and hid him deep in her closet.

She never spoke of it to Lili, but when neighbors or relatives came round to visit Kobra would pull the jar from its hiding place. "His eyes are blue!" she'd tell them. She traced the glass with her forefinger, out-lining the curve of his spine, his head, his tiny fists. "Blue, blue, blue!"

"She thinks it's Omid," her cousins and sisters whispered to one another, recalling the madness that had gripped her when she'd found her own little boy dead at the foot of the pool. "She thinks she's lost him again." They were kind; they were indulgent. They nodded and they smiled, and when she grew quiet, they took her arm and led her gently away from the jar.

Five weeks later, when Lili herself had managed, mostly, to submerge her grief in work, the stillborn fetus was just as beautiful, just as perfect, and Kobra just as unwilling to part with him.

"His eyes are blue," she murmured, touching a finger gently to the glass. "Blue, blue, blue..."

"But his soul!" her sisters reasoned. "You must bury him. God will not take his soul until you bury him."

Kobra narrowed her eyes, puckered her lips, and began contemplating the fate of the stillborn's soul.

She buried him in the sixth week. She went alone, told no one her plan. She pulled on her chador—reserved in those days for pilgrimages to Mashhad or the holy days of Ramadan—bundled the stillborn back into the white hospital sheet, and carried him to the cemetery. She performed the ablutions herself, swaddled him in a funeral shroud no bigger than a pillowcase, and buried him in the children's section of the graveyard.

"The child's name?" they asked her that day.

Kobra lifted her eyes. "His name?"

Later it would seem that only the blank expanse on the gravestone could contain her grief, but for hours Kobra would sit by herself, desperate to think of a name to give Lili's baby. Long after the other mourners had filed out of the cemetery, Kobra sat cross-legged beside his grave, rocking herself back and forth, weeping and praying until at last she felt her madness lift and she imagined salvation descending to take its place.

★   ★   ★

As Kobra recovered from her grief over the stillborn's death and Lili diverted hers by seeking out yet another series of fertility treatments, Johann dedicated himself to his own cause: Iran's infrastructure. "I know what this country needs!" Johann declared to Lili one day, handing her a thick pile of sketches. "Ready-mix concrete!"

For all the feverish construction of those years, concrete was still mixed by hand in Iran. It was a costly and time-consuming, not to say backbreaking, process, and one for which Johann, bent over the dining table with his drafting tools and maps, sketching and calculating through packs of cigarettes and a bottle of English whiskey, had finally managed to find a solution. That the project might distract Lili from the agonies of infertility had made him doubly sure of its necessity.

"But how much will it cost us?" she asked him.

"Just thirty thousand *tomans* to start, and we're sure to get a loan for the rest."

Lili cast her eyes up to the heavens. At that moment they had less than a thousand *tomans* between them, but the project's merits were immediately obvious to her. She lowered her gaze and looked about her. "We'll sell the condominium," she sighed.

With that they moved into a smaller apartment farther south on Avenue Pahlavi. Johann procured a loan from a German bank the following month, quit his job at Etco, and struck out some sixty miles northwest of Tehran, to a place so forlorn that not even a dog could recognize its master, as the saying went, and there he bought a thirty-acre parcel of land. A quick survey of the closest village put him in contact with a copper-skinned, broad-faced Azari Turk named Fato'allah. A long-unemployed father of three, Fato'allah took one look at this lanky, blue-eyed foreigner and cheerfully attached his fate to the venture.

Johann bought a clanking, sputtering, weather-beaten pickup truck and then he and Fato'allah began filling its bed with bricks. They spent several weeks working side by side, building a low brick wall to demarcate the property line from the neighboring wasteland. In the middle of the day, with the sun at the height of its mercilessness, Johann and Fato'allah spread out a carpet under the parcel's lone date palm, shared a tobacco pipe, poured two cups of tea from a canister, and proceeded to eat the flatbread and walnuts Lili packed for their lunch each day. At the start of the project, Johann could not make out much more of Fato'allah's Azari accent than *"salaam"* and *"merci,"* but in their many months together under the date palm Johann would learn to speak a more or less fluent Persian tinged with the same sweet Turkish accent as Fato'allah's.

Next Johann built Fato'allah a house on the property, a simple two-room structure with an adjoining privy. Fato'allah, speechless with gratitude, rounded up his family from the village and brought them to live in the cottage. Every night Fato'allah's wife, Samira, unrolled a mattress onto the center of the floor, and every morning she rolled it back up against the wall. Whenever Lili came along with Johann to survey the factory's progress, she'd find Samira by the door to the cottage, smiling shyly from behind her flowered kerchief while her children played nearby. Samira was perpetually pregnant. *Dear God, how can another body possibly fit in there?* Lili thought each time, but still the family grew. Lili improvised checkups for Fato'allah, Samira, and their children, and even if they had but three cookies and one melon in the cupboard, they would always offer everything they had to Madame Doctor alongside a freshly brewed cup of cardamom-spiced tea.

When the brick wall ran all the way round the property, Johann and Fato'allah began to build the factory itself. The mixing machines began to rattle, churn, and hum. Together Johann and Fato'allah kept the machines working through the crushing heat of summer until, finally, the two ready-mix concrete trucks arrived, at enormous expense, from Germany, and with that the pair at last made their maiden voyage to the capital, Johann manning the wheel and Fato'allah exultant at his side.

On Lili there now fell the dual functions of the corporation's president and its secretary. She propped a poster in the parlor window, acquired a desk, and began negotiating the company's contracts. Mostly her work was conducted over the phone and in the hours between her hospital shifts, but whenever signatures were required Lili pulled on a suit and drew a chair opposite her desk.

This arrangement worked well enough until the day the landlord's wife, Khanoom Nabavi, caught Lili's arm in the hallway. "You have many gentleman callers, *khanoom,*" she murmured, averting her eyes. "Many, many men..."

It took a moment for Lili to grasp her meaning. Khanoom Nabavi had mistaken her for one of those women whose profession could not even be named. Lili led her to the window. "You see, *khanoom,*" she said, pointing to the sign, "we have a company. Ready-mix concrete. My husband's company and mine."

Khanoom Nabavi stared at the sign and shook her head. "Too many men...," she murmured.

All-merciful God, Lili thought to herself, *the woman is completely illiterate!* How could she get Khanoom Nabavi to understand that her and Johann's venture was a legitimate one?

When she next spied Khanoom Nabavi's grandson mounting the back stairs, Lili quickly poked her head out the window and called him into the apartment. "Please," she said, handing him some contracts and a stray pile of receipts and pointing out the poster in the window, "can you explain to your grandmother?" She specified the profession for which Khanoom Nabavi had mistaken hers.

The young man blanched, dropped his eyes, and mumbled an apology.

"Surely an honest mistake, *agha,* but should you or any of your friends or associates need any concrete," Lili added when showing him the door, "you now know who you're obliged to buy it from!"

One day a woman approached Lili as she was making her way out of King's Serenity. She wore a chador, a full, black veil. "I beg your pardon, *khanoom*," she said with a nervous glance at Lili's uniform, "but are you a nurse?"

"A midwife."

"Thanks be to God!" the woman cried, and clutched Lili's hand. "My sister, she is pregnant." She turned her palms up and tilted her head. "But they wanted two thousand *tomans* there," she said with a nod toward the hospital, "and it's too much for us...."

"And the public hospital?"

"No room. They told me to bring her here, but—" She lowered her eyes.

"But what can I do for you, *khanoom-jan*?"

"Will you come to our house?"

The woman's hand, as she held Lili's, trembled.

"And where is your house?" Lili asked her.

The woman lowered her eyes. "Tayeh Shar," she mumbled. The Bottom of the City, the poorest district in Tehran.

Seeing the woman's shame only hastened Lili's reply. "Yes," she answered, "I will come with you, *khanoom-jan*."

They drove south by taxi, past the train station, past the vestiges of Tehran's caravanserai, the old way station for travelers, until at last they reached a cluster of tin-roofed buildings set against a muddy slope. She'd lived not far from here once, many years ago when she'd been Kazem's wife. Her sadness, exhaustion, and terror had prevented her from grasping the poverty of her life back then. It struck her now like a blow, but she would not let her face betray her for fear of offending the woman at her side.

Together they climbed out of the taxi. Lili let herself be led up a mud-packed path until her companion stopped before one of the shanties. In place of a door, a sheet of sun-bleached burlap had been nailed to the wall. She lifted it gingerly, entered, and then watched a dozen pairs of eyes turn to her with fear and then relief.

"Thanks be to God!" the women cried, and pulled her inside.

Lili squinted against the dark. The room, she gradually saw, was just ten feet wide and ten feet across. It had no window and no carpets. In the center of the room a girl of no more than seventeen lay tucked under the *korsi*, moaning. Her face shone with perspiration. Her patient.

"*Salaam, dokhtar-jan*," Lili said. Hello, dear girl.

Lili set down her work bag and then turned to the oldest woman in attendance, a heavyset matron with gray braids that fell to her hips. "Her water sac?" she inquired.

"Broken."

"When?"

"Last night."

"Last night!"

Lili sucked in her breath and began unpacking her tools. "Boil water!" she ordered. "Boil water at once!"

She reached for the girl's hand. Her pulse was regular, her temperature normal, but when Lili pressed her fingertips to the girl's belly, just above the girl's pelvis, she felt an unmistakable sign of trouble: she could not feel the baby's heartbeat. The birth could be risky, fatal even, but with the girl's contractions at less than a minute apart, there was no chance they'd reach the hospital in time.

For the first time in many years, Lili felt her hands begin to shake as she prepared to deliver a child.

For a quarter of an hour the girl leaned against her grandmother's shoulder, groaning and crying and screaming by turn. Lili meanwhile scrubbed her hands and forearms in a pot of hot water, calculating the contractions as they came. When she checked the girl's pelvis again, Lili still felt no heartbeat. She drew a breath, pushed up her sleeves, and told the girl to lie back down by the *korsi*.

The baby came fast. Lili pulled him clear, checked his color, pressed her mouth to his tiny lips, and then gave him a slap against the buttocks. He let out a ripping scream. *"Pesareh!"* one of the women shouted. "It's a boy! A boy!"

With that the event was at once transformed into a celebration. Tears spilled from the girl's cheeks, someone began to sing, and even the neighbors crowded into the room and let out whoops of joy.

When she'd stitched the girl's wounds and quelled her bleeding with ice, when the basins and bloody sheets had been hauled away to where she did not know, Lili packed her implements, reached into her purse, and counted out two hundred *tomans*.

"For your baby," she said as she placed the money on the mantel.

Her hand was already on the burlap when the women swept her back inside. "But we can't accept this!" they pleaded. They tried to press the bills back into her hands. Lili shook her head and made ready to leave. "Then you must stay now as our guest! You absolutely must!" A candle was lit on the mantel, an embroidered cloth unfurled on the floor, and it was many hours later that they sent her off with kisses, blessings, and a small but very full basket of quince fruits.

"But we must do something!" she told Mariam the next day.

Mariam only laughed bitterly. "Those districts are teeming with such stories," she told Lili.

With the advent of modern hospitals and licensing regulations, the old informal networks of midwives had grown thin. A number of large public facilities struggled to fill in the gap, but many traditional families were not keen that male doctors should examine their daughters and attend them in childbirth.

"That girl," Mariam said, "was lucky her family brought her anyone at all."

"But we must do something!" Lili cried again.

Mariam made no answer, but then she narrowed her eyes in a manner Lili had come to recognize well. Mariam was scheming.

Within a week of that exchange, Lili and Mariam had rented a space in the Bottom of the City. Their "clinic" consisted of a single examination room, with a sink, a cot, a chair, and a small wooden side table. Though they charged a nominal fee of one hundred *tomans*, the enterprise was subsidized in large part by their own salaries and staffed by just the two of them. Lili and Mariam's patients ranged from factory girls of fourteen or younger to fifty-year-old housewives with eleven children. As they labored in the clinic's one room, their sisters and cousins and mothers sat cross-legged in the corridor. They brought their knitting and embroidery, passed around their pots of stew and jars of pickled onions and beets, and, invariably, fell into each other's arms with joy at news of a boy's birth and wept and consoled each other at news of a girl's.

As word of the clinic spread, the Bottom of the City families also brought their nine- and twelve- and fourteen-year-old daughters, skinny and pudgy, flawless and blemished, rich and poor, mostly Muslim but also Jewish and Christian—dozens and dozens of young girls alike only in their fear. The girls appeared at the clinic to have their virginity confirmed, most often on the eve of their weddings but also when their parents suspected them of having boyfriends or, less frequently, of having been raped.

The ten years that stood between Lili and most of these girls could not close in on the memory of the day she'd had her virginity examined and everything that had followed. She knew, from the first, that whatever it cost her, in money and in grief, she could never turn these girls away. But over time she developed her own methods for these examinations. She always started by meeting the girls' eyes. "Tell me," she'd begin. They confided as much of their stories as they could. "My father will kill me," they whispered, or, "My brothers will kill him." Most, though, said nothing at all.

Whatever they told her or could not tell her, Lili always nodded, patted their hands, and smoothed their brows. She checked the girls for bruises and scars, and if she found none, she released them to their families with reassurances that all was in order. The result of all this was that Lili sent out far more "virgins" than came through her doors in those years. She counted on people's pride to keep them silent, and, so far as she knew, it always did. The declaration of chastity was made and its documentation delivered, and if subsequent events indicated a girl's virginity lacking, they sought their revenge elsewhere, far away from Lili.

By the late sixties Kobra had been working as a seamstress for well over two decades, and though she was still young, still in her forties, she swore that another year spent hunched over her sewing machine would find her both completely blind and crippled with arthritis.

Business had been falling off since the introduction of department stores to Iranian life, and her income, while more or less sufficient, could no longer justify the sheer physical sacrifice exacted by her profession. Kobra's sisters urged her to stop working at once and move in with Lili and Johann, but after so many years she was accustomed to earning her own money and living in her own house. She was also totally incapable of idleness.

But what else could Kobra do besides sew?

The answer came to Lili when, on her way to King's Serenity one day, she noticed a newly erected Western-style beauty institute. A glorious spectacle of mirrors and marble and brass, the institute proved an instant hit among office workers and salesclerks, who now made up the majority of Iran's female workforce. Lili looked it over, inside and out, and formulated a plan, which she wasted no time in presenting to Kobra. The modern Iranian woman, Lili explained, required manicures, pedicures, shampoos, tints, cuts, highlights, perms, and blow-outs, all of which demanded a corresponding army of professionally trained beauticians.

These, Lili went on, were just the needs of ordinary working women—the real money lay with the brides. While once they had been tended in the bathhouses by their own relatives, it had became fashionable among all but the most destitute *Tehrooni* families to send brides to the beauty parlor before their weddings. It hardly needed mentioning that a bride was the most lucrative of clients, for she always brought along her mother, sisters, aunts, and cousins—some two or three dozen females all requiring a complete overhaul before the wedding.

Kobra's eyes brightened when Lili put forth the proposition, especially when she reached this last part about the brides. Lili congratulated herself on the plan and put down the money for a complete course of study, but Kobra was to be sent home the next day. A teacher had ordered her to read the directions on a bottle of dye and discovered that Kobra could not make out a single word. She was totally illiterate.

Lili intervened on Kobra's behalf, offering to enroll her in night school if she was allowed to stay on and watch the instructors. Kobra now found a single page from her first-grade reading primer could pitch her into a fit of tears. Lili hired a private tutor for her, Kobra made slow gains toward literacy, and some months later she matriculated in beauty school.

A European certificate, Lili contemplated, would be just the thing to launch Kobra into this new career as a hairdresser. Lili conferred with Johann, and Kobra was sent to Hessisch-Lichtenau, where for one year she would occupy Johann's old room. Presenting a translation of her Iranian beauty school certificate, Kobra offered herself as an apprentice at the village salon. She was, from the first, a brilliant success. The likes of her depilatory methods had never before been seen in that German village. "*Wunderbar!* Wonderful!" They beamed as she worked a length of string over their eyebrows, upper lips, and chins.

On Saturday mornings Mutti and Kobra made trips to the nearby town of Kassel. Whenever a man eyed Kobra on the bus or flashed her a warm or faintly suggestive smile as they passed her on the street, Mutti pulled her close and whispered, "*Nein, nein, nicht gehen!* [No, no, don't go!]" Kobra averted her eyes and stayed put at Mutti's side, and as a reward for her obedience Mutti spoiled her with a gift from one of the village shops.

A little over a year after its inception, the ready-mix concrete company began running aground. They did not lack for contracts, but to pay off the German creditors Johann and his assistant, Fato'allah, would have to work twice as fast.

"What can we do?" Johann asked Lili.

In less than a minute she found him the solution: "Night shifts."

As this would require a permit, she set off for the city's central business registry one morning wearing a crepe navy dress, matching navy heels, and a lace-trimmed hat. Her best. At the registry a uniformed officer glanced up, shot her an appraising, then appreciative glance, and led her up a curving marble staircase and deposited her in a private office.

Lili stole a look about the room. It was handsomely appointed, with a large inlaid desk and leather chairs. The floors were covered from one end to the other with silk carpets. Lili made a quick study of the patterns, noted their provenance (Shiraz and Tabriz, Iran's finest), and then she smoothed her skirt, tidied the sheaf of papers in her lap, and waited.

Ten years had passed since the day she'd last seen him. His hair had turned white at the temples, he'd grown a mustache and a paunch and had traded his much-decorated military uniform for a suit and silk cravat, but as soon as he turned his green eyes to her she knew him. The General.

He was the first to speak. "They told us this company belongs to a foreigner."

"It's true," she stammered. "The foreigner is my husband."

"Ah," he said, raising an eyebrow and considering her more carefully. He walked behind his desk and opened a drawer. Her heart lurched. *He's reaching for his pistol, he's recognized me, I'll die right here, in this office, and no one will ever know.*

It was, however, a box of Swiss chocolates that he held out to her. She shook her head.

The General shrugged, took a chocolate for himself, and then set the box back into the drawer. "And what is it you need from us?"

"A permit," she stuttered.

"I see," he answered. "But this is no trouble whatever, *khanoom-jan*, provided you'd be willing to resume our conversation at a private meeting."

"And my husband?"

"But surely he does not understand Persian, this foreign husband of yours?"

"Not a word."

"Leave your telephone number with my assistant, *khanoom*," he said as he rose from his desk. "We're sure to find an answer to your problem."

He drew his hand from his pocket and smiled. She extended her own hand and let him squeeze it. Still she kept her eyes cast down. There was a moment, then, when she felt sure he would remember her, but his smile was warm to the last.

"A pleasure, *khanoom*," he said as he showed her to the door.

As Lili walked out of the General's office that day, she kept her eyes down and her steps slow and steady. All the way down the hallway, past the uniformed officers and suited businessmen, down the enormous circular marble staircase and through the main doors, she kept her pace slow and even. It was only in the streets, in the open air, and surrounded by crowds of people that she doubled over as if struck by a blow, threw a look over her shoulder, and broke into a run.

"They won't authorize a permit," she told Johann that night.

It was the first outright lie of her marriage, and despite the ruin it would cause them, it was neither a lie she hesitated to tell nor one she would ever regret having told.

All through that autumn and winter the two ready-mix trucks rumbled back and forth between the factory and Tehran. Johann and Fato'allah began working sixteen- and eighteen-hour shifts and finally twenty-hour shifts, but still they could not work fast enough.

The bills came daily now. Official letters from the bank, invoices from shipping companies and cement suppliers and subcontractors. The German creditors rang each morning (5:00 A.M. Tehran time), pressing for satisfaction, first with warnings and then, increasingly, with threats.

In the end, there was no choice but to sell the factory, the two trucks, and every last sack of cement, until they owned nothing but the parcel of land on which it all sat.

It was then that Johann's drinking really began.

At night he'd come home with a case of Shams beer under one arm and a bottle of English whiskey under the other. He spent days holed up in the apartment on Avenue Pahlavi, drinking and playing the same record on the turntable until he passed out and finally the needle ran off the edge and scratched at nothing.

She'd return from work and find him dead asleep in the middle of the day or slumped in a chair with his face buried in his chest or in his hands. When she called out to him, he'd turn his face to her and wrinkle his brow, as if struggling to place her—or himself. She'd slip his shoes from his feet, pull a blanket over him, and draw the curtains. There were bottles in every room, in every corner, and even at the foot of the tub. In the summer the heat sharpened the scent of the beer and whiskey, and in her desperation she'd throw open the windows and sleep curled up in a chair on the balcony.

She cajoled; she pleaded; she reasoned. She used every endearment, German and Persian, that she knew and more than a few curses, too. Often she refused to speak to him at all.

"I won't drink anymore; I won't," he'd swear, clasping her hands in his own. "I promise you. No more."

However heartfelt, however earnest his promises, within an hour his hands would start shaking, and then instead of the bottles of whiskey and Shams beer it would be dinner plates brimming with cigarette butts, ash smeared on the carpets and the couch, smoke in her hair and on her skin until once again bottles lined the mantel, cluttered the dining room table, and lay by the sink and at the foot of the tub.

She tore through the Armenian deli so many times and with such fury that the owner began throwing his arms in the air as soon as he saw her coming. "Why did you sell him so much?" she'd demand.

"But what can I do, *khanoom*?" he begged to know. "What can I do?"

In the evenings, at the end of her shift, she would stand waiting for Johann in the street outside King's Serenity. Half an hour, then an hour would pass, and still he did not come. She'd turn back to the hospital to call him on the phone, and if he answered at all, it was always in a voice thick with liquor and sleep. She'd return to the street and pace the sidewalk until finally she'd glimpse him weaving down Avenue Pahlavi, the front wheel of the car careening over the edge of the sidewalk until he jerked the clutch and greeted her with a look that was the perfect confluence of helplessness, exhaustion, and mischief.

When, finally, the German creditors were paid off and a small sum of money came in from the sale of their company, Lili marched to the bank, put half the money into an account in her own name, and then cut Johann a check for the other half. "You're free to go back to Germany," she told him. "In a plane or car or in your bare feet—however you prefer."

Johann sobered up, put aside ten thousand *tomans* for Fato'allah and his family, deposited the rest of his share into Lili's bank account, and took a job building villas for the rich in Shemiran. It was neither his first, nor his last, wholehearted and wholly unsuccessful attempt at reform.

Established soon after her return from Germany, the Lady Diola was Kobra's brainchild, and it was born the moment she chose its name. "Lady Diola" was both fantasy and fiction—invented by Kobra to sound both French and modern. For two decades *Tehrooni* women would pass through her doors, calling out, "*Salaam*, Diola Kha-noom! [Hello, Mrs. Diola!]" Year after year Kobra indulged them, smiling silently over her pots of dye and tucking away the bills that would prove her salvation many times over.

To finance the venture, she hauled Lili's best carpets to the bank and signed them over as security for a loan. Kobra then acquired the deed to a new apartment on Avenue Geisha. The living room was outfitted with three gleaming pink sinks, a row of matching pink hair dryers, and pale green floor-to-ceiling carpeting. The larger of the apartment's two bedrooms she'd turned into a waiting room complete with a pair of gold-footed Louis XIV chaises and a steady supply of French and American fashion magazines. The third room in the apartment was Kobra's bedroom, with its single bed and white coverlet and latticed window frames, and this room she always kept locked.

Since opening the Lady Diola, Kobra had undergone a striking transformation. Though she favored styles far more conservative than those in fashion—long, flowing skirts and flowery blouses—they were now invariably cut of the very finest silks. To bolster her diminutive frame, she also began wearing cork-heeled wedges. Kobra and her assistant Hovick, a slender, mustachioed Armenian gentleman with a genius for highlights, could be found every night together at the Diola, experimenting on her hair with the latest tints and hairstyles. And on the eve of her fiftieth birthday she submitted her face and nose to the hands of one of the most famed plastic surgeons in Tehran—to wonderful effect.

As Kobra's fortunes, and beauty, increased, so, too, did the number and quality of her suitors. For a time they had been confined to a thin assortment of aging, often senile, widowers, and Kobra had not hesitated in refusing their advances and dismissing them as a band of gold diggers. Then, in her third year as Lady Diola, she was introduced by one of her neighbors on Avenue Geisha to a very good-looking young man with no visible defect apart from his inability to hold down a job. To everyone's astonishment, Kobra entertained him with a coquetry she'd never, to anyone's knowledge, even vaguely exhibited in her youth.

"Have I mentioned," Kobra confided to Lili one day, hiding her smile behind her hand like a girl, "that my suitor is just thirty years old?"

"But you cannot really mean to marry this gigolo?" Lili inquired.

Kobra blushed; she giggled; she refused all counsel.

The affair continued until at last Lili and Johann were invited to the Lady Diola to formally meet Kobra's suitor. For this occasion Kobra had draped the sinks and hair dryers with white tablecloths and hauled the Louis XIV furnishings from the waiting room to the parlor. Upon arrival, Kobra's suitor was directed to one of the chaise lounges, while Lili and Johann were ordered to sit side by side on the second one. Kobra, dressed in a pink chiffon dress and pink pumps, had never looked as radiant. In this period, she wore her hair in a blond bob that she liked to pull back on one side with a tortoiseshell clip, but that day she'd pinned it into place with a rhinestone barrette. When all parties had assembled, she retreated to the kitchen to prepare tea, which she then proceeded to serve between sweet sidelong glances to her suitor. The pastries were sublime.

Lili narrowed her eyes and appraised her mother's suitor. He was a completely amiable fellow, well mannered and much more handsome than Lili had expected. Most disarmingly, his affection for Kobra seemed completely genuine. Why shouldn't Kobra entertain his attentions? What harm was there in this "second spring," as Johann had dubbed Kobra's midlife affair?

But not long after this meeting Kobra herself began to waver. Her suitor's trousers, she claimed, were always too short, while his fingernails were always too long. When she had finished chronicling his thousand other defects, Kobra sighed and told Lili, "He's nothing next to your father." Lili took it upon herself to remind Kobra that her years with Sohrab had hardly amounted to a happy marriage. Kobra shrugged off the comment. "Your father was a gentleman," she continued. "A perfect gentleman."

The years had worn away at the truth of things, and to Kobra, Sohrab was now not only the husband she'd always longed for and loved but also the husband who'd always longed for and loved her.

Perhaps, Lili reflected, it was not so much this fantasy that Kobra coveted but her independence. In any case, Kobra's courtship with the young suitor came to a decisive end when Kobra, for the very first time in her life, signed her name as Sohrab's wife to an unwitting government clerk and thereby claimed the grave beside his in a cemetery outside Tehran. The previous year Simin, Sohrab's blue-eyed jinn, had died of cancer—a quick though by all accounts tortuous death. With Simin dead, there'd be no one to challenge Kobra's claim to Sohrab's grave. Kobra would, for the rest of her life, be exceedingly proud of this plot of earth, and would be known for many years afterward to hire a taxi to drive her to the graveyard and visit it from time to time.

In the early seventies, Lili alighted on a certain Parisian arrondissement and swept into the offices of a certain celebrated French fertility doctor. She had no appointment and only broken English with which to plead her case, but in one hand she held a gigantic, beribboned metal tub of caviar, and just as she'd predicted, this would serve her better than any letter of introduction.

"Tubes," the celebrated French doctor told Lili with a deep and decisive frown.

The diagnosis did not square with any of the hundreds of others she'd received over the years, but by the time she'd opened her mouth to protest the doctor had already plunged a needle, thin and pliant, into her navel until it disappeared.

"Nothing the matter but your tubes, Madame," he told her as he pulled the needle clear.

No sooner had she acquired the laboratory slip confirming her pregnancy than Lili resigned from King's Serenity and took to her bed. Kobra came to her once a day bearing clay pots of stew and silver platters of potato cutlets, her purse stuffed with herb sachets and wild rue. She attacked the rooms with buckets of ammonia, dusted and swept and polished, and before she left she always circled smoking pots of herbs over Lili, first over her head and then over her belly.

> *Wild rue, wild rue, kernels of wild rue,*
> *Hundred and thirty seeds of rue,*
> *All-knowing rue,*
> *Blind all jealous eyes.*

In the fall and winter Lili buried herself by the *korsi*. She ate persimmons by threes and fours. Twelve weeks into the pregnancy, she had the mouth of her uterus stitched tight to keep the baby from slipping loose. She would not leave the apartment or even stand for fear it would slip loose anyhow. When the weather grew warmer, she abandoned the *korsi* and instead reclined on a carpet on the balcony with a wide-brimmed straw hat pulled over her eyes, eating whole watermelons and reading her way through the classics of nineteenth-century Russian and French literature—Dumas (père and fils), Balzac, Dostoyevsky, and Tolstoy.

One day Mariam planted pots of geraniums along the balcony for her. "For good luck," Mariam explained as she worked the seeds briskly into the soil. The leaves of the geraniums, when they grew, were fleshy, fan shaped, and when the wind blew the petals and scattered them across the balcony they looked just like pomegranate seeds. By No Rooz, Lili felt strong enough to stand, to walk the length of the balcony and dip the nose of her watering can into the flowering pots. Her belly was pleasingly enormous. Slowly, secretly, she let herself imagine her baby's face.

That June, in a first-class hospital suite with a view onto Mount Damavand, Lili lay waiting. She wore a pretty new nightgown with lace at the wrists, collar, and hem. To better remember the day, she refused even a whiff of chloroform. For twenty hours, while Johann paced the corridors, smoking cigarette after cigarette to calm his nerves, her colleagues joked and soothed and cajoled her through labor, and when I appeared at dawn with an umbilical cord wrapped tightly round my neck and the doctor unfurled it and I took my first gulp of air, there were even champagne flutes to greet me.

Aroosak farangi, Lili called me, the foreign doll, her eyes filling with tears even as she laughed and took me into her arms. She pressed her nose to my skin and brushed her lips against my forehead. On the occasion of our first photograph together that day, she piled her hair high on her head, teased up the front, and pinned a gardenia behind her ear.

Every morning Kobra arrived at the apartment on Avenue Pahlavi, touched a forefinger to my eyelids, and gently forced my eyes open. Frowning, lips pursed, she surveyed their progress from gray to blue to black. Then one day she found a near-perfect match for her own honey-colored eyes. "Beautiful," she crooned, sweeping me from my canopied crib with one hand and reaching for her wild rue sachet with the other.

As for Johann, fatherhood would draw forth all his native kindness. He rolled up his sleeves and changed my diapers and bathed me. He stood over my crib and sang me Iranian lullabies in his Azari-tinged Persian. Lili's relatives looked on, dumbfounded. Of course every father loved his child, but no father they'd known had ever proved of such practical use. "Yes, Lili's bread's been drenched in oil," they noted to one another, and once again shook their heads in wonder.

When I passed my fifth month, Lili, Johann, and Kobra took me north to Mashhad, to the shrine of Imam Reza. It was Ashura, the holiest day of the Shiite Muslim calender, the day commemorating Imam Hossein's martyrdom. Thousands of pilgrims had descended on Mashhad to beat their chests and cry out to God as they circled the shrine.

"Take her inside!" Lili called out to Johann over their cries. "Take her to the shrine!"

The turquoise dome of the mosque shimmered in the late-summer sun. Johann, dressed in a denim shirt and jeans, his blond hair to his shoulders, nodded, lifted me high over his head, and fell in with the pilgrims. In addition to drawing forth his native kindness, fatherhood had brought on a protracted period of sobriety. This would not last, but on that day in Mashhad it would still be something for which both Lili and Kobra could give their thanks.

"Give her here, Mr. American!" a man called out in English to Johann when he reached the shrine.

"But I'm not—," he started to call back in Persian. It was useless. The din drowned out his voice. He shook his head, lifted me up in the air, and passed me into the stranger's hands. One by one the pilgrims passed me over their heads, touched my forehead to the doors of Imam Reza's tomb, and then, very gently, they passed me back into my father's hands.

And in this way, I was blessed.

Nine

Revolution

"First the shoolooqi and then the war," Lili said into the tapes.
*"Who knew how long it would last? Nobody could be sure of
anything in those years. As for me, I knew only this: I had to keep
you close and I had to keep you safe."*

IN MY IRAN EVERY story always began the same way. *"Yeki bood;
yeki nabood.* [One was all; all was one.]" It was a riddle, an incan-
tation, a summons. It was my grandmother's honey-colored eyes
narrowing in the dim back room of the Lady Diola whenever she
began to remember or to imagine a story.

Yeki bood; yeki nabood.

One was all; all was one.

We lived then in a high-rise apartment building, one of the many
that were rising up almost daily to permanently alter the shape and
contours of Tehran. Except for its mirrored walls, our apartment on
Avenue Pahlavi was decorated completely in white—white leather
couches, white Formica dining table and dining chairs, white plush
carpets. When I think of Iran I can still hear Elvis' voice echoing
through the all-white rooms of that apartment and can still see
Charlie's Angels sashaying across our TV screen in their bikinis and
their evening gowns.

I was *doh-rageh*, a two-veined child. Not "half" or "mixed," as
they say in America and many other countries besides, but double.

Two. For Iranians, such legacies are carried in the body, intimate as blood and unopposable as destiny.

Every day my mother Lili dressed in a white shirtdress and stacked heels, twisted her hair into a bun, and pulled on her fancy white headdress. She was the only woman in her family with a foreign diploma and the only one who worked outside the home. She called me her *aroosak farangi,* her foreign doll, and she liked to dress me in white to match her own white uniform.

In the mornings she'd drop me off at my grandmother Kobra's salon on Avenue Geisha and from there she'd call for a taxi to drive her to the hospital. In memories it is, somehow, always a summer afternoon at the Lady Diola, the kind of summer afternoon when heat rippled off the rooftops and forced a stillness over the streets of Tehran. I'd toddle through the salon, clawing at the women's hosiery, seeking out my grandmother's long skirts, and begging to be picked up. "Dear God, what will become of this one?" she'd sigh, scooping me up and balancing me on her hip as she washed and tinted and blow-dried her clients' hair.

There was a girl who used to visit the Lady Diola sometimes. She had long black hair that fell like a veil all around her. Months could pass between her visits, and I didn't know whom she belonged to or why she came at all. She'd sit with me in a room behind the salon while my grandmother Kobra worked. Sometimes the girl played dolls with me. Sometimes she drew me pictures. A sweep of blue for the sky. Roses and irises and peonies, all growing alongside one another. I can still see the flowers and the exact shade of blue of her sky, but hard as I try I can't remember the girl's eyes, and it's only like this—faceless—that I know her now.

When the last of the women left the salon, Kobra and I retreated to the kitchen and there she would trade her smock for an apron. She whipped up pancakes spiced with a pinch of saffron and drenched them in sugar and rose essence. She plucked pomegranate seeds

from their honeycombs and fed them to me from a bowl. She pried
the skins off kumquats so that I could pop them into my mouth like
grapes. Her fruits always tasted, faintly, of the mint and parsley she
trimmed for her stews.

Then Kobra would take me to her bedroom, and there she sewed
me dolls with velvet tunics, satin slippers, and real golden hoops
pierced through their tiny cotton ears. She lined both my wrists with
rows of thin gold bangles and strung a blue-eyed amulet around my
neck just as, she told me, her mother had once done for her. We'd lie
down side by side on her narrow bed and she would tell me tales about
a rapacious *deev* and the princess who bewitched him with a dance.

While I napped on those afternoons in Tehran, she would sometimes steal away to the bathroom and with eyeliner and lipstick draw
on her stomach a set of enormous eyes, a pair of thick, vermillion
lips, and a black beauty mark as round and as fat as a coin. She'd sit
on the edge of the bed, waiting for me to open my eyes, and then
she would begin her dance.

Kobra strained and stretched her belly, let it loose and drew it in,
arranged and rearranged the painted features so that her stomach
turned into a live, wriggling kaleidoscope of expressions. I'd sit up,
wide-eyed, clapping my hands and following her with my eyes as
she danced.

I didn't know this yet, but it was a dance that Iranian women
had performed for each other in the *andaroon*, or women's quarters,
for hundreds of years, a vestige of the all-but-vanished country to
which my grandmother had been born and the place she conjured
for me in the stories and songs that would always make up my own
best memories of Iran. What fascinated me most, though, was neither the dance itself nor the face of the woman Kobra drew but the
canvas of my grandmother's skin. Dimpled and slack in the middle,
the peripheries of her stomach were streaked with what looked to
me then like claw marks.

But of all that I can still remember about this "land of jewels"—the final years of the Pahlavi dynasty and also our final years in Iran—it's the girl, the one with hair like a veil falling all around her, whom I think about most often now. One day when I was three years old, my grandmother stepped out of the Lady Diola to meet the postman. The girl lifted me up and smiled into my eyes. At this my memory dissolves and recedes, and I know only that it was my screams that brought my grandmother running in from the street. Kobra pulled me to her. I'd cut my lip and my blood splattered onto her white smock. Turning to the girl, my grandmother shouted words I'd never heard before and drove her away with her shrieks and her cries.

The girl never returned to the Lady Diola after that. I missed her for a while and asked my grandmother why she'd disappeared. But no one spoke of her again and then, for more than twenty years, I would forget that the girl had ever been there at all.

At the gates of the boarding school by Sa'ad Abad, Lili would reach into her purse, count out Sara's pocket money for the week, fold it once, twice, four times, and then finally press it into Sara's palm. "Promise me you will study," she'd say. "Promise me you will be a good girl, that you will be my very own good daughter."

Usually Sara would bundle her packages together, offer Lili a cheek to kiss, and slip quickly out of the taxi, but one night she crossed her arms over her chest and refused to leave.

"I don't want to go back there," she pleaded. "I want to stay with you. I want to live with you and the baby! Why don't you take me to your house? Why can't I live with you?"

"Just another year," Lili promised. "Just one more year."

The words were meant honestly—she had not quite given up hope yet—but before the year was out Lili would be pregnant again and Sara would be a married woman.

It was Zaynab who brought news of Sara's wedding. "She has a suitor!" Zaynab announced. Kobra had put me down for a nap in the back room of the Lady Diola and they were sitting cross-legged on the carpet, taking their afternoon tea. "Her father's already consented to the match," Zaynab continued. "They'll be married in the spring, after the New Year, and they'll live near the groom's family in the countryside."

"Thanks be to God!" Kobra exclaimed, raising her hands to the sky. "Marriage will settle that girl at last!"

Lili, confined once again to her bed, pulled herself onto her elbows and considered the news. That Sara should have a suitor did not surprise her. No pretty girl would want for suitors, and Sara was certainly prettier than most. Still, no one, not Sara and certainly not Kazem, had given Lili reason to think a proper courtship was actually under way.

She frowned. "And just who is this suitor?" she asked.

Zaynab brightened. "Such a nice young man!" she exclaimed. "Handsome, too! Looks just like Elvis Presley—"

Kobra threw her hands up into the air again. "All-merciful God! A suitor and he even looks like Elvis Presley!"

"But it's true!" Zaynab insisted. She turned to Lili and lowered her voice. "She wants to know if you'll come to her wedding."

Kobra stiffened. "Don't you dare!" she hissed. She nodded toward Lili's belly. "You'll lose that baby if you so much as stand on your two feet!"

"May your tongue grow mute, Kobra Khanoom!" Zaynab cried out at this terrible thought.

Once, not long before this day, Sara had called Lili on the telephone from the boarding school. The conversation had been brief. "It's true what they told me about you," Sara said. "You are *kharab*." The word meant "broken" but also "bad." A prostitute.

With this one word, *kharab*, Lili had finally understood many things: That no matter what she promised or sacrificed, she would always be "broken" to her daughter. That my birth had undone what little affection she'd earned from Sara in the last few years and had returned Sara's rage to her. That the pain of this would always be equal to her will to not feel anything. And, too, that there is a mercy in forgetting and also in letting one's self be forgotten.

For some minutes there'd been silence as Sara waited for Lili to answer. Slowly, almost tenderly, Lili had set the phone down, lifted her hands to her face, and cried.

On the eve of Sara's wedding, Lili sent her a set of embroidered bed linens, a white sharkskin suit for Sara's groom, and a gift of seven thousand *tomans*, all her savings. But Lili could not go to the wedding, she could not steel herself to face Kazem and his family, nor could she bear to meet Sara's eyes on the day she became a bride. And when Lili miscarried again that summer, she pitched her grief onto the many others, the previous miscarriages, Johann's drinking, and her in-laws' cruelties, went back to work, and surrendered all of her love and hope to me.

In those days no one spoke of "addiction," much less of "treatment." For Lili the Persian word for addiction, *mohtad*, conjured images of opium dens, those dark, ancient caverns where men wasted away in a thick, sweet haze. Or else it made her think of the cocaine and heroin that now circulated in the back rooms of the city's discotheques and bars. She'd seen dozens of celebrities and socialites spirited away to the birthing clinic for a discreet, if tortuous, course of detoxification. Their screaming was terrible, far worse than the cries of women in labor. Sometimes they'd have to be tied down to their beds until their bodies were free of the drugs. That, Lili told herself, was addiction.

Meanwhile, Johann's face turned haggard and he grew so thin

that his pants sagged and flapped against his legs. He was never violent, he never spoke a harsh or unkind word against her, but many
days his boss would call Lili at the hospital with complaints. "Please
understand, *khanoom*," he begged, sounding on the verge of tears.
Johann had come late to work on Monday. He'd been drinking at
his desk; he'd insulted a client; he hadn't come to work at all for
three days. "If it weren't out of respect for you, Khanoom Doktor, I
would fire him, please understand, Khanoom Doktor...."

Worse still were the days and weeks when he disappeared. She did
not know where he went, whether as far as the provinces or just to
some corner of the city. When he came back home, his clothes were
always soiled and wrinkled, his pockets empty, his face and chest
ruddy from the sun, and his eyes dull and bloodshot.

Mostly her family pretended not to notice Johann's drinking, but
these absences so terrified Zaynab and Kobra as to shake them from
their reticence. Zaynab, fairly trembling with worry, would pull
Lili aside at family gatherings and tell Lili the story of a foreigner,
a poor *bandeh Khoda*, creature of God, who'd been found dead and
half-naked at the edge of the Dasht-e Kavīr, the vast salt desert that
stretched across the Iranian plateau. "Keep him close," Zaynab whispered. Kobra favored a more direct approach. "You are a good man,
Mr. Engineer," she'd tell Johann, taking him by the arm and speaking softly to him, "a true gentleman. I don't tell you not to drink,
just to drink here, in the house, where you will be safe...."

But whatever name Lili and her family gave his drinking, or would
not, there would be many months now that she had no money to pay
rent. Once she laundered and ironed all her clothes—her flowered
sundresses and wool skirt suits and even her silk stockings—hung
them along a string in her bedroom, and prepared to sell them to the
neighborhood women.

"And just how much do you think you'll get for all this?" Mariam
had asked her.

"Three thousand *tomans*."

"Three thousand! You'd let people steal your clothes from you for three thousand *tomans*?"

"Fine. Six thousand."

"That's better," said Mariam. She reached for her purse. "I'll buy it all, but I won't pay you less than seven thousand."

"You!" Lili exclaimed. "But none of it will fit you!"

"That, *dokhtar-joon*, is my business, not yours!"

With the money Mariam gave her for the clothes, Lili paid the back rent on the apartment on Avenue Pahlavi and bought a bottle of whiskey that would at least keep Johann home the next time he started to drink.

"I can't make him stop. . . . ," she once confided to Mariam.

"You stupid girl," said Mariam with rough affection. "Of course you can't."

There was talk sometimes of trouble in the holy cities of Qom and Mashhad, of an exiled cleric named Ayatollah Khomeini smuggling cassette tapes into Iran from abroad. No one seemed to pay much attention. The shah's soldiers were everywhere. Twenty billion dollars of oil revenue streamed into the coffers of the Peacock Throne each year. Nearly a million foreigners were living in Iran by then, and with the city's hotels booked solid for much of the year, there were even rumors of tourists renting bathrooms and hospital beds. "The very gutters of Tehran are lined with gold!" it was said in London and Tokyo and New York. What, many Iranians reasoned, were an exiled cleric and his cassette tapes beside all that?

Still, there was talk; there were signs. Once, on Lili's way back home after a delivery in the Bottom of the City, a woman in a long, black veil, a *chadori*, eyed her as she stood on the curb waiting for a cab. Every time Lili looked in her direction, she caught the woman staring at her. Lili turned her face away, pretended not to notice or care, but then the woman brushed past her and whispered, "You should cover yourself, sister."

She had only meant it kindly, Lili told herself, and so she'd just nodded and gone on her way. But then, not long afterward, Johann told her that his clients had started reneging on their villas in Shemiran. "They're sending their money out of the country," one of the project's Iranian engineers told Johann one day before confiding that he'd started doing the same. "Did you know that just a hundred thousand dollars buys a house, a business, and a green card in America?" Johann did not, but suddenly it seemed that everyone knew someone who'd left Iran for America or Europe and many others who were planning to leave the country soon.

For all this, in later years Lili would trace the end, or rather her end in Iran, to Mariam's death.

One August evening Mariam went to visit her father, Shahryar Khan, at his ranch an hour outside Tehran. A country gentleman of vast estates, Shahryar Khan had long indulged a passion for hunting. At eighty, he still took weeklong treks through the countryside with his friends and their female consorts, returning, invariably, with carcasses slung over both shoulders—rabbits, antelope, and eagles. These he skinned, stuffed, and mounted on the walls of his house alongside his rifles, pistols, and antique swords.

For years Mariam had pleaded with him to show greater mercy. "Blood brings blood," Mariam had warned her father, with much sincerity and far less success.

When Shahryar Khan woke one night to noises outside his house, he reached for the pistol he always kept by his bed, flung the door open, and shot into the dark. His eyesight was poor, his hands palsied, but with one bullet he met his mark. It was not until the next day that his second wife, the young country girl, found Mariam's body bleeding and laid open to the sky.

For Lili, Mariam's death belonged to a class of grief so deep it foreclosed the possibility of tears. One day Lili went to the clinic, pulled the sign from its place by the door, and drew the curtains closed. For many weeks the Bottom of the City women would arrive with their sisters, daughters, aunts, and cousins, their pots of stew and their knitting, only to find the clinic's windows shuttered and its door locked. Inside, Lili would sit cross-legged on the floor, praying, and as she prayed she'd hear Mariam's voice, as clear as it had been in life. "Blood brings blood," Lili murmured as she rocked herself back and forth, though sometimes she screamed the words, too.

Now she began to dream.

Thousands had gathered in the streets of Tehran. Shoulder to shoulder, from one end of Avenue Pahlavi to the other, they stood with their faces turned up toward the sky. The shah's plane circled the city. Then came the smoke. It began, always, as a thin black stripe, but this smoke, the smoke of Lili's dreams, didn't dissipate but instead grew thicker and blacker until finally it had swallowed the whole sky.

It was dreams, always dreams, by which Lili and Kobra took measure of both past and future. When Kobra dreamt, it was mostly of her dead, and her dreams invariably guided her toward acts of piety. When she dreamt of her mother, Pargol, she fasted. When she dreamt of Sohrab, she gave alms to the poor. As for Lili, long after she'd learned to spurn most all of Kobra's superstitions, she still took close counsel from her dreams.

"We must leave Iran," Lili finally told Johann one day.

Fifteen years had passed since he'd first come to Iran to marry her, and in that time he'd learned the futility, and often the peril, of dismissing such pronouncements. When Lili told him about her dream and announced that "we must leave Iran," he claimed to have been visited by a dream himself.

"I dreamt we were in America and that I died there in a tall building."

"But there's trouble. They say—"

"Let's just wait another year," he pleaded, but it was Lili's dream that would guide us—that night and in all the years to come.

We left Iran on Shab-e Yalda, the first night of winter and the longest night of the year. For centuries Iranians had celebrated Yalda with a midnight feast of pomegranates, wine, and poetry, but on our final night in Iran, while Lili and Kobra packed the two maroon leather suitcases we would be taking with us to America, Zaynab and I celebrated the solstice by watching a Yalda special on television.

At midnight Googoosh, the diva of 1970s Tehran, appeared in a golden chariot. Zaynab pulled on her glasses and sat me on her lap, inches from the screen. Googoosh tossed back her blond hair and began to sing and dance. Every few minutes she floated away on her golden chariot, and when she came back she was always wearing a different dress, her hair had been restyled, and her heavy-lidded eyes had been painted with a different shade of pastel eye shadow.

"She's changed her outfit again!" Zaynab would call out breathlessly. "Come see; come see!" she'd call, and from time to time Lili and Kobra would poke their heads into the room to admire Googoosh's latest look.

A light snow had begun to fall earlier in the night. By the time we reached Mehrabad Airport, it was four in the morning and large, heavy snowflakes filled the still-dark sky. We trudged across the icy tarmac. The plane's engines roared and hummed and the lights on its wings began pulsing.

"If you don't hurry," a woman called out to us, "it will be too late for you to board!"

At this, Lili, Kobra, and Zaynab fell into each other's arms, crying. I caught a snowflake on my tongue and ate it, then caught another and another.

Zaynab broke free from Lili's and Kobra's embrace and brushed her tears away with the edge of her veil. "America," she said suddenly. "It's a wonderful place, they say. Everyone says it's a wonderful place...."

This only made Lili cry harder. For weeks she'd been telling everyone—her cousins, aunts, colleagues, and neighbors—that we'd soon be back in our apartment on Avenue Pahlavi. "We're only taking two suitcases!" she told them. "How long could we stay away with just two suitcases?"

But in these last minutes a terrible apprehension overtook her. She turned to her aunt and clasped Zaynab's hands in her own. "What if we can't come back?"

"But of course you'll come back!" Zaynab and Kobra cried out together.

Lili nodded and drew in a deep breath. "But you'll keep an eye out for her, won't you? Just sometimes, so I know—"

"Yes, yes," Kobra said quickly. "You just watch out for that one," she said with a nod toward me. "And your husband, too."

"But I'll have no one to talk to over there!" Lili wailed.

"You'll have her!" Zaynab exclaimed, giving my cheek a pinch.

"Her? What will she understand? She won't even remember any of this. She won't remember any of you!"

This would prove just as true as her dream. Until Lili told the story in the tapes twenty years later, I'd forget almost everything about that last night in Iran. The two suitcases, the pretty lady in the golden carriage on television, all the cries, prayers, and promises, Kobra as she held the Koran over our heads, and Zaynab burying her face in Lili's chest and then wrestling herself free and walking away so that there was no choice for us but to go. One by one my memories of that last night in Iran fell away until finally I remembered nothing but the snow.

Later it would be called the Islamic Revolution, but for a long time the hopes and furies that gripped Iran in the late seventies would be known to Iranians only as the *shoolooqi*, "the busyness." In the first months of the *shoolooqi*, when the streets of Tehran were overrun with mobs, tanks, soldiers, and snipers, Kobra would sit in the dark back room of the Lady Diola until the cries of *"Allahu Akbar!* [God is great!]" rose from the rooftops of the city.

My mother, father, and I landed in New York with two suitcases. Lili and Johann bought a silver Buick sedan and headed south and then westward across the United States. I sat cross-legged on my mother's lap in the front seat, chattering to myself and playing dolls. Lili, lost in her thoughts, braided and unbraided and rebraided my hair. From time to time her eyes would seize on some detail of the landscape and she'd point out the window and tell me to "look at America." I was five years old and "America" meant nothing more to me than the plush maroon seats and gleaming hood of that Buick. Persian was just the sound of my mother's voice and German was my father's.

We stayed at roadside motels, slept three to a bed, woke early, and drove all day. In New York, in Fort Lauderdale, in Houston and Las Vegas, Lili stayed up long past midnight, dialing Kobra's number and then Zaynab's. No answer. Lili would let the phone ring ten, twenty, thirty times before setting down the receiver. Sara had no telephone in the countryside. She might be safer there than with relatives in the city, but Lili couldn't be sure. She paced the motel room, cursing or crying or both. Ten minutes later she'd dial Kobra's and Zaynab's numbers again. No answer. Every night Lili lay in bed, staring at the ceiling, desperate for sleep. It rarely came. By the time we reached

Texas, her eyes were ringed with dark circles. When we stopped at gas stations she bought packages of pink doughnuts, and when she felt her waist start to thicken she found she did not care.

In Tehran, meanwhile, Kobra began to hoard flatbread, beans, and nuts. Twice a day she moistened a sheet of *nooneh sangak* with a sprinkle of water, pressed some feta cheese and walnuts on top of it, and ate it in one bite. Whenever she came by an orange or an apple at the marketplace, she'd wrap it in a sheet of newspaper and bury it deep in her refrigerator. Just before the fruit reached the point of rotting, she'd pull it out and eat it as a treat.

The shah left the country with a small box of Iranian soil tucked under his arm. Ayatollah Khomeini returned from exile to kneel on the ground and kiss the source of that same soil. *"Allahu Akbar! Allahu Akbar!"* came the cries across the rooftops of Tehran night after night—God is great! God is great!—and all through the *shoolooqi* Kobra, too, put her faith in Him.

We crossed into California and spent an entire day circling Los Angeles, looking for Hollywood. Failing to find it, we settled for a tour of Universal Studios. The Santa Ana winds set the palm trees swaying, mixed the scent of the desert with the scent of the sea. My father took me to Disneyland and Lili, alone in a motel room in Anaheim, watched the news from Iran and wept.

From Los Angeles we continued north along the California shore, down Highway 1, until we reached San Francisco. When we crossed over the Golden Gate, my mother narrowed her eyes at a strip of coast just beyond the bridge. The light brushed the slate gray water silver and the hills that skirted the ocean were unlike any she'd ever seen, blond and rounded and endless.

"Here," she told my father, because by then she understood that there'd be no going back to Iran, or no going back yet.

Like most immigrants, my parents found their degrees and work experience did not count for much when they came to America, and so they used their small savings to buy a run-down motel on a frontage road off Highway 101 ten miles north of San Francisco. The Casa Buena, the Good House. It had twenty rooms, doubles and singles, on two floors, and a small cottage, the "manager's suite," attached to the motel on one end. The parking lot was pitted with potholes, the beds all sagged and creaked, and the carpets and curtains stank of mold and cigarettes, but in those ruins they willed themselves to see their future. To begin again.

They worked in shifts, day and night, seven days of the week. My father took the night shift, snatching at sleep on a tattered powder blue couch in the office. His eyes, too, would soon be ringed with dark circles and his face would soon take on a look of permanent confusion but in the beginning he held fast to his gentlemanly ways. At six in the morning he rinsed his face, splashed on some cologne, then combed his hair and set it with hairspray. He wore dress slacks, not jeans, dress shoes, not tennis shoes. He boiled himself a full pot of coffee—twelve cups' worth to last him through the day—fried two sausages in a pan, and ate them with a knife and a fork, and then he returned to his desk behind the plastic window of the manager's suite.

At noon—checkout time—Johann napped in the back room and Lili began her own shift at the Casa Buena. She piled the day's clean sheets and towels onto an ancient, battered olive green trolley, checked her supply of bleach and Windex, and began making her way through the motel rooms. She emptied and polished the plastic ashtrays, then collected the beer bottles, soda cans, and pizza boxes from the floor. She stripped the beds, taking care to air out the mattresses before pulling on the new sheets, dusted the nightstand and the television, and vacuumed the carpet. Then, with one ear to the parking lot in case someone came looking for a room, she splashed the tub and the toilet with bleach, and to save time she threw rags on the bathroom floor and mopped with her feet as she wiped down the sink.

Mostly we rented to truckers on their way to Los Angeles. They'd stay the night and leave before dawn, and though they could be gruff or outright rude, it was the locals who always gave the most trouble. They'd stagger into the office when the bars closed, hollering and cussing and slamming their bills onto the counter. When they got to their rooms they'd send the lamps and tables crashing against the walls. Once a man dragged a half-naked woman into the parking lot and began whipping her with his belt, and by the time the police came the woman's face and shoulders were covered in bloody welts and the man had made off into the dark.

We had long-term lodgers, too. One man stayed the better part of that first year at the Casa Buena. Every morning Lili would find the carpet in his room covered in strange white flecks. "What is it?" she finally asked him one day. "Skin condition," he told her. "It's not contagious, I swear. I've even been to a doctor." He lowered his voice. "My wife's put me out," he confided, his eyes filling with tears. There were out-of-work migrant farmers who spread blankets on the floor and slept their families six or eight to a room. There was a rail-thin, bent-backed elderly woman who rented three or four times a year. She arrived on foot, her long, gray braids messy and oily. She carried no bags, not even a purse, stayed one or two nights, and then disappeared. It was a long time before Lili discovered that Americans had a name for such people. Homeless, they were called here, and she could never stand to turn them away.

Our first home in America was a tract house in a working-class neighborhood of Terra Linda. A small box of a house, it sat on a winding street of brightly colored houses—green, yellow, pink, and blue—each with an identical eight-by-eight-foot lawn in the front and a single cherry tree in the backyard. We wouldn't stay long (of this Lili was sure), but it was here that she unfurled her best carpet, a pistachio green Tabriz that had taken up most all the space in one of the two suitcases we brought from Iran, and hung it from the wall like a tapestry. With the first earnings from the motel she bought a pair of green velvet couches to match it, but apart from the carpet and couches, for a long time the only other pieces of furniture in that house were the mattresses in our bedrooms.

It was Lili's house and mine, really, because my father always slept at the motel, in the manager's suite, and he spent most of his days there, too. He sat at his desk behind the plastic window, his small portable radio tuned to a classical music station, and he left the office only to make repairs around the motel or to nap in the back room.

Every few weeks, though, he'd take me to the bookstore in town. When we walked together in the street, he clasped his hands behind his back and lifted his face to the sun. "I'll only buy as many as you can carry," he'd tell me before letting me loose. I'd pile books up to my chin, two and three bags' worth, and present myself to him. "Sure you can carry them?" he'd ask me. I never could, but it only made him smile to see me try.

Those first few months in America, my mother Lili and I walked everywhere together: to my school, to the mall, to the community pool. Terra Linda was hot and dusty. We were the only pedestrians for miles. I dragged my heels and kicked up such a fuss that one day she had just had enough. We got on a bus and headed straight for the DMV.

The day she passed her driving test, we walked to the car dealership just down the road from the motel. Lili circled the lot, taking careful measure of the inventory, and I trailed along behind her. She settled finally on a pale yellow Cadillac convertible with tan leather seats, chrome details, and windows that went up and down at the push of a button.

"Ready?" she asked me before pulling out of the lot that day.

"Ready!" I squealed.

We'd gone no farther than a mile when black plumes began to drift up from the hood. Lili's Cadillac would spend at least one week out of every month at the repair shop, and then we'd have to go back to walking, the two of us on those empty California sidewalks, she in her denim bell-bottoms and huge tortoiseshell sunglasses, me in my flounced summer frocks and black patent-leather Mary Janes.

When Lili first narrowed her eyes at San Francisco Bay, turned to my father, and said, "Here," she could not guess that many other Iranians had already staked the same claim. But by the late seventies there were already hundreds of Iranians in the area. Many had arrived several years before the revolution with substantial fortunes in several countries. Some claimed close ties to Mohammad Reza Pahlavi, the last shah of Iran. They filled the walls of their homes with photographs of fathers, uncles, and grandfathers in heavily decorated military costume, receiving medals of honor from the king's own hands. Others traced their lineage to the Qajars, the previous—and they would have said true—dynasty of Iran. Their green-eyed wives and daughters had been known for centuries as the most beautiful of Iranian women, and they could be identified easily even in exile.

These were the "good" Iranian families, the ones whose names were firmly planted in the roster of the Iranian elite. They did not think of themselves as immigrants, but as émigrés, and they called themselves Persians, not Iranians. The wives of such families could be found every day at Nordstrom, immaculately dressed in pencil skirts and twinsets, pearls at their necks and Chanel sunglasses perched on their heads. Their husbands often didn't work in America, as it was understood that here there were no positions commensurate with their pedigree.

We were not that kind of Iranian family, but with American money and a certain guile we would soon take on many of their airs. It was a performance in which we were hardly alone; it was a way, common to so many Iranians back then, of imagining new lives in this country.

"*Irooni!*" my mother Lili would whisper whenever she saw Iranians at the grocery store or at the mall, and then give my hand a squeeze. "Do you see them? *Irooni!*" In those days a phrase of Persian overheard from a distance could fill her with terrible longing, and she'd follow them with her eyes until they disappeared.

It was in springtime, on *SeezDeh Bedar* or the last of the New Year's celebrations, when she finally found her way to them. *Tehroonis* always spent this day by the streams and rivers north of the city. Families packed their carpets and water pipes, their pots of rice and stew, piled into their cars, and drove, caravan-style, up through the mountains. All day they picnicked on the riverbanks. They played music and they danced. At dusk young girls knelt in the grass, knotted two blades together, and wished for suitors in the coming year. Before leaving for the city everyone always tossed their swatches of *sabseh*, or greens, into the water for good luck.

Lili had started her greens late that year. The lentils had barely sprouted, the shoots were just tender white curls, but it would be bad luck not to throw them to the waters. Here there were no rivers, or any rivers we knew, so Lili packed a picnic for the two of us and drove us toward the ocean.

She saw them as soon as we climbed out of the car and reached the shore: dozens of lush, round swatches of greens bobbing along the waves. Many more had gotten caught in the eddies or lay tangled in seaweed. Lili turned and looked about her and there, in the shade of a eucalyptus grove a hundred feet from the beach, she found the source of the miracle. "*Irooni!*" she exclaimed, and gave my hand a squeeze. Not one or two, but numerous Iranian families.

Grandmothers and aunts hauling pots of rice and stew still warm from their ovens; fathers and grandfathers and uncles playing backgammon at the picnic tables; and wives sitting cross-legged in a circle, taking tea and cracking sunflower seeds between their teeth. They'd spread their silk carpets on the grass, and to Lili it seemed as if the beach were theirs and had always been.

"*Salaam!*" she called out to them, a smile breaking across her face as she made her way forward.

"*Salaam, salaam!*" they called back.

"And when," they asked her after the preliminary pleasantries had been exchanged, "did you come, *khanoom*? Before or after?"

This was the question no two Iranians failed to ask each other when meeting in America back then. It was a nearly discreet way of discerning who hailed from the "best" families in Iran. The "best" Iranians were almost always the ones who'd left months or years before the revolution; everyone else was presumed to have escaped the country in various states of economic and legal hardship. It might not seem that such things could matter here, so far from Iran, but they did—mostly because in America Iranians were suddenly thrown together in ways that wouldn't have been possible in Iran.

"Before," Lili answered quickly. "We came before."

They passed her a fresh cup of tea and sent me off to play with their daughters. "Tell us, *khanoom*," they entreated her. "Tell us your story."

They were kind, they were generous, but neither eight thousand miles nor all the privations of exile would ever be sufficient to loosen Lili's tongue in their company. "*Vah, vah, vah!*" she imagined they'd say of her. "A divorcée?" By the time her story circulated among these women, she'd have abandoned not one husband, but three, not one child, but ten. Lili took her tea gratefully, found a place at their picnic that day and later on their leather couches and Louis XIV settees. They'd invite her to their tea parties and their dinner parties, their No Rooz celebrations and their children's weddings. She'd fall in with their gossip, grow familiar with their rivalries and losses and aspirations, and even confide some of her own. A few of the women she met on the beach that day would eventually become as close to her as sisters, but from the moment she took her place among them she knew she would never tell them anything about her first marriage or her daughter in Iran. For thirty years, she would tell them nothing at all.

What she'd tell me she dismissed as another day's trouble.

It was the new language that led me astray, cut off my mother tongue and carried me off in a jumble of strange but wonderful words. "Whisper," "marshmallow," "tumble." I shaped my mouth around each one, finding my way to its cadence. Slowly I learned to look at the world backward, trained my eye to move left to right instead of the Persian way around the page. The lines of my first penmanship—a script that flows down and across every boundary—fell to waste. In their place I traced stocky letters easily contained between dotted lines. When I finished, I'd hold the paper up and admire my handiwork.

My mother prided herself on the ease and speed with which I picked up English. In public with Americans, she'd nudge me and whisper in Persian, "Show them how well you can speak! Even better than they can speak their own language!" At home, though, I could expect nothing but reprimands for speaking "that" language instead of "ours." "Don't use your big English words on me!" she'd chide.

When she dragged me along to the mall or the grocery store, I'd stand by mutely as she struggled to communicate with Americans. Very soon I could tell that hers was not a fashionable or exotic accent but rough and ugly to these strangers' ears. One word out of her mouth and Americans would stare her down, hard and long. "What'd you say?" they asked her. My mother seemed not to notice or care; if anything, she pitied those shopgirls for their apparent stupidity. But not me. Whenever my mother spoke English, even a word of it, I cringed. I'd inch away from her and quietly disappear behind a rack of clothes or scramble down the next grocery aisle.

When I was a child, shame was my first, true, and native instinct. Nothing about me was right in America; nothing about me "fit" here. In Iran I'd been coddled and fussed over as a "two-veined child," but here my "gold" hair and "honey-colored eyes" were just plain old "brown." Worse, in America my mother's ways were strange and shaming. Day after day she sent me off to school in party frocks and two-piece suits in miniature. She filled my lunch box with cucumbers and sliced quince fruit. I'd peel off my jacket, hitch up my skirt, and toss her offerings into the trash before school even started. Shy and sullen among the swarm of blond ponytails in the schoolyard, I took to hiding out in the library at recess and lunchtime. If I could not be ordinary (and already I knew I could not), then I would be invisible.

Still, my shame in these years inspired in me certain abiding talents. Shame gave me English. At school I filled my writing primers and earned my teachers' praise, and in the afternoons I sat on the floor of the manager's suite in my parents' motel with the heaps and heaps of books that made the hours there bearable, or nearly so.

When the news from Iran came on the television now, there was always a number that ran across the bottom of the screen. Ten days, forty-two days, a hundred days. The number rose and rose. The *shoolooqi* had a proper name by then—the Islamic Revolution—and the blindfolded men on the screen were called hostages.

The news was always on at our house in those days, but for me the Hostage Crisis only really began with a girl named Ziba.

"We have a new student," my teacher, Miss Stevens, called out one morning. She gestured for the new girl to come forward. The girl hesitated, then walked slowly to the front of the room and faced the class. Her cheeks were bright red and very big and she had black eyebrows that met in the middle of her forehead. "Ziba is from Iran," Miss Stevens told the class.

I cringed. She pronounced Iran the way they did on television. "Eye-ran."

For a moment everyone in the class seemed to consider Ziba. Then the first paper airplane of the day arched over our heads. To my relief, no one seemed to care much about Ziba or Eye-ran.

When I walked into the classroom the next morning, I saw that Miss Stevens had pulled Ziba's desk so close that its edges touched mine. "It'll be so nice for her to have a friend from her own country," Miss Stevens explained.

Ziba sat down next to me. She turned her face toward me and smiled. It was a pretty smile, trusting and kind, but I didn't smile back.

Ziba's English was awful. She couldn't even say "the" properly, she was always mixing up her pronouns, and her penmanship was worse than a kindergartner's. Just as I started to think she'd get sent back a grade, or maybe even two, Miss Stevens discovered that Ziba was very good at math. She was, in fact, a math genius. Every time Miss Stevens called on Ziba with a math problem, Ziba would cup her hands under her dimpled chin, chirp out, "I tink...," and then give the perfect answer.

Somehow this high-pitched "I tink" became Ziba's trademark. The class seemed charmed by it. All day long kids begged her to say it. Ziba always obliged and laughed along with them.

Then one day they forced her to say it over and over until her eyes welled up with tears. "Hey, listen to unibrow!" someone called out, and everyone burst out laughing.

Within a few weeks kids stopped calling her unibrow. Instead they called her a sand nigger. Nazi. Smelly A-rab.

The news from Iran had finally reached our elementary school.

Ziba and I made it through the next months of the Hostage Crisis together. We stopped eating in the schoolyard with the other kids. Instead we ate our lunches on the bench outside our classroom. Ziba's mother always packed her things like dried garbanzo beans, but Ziba didn't seem to care. She'd swing her legs under the bench and smile at me as she crunched on her dried beans, and I'd sip my Capri Sun and wonder just how long it would be before Ziba was sent out of the country.

But before the Hostage Crisis ended I managed to ditch Ziba for a tall, kinky-haired American girl who wore a silver cross around her neck and Ziba had befriended two other, much kinder Iranian girls from another class.

Kindness, my mother taught me when Mutti, Elsa, and Maria came to visit us in America, depended on certain fictions.

On their first day in this country, Mutti, Elsa, and Maria woke at five o'clock, dragged the table from the kitchen to the office, draped it in one of the embroidered tablecloths they'd brought as a gift, set a large ashtray in the center, and began smoking cigarettes. At seven thirty they walked down the road and across the freeway to Safeway and returned with several bags of groceries, two cases of beer, and a bottle of vodka. By nine o'clock they stood in the kitchen in their matching aprons, cigarettes dangling between their lips, and started in on the day's cooking: pots of goulash, cauliflower, and potatoes, pans of sausages and pork loins. By nine thirty the windows had all steamed up and the manager's suite smelled of onions.

When Lili finished cleaning the motel rooms, she'd find them smoking in the office and speaking their language to one another while Johann stretched out on the couch with a bottle of beer in one hand and another bottle already open and waiting for him on the table. The lunch plates would already be drying by the side of the sink and not one potato had been put aside for her.

She'd press her lips together, toast a slice of pita bread, and eat it standing over the sink.

"You have a lot of work here," Mutti told her on the third day.

Lili rubbed her forehead with the back of her hand. "Yes, Mutti."

Mutti waved at the walls. "It's not so good here for a child."

"No, Mutti," Lili sighed.

Lili drew a deep breath and prayed for *sabr,* forbearance. It did not come. At the end of the week she pulled Johann into the back room of the manager's suite.

"No more," she told him. "If they want to stay here, they have to stay in the house."

Johann hung his head and nodded. "I'll tell them in the morning."

But there would be no need of that, because when Lili opened the door they fell, one on top of the other, onto the floor. They'd heard every word.

"*Hexe!*" Elsa shouted as she scrambled to her feet. Witch!

Again Lili prayed for forbearance. Again it did not come.

In the second week, they moved into our house and took me with them. They walked me to school in the mornings. They waxed the floors and filled the cupboards with jars of herring and pickles. They planted tomatoes and sunflowers in the garden. They trudged down the street in their flower-print dresses and kerchiefs, plastic shopping bags swinging from their hands, and walked me back home from school. Whenever I asked after Lili, Mutti would pat my head and bring me a plate of Linzer cookies from the kitchen or reach into her apron pocket and give me a handful of lemon drops.

Every few days Mutti pulled me onto her lap and they'd all search my face for any resemblance to my father or to themselves.

"Her nose?"

"Her forehead?"

"Her cheeks!" they finally decided, and immediately began pinching my face.

It was not long before I started pinching them back.

I'd sneak up to them when they were working in the kitchen or hanging the laundry in the backyard and then pinch them on their backsides. Mutti and Maria only laughed, ruffled my hair, and gave me a playful pinch on the cheek, but one day when she was sitting on the couch, darning a pair of socks, Elsa decided to cure me of my tricks.

"Come here," she told me, hooking her index finger and wriggling it at me.

The pain of it was awful, but it took me a moment to realize what she'd done. I looked down at my arm. A trickle of blood had appeared where she'd pricked me with her needle. Suddenly my throat felt very hot and very tight. When I looked up again, Elsa was waving her needle and smiling. "Did you like that?" she asked. "Did you like how that felt?"

I never pinched any of them after that, not even kindly Mutti with her Linzer cookies and her sweet lemon drops, but I would never let them take me into their laps, either, and I was not at all sad when they left the next month. Still, for many years Lili made me write them letters, in German, telling them how very much I missed and loved them all.

The new house in Tiburon was at the top of a hill, in a cul-de-sac of three large homes, and it had a view of San Francisco, Alcatraz, and Angel Island. In just a few years the interest on the loan that had made its purchase possible would reach nearly 30 percent, but for the moment the house seemed not just a bargain but a coup. The day of our move my mother and I pulled into the driveway in her buttery yellow Cadillac, boxes and plastic bags crowding the tan leather seats, both of us giddy at our great luck.

Over time my mother would furnish every room of that house in Tiburon with antiques; adorn the windows with folds of real silk; decorate my bedroom with a white canopied bed and her own with a king-size waterbed, purple velvet coverlet, and piles of purple cushions; and line the living room mantel and all the walls with black-and-white photographs of herself as a young woman in Iran.

Of all these photographs, the most prized would always be the one in which she stands beside a vase of white gladiolus on her wedding day. With one hand she holds the train of her wedding dress. Her other hand is set jauntily at her waist. Her dress is pulled taut across her torso and seems of a piece with her chest. In this picture her face is turned away from the camera and she smiles graciously, as if to a crowd of admirers. She is exceptionally beautiful.

In Tiburon Lili would recover some measure of that beauty, though never with the same effect.

For her first PTA meeting, she pulled on her best outfit: a fuchsia skirt suit, silk ivory blouse, and black open-toed pumps. She painted her lips pink, pinned her hair into a chignon, and dabbed perfume behind her ears and her wrists. She pulled on a black broad-brimmed hat and looped a string of pearls around her neck. She would have worn gloves, but the day was warm and so, thinking twice, she'd left them behind.

Most of the other mothers—the American mothers—present at that day's PTA meeting wore polo shirts, jeans, and penny loafers. A few, however, wore pleated ankle-length flower-print dresses, and the most lithesome among them flashed taut, tanned thighs from underneath tennis skirts. They were lawyers' wives, doctors' wives, executives' wives. In just ten years these Marin moms would survey their ranks for the few Chinese American, South Asian, and, eventually, even Iranian families, all of whom they'd suddenly embrace according to a new ethic of "cultural diversity." But not yet. This was 1981, Ronald Reagan was president, and "immigrants," when these women thought of them at all, were the brown-skinned "Mexicans" who loitered in the canal down in San Rafael. Iran was "Eye-ran" and hospitality, where Lili found it in Tiburon, extended no further than a thin-lipped half smile. Here her fine clothes were absurd, her pleasantries incomprehensible. In consequence, there would be no invitations to their cocktail parties or their sailing cruises or their ski cabins up in Tahoe. And for her part, Lili would never forget their barely perceptible but still unmistakable cruelties, or, for that matter, their stunning absence of style.

My father had a habit of suddenly leaving his post behind the plastic window at the Casa Buena and disappearing. Usually he'd just slip over to the Italian diner next door for a few hours in the middle of the day. When she finished cleaning the rooms, Lili would make her way back to the office only to find the manager's suite abandoned and the cash register empty. She'd storm over to the diner and find Johann slumped over the bar with handfuls of bills spilling from his pockets. In the beginning, her cheeks burned with the shame of it and she'd lower her eyes and speak softly as she took him away by the arm, but eventually she'd haul him back to the motel so many times as to be cured completely of shame.

Sometimes, though, he'd disappear for nights or even weeks and she could not easily lure him back to the motel. One time it was to Hawaii, another time a hundred miles up the coast to Gualala, where he drank until his money ran out and he had no choice but to come back home. Whenever he disappeared like that, my mother and I just threw our clothes into some plastic shopping bags and moved into the Casa Buena.

"We'll go back home soon," my mother would tell me then, setting her mouth in a smile. "He's just gone on a vacation."

At the motel, odors from the Italian diner mixed with the candied-eucalyptus scent of the disinfectant Lili used to clean all the bathrooms. The only window of the manager's suite faced the highway, and the curtains were always drawn against the whizz and hum of cars on their way to San Francisco. The shower stall in the bathroom was lined with pale pink tiles, and over the years a leaking faucet had etched thick brown lines in the sink. Cockroaches lurked in every corner of the kitchenette. They terrified me until I learned to scare them away by banging on the cabinet doors before reaching inside for a bag of cookies or crackers.

In the afternoons, just before three o'clock, Lili hung the "Will Return By" sign in the window of the motel office, changed her clothes, and drove to Tiburon. As all the Mercedes and the BMWs filed out of the school parking lot and the other girls went off to soccer practice and play dates, I'd sit cross-legged on the curb, head buried in a book, until Lili pulled into the lot and honked the horn.

Now it was time for my after-school classes.

There were ballet lessons, piano lessons, art lessons, French lessons, and Persian lessons. Ice-skating lessons in the winter and swimming lessons in the summer. I had at least one class and often two every day of the week, Monday through Friday, and on Saturdays, from eight until noon, I went to a German-language school where the only other half-German girls were two green-eyed, coppery-skinned sisters with a Guatemalan mother.

"I hate after-school classes!" I whined, but Lili would have none of it. None at all. She could do without her beautiful house in the Tiburon hills, her tea parties, and her dinner parties, but she'd never give up my after-school classes. "You have to make yourself something in this country!" she'd tell me, lifting her chin and waving toward the window to indicate America. "Or else you are nothing, nothing at all!"

We'd sleep in the back room of the manager's suite, Lili and I, in a double bed with a scratchy, flower-print comforter like the ones in all the motel rooms. "I'll stay until you go to sleep," she'd whisper. Some nights she fell asleep before I did, and I'd stare at the twinkling asbestos ceiling and listen to noises in the parking lot or else watch her as she slept.

She was always so tired, my mother. I had never known her any other way, but still it confused me and scared me sometimes, too.

Once when the Cadillac was in the repair shop, she hung the "Will Return By" sign in the window and took a taxi to pick me up from school. Usually she wore her hair pulled back in a low bun, but that day it was loose about her shoulders and very frizzy. Even from a distance, she looked exhausted. And sad.

When we returned to the motel that afternoon, Lili pulled me into the back room of the manager's suite and locked us in the bathroom. She sank down to the floor, leaned her head against the sink, and closed her eyes.

I looked out the window toward the dumpsters of the Italian diner.

"Why are we in here?" I asked her.

A deep crease sprang up between her eyes. I was afraid I'd made her mad, but suddenly her expression softened and she smiled. She pulled me to her, hard, and held me against her chest. I raised my head, and when I saw that she was crying I tried to brush her tears away with my hand. She started laughing then, and crying, too, and kissing my hands, one and then the other, again and again.

Suddenly, she stood up, washed her face, and pinned up her hair. "No more crying now!" she told me as she pulled the door open.

She moved the clock hand on the "Will Return By" sign and hung it in the window. She held my hand tightly as we crossed from the parking lot to the sidewalk. She was quiet now, very calm. When we reached the pizza parlor with the triangle roof at the end of the street, she bought me a personal-size pizza and an extra-large Coke. She smiled at me as I ate.

The next morning at school the principal called me into her office.

"Did your mother pick you up yesterday?"

"Yes."

"In a *taxi*?"

I nodded.

She raised an eyebrow. "Where do you live?" she asked me. Her voice was kind, her eyes were kind, but I would only shake my head no.

"You can't tell me where you live?" she asked.

I shook my head again and round, hot tears spilled from my cheeks until finally she let me go.

Back in Iran, when the worst of the *shoolooqi* was over, Kobra drew on her veil with as little fuss as she'd put it aside twenty years earlier. Veiled or unveiled, women's vanities, she predicted, could be counted on to survive every calamity. She reopened the Lady Diola and once again she set about her work.

Every Friday morning she took a taxi to our apartment on the onetime Avenue Pahlavi (now the Avenue of the Revolution). She cracked open the windows, laundered the sheets, dusted the shelves, cleaned the white leather couches with a special cream, watered the geraniums on the balcony, said a prayer for our homecoming, and then, with a last look about the rooms, she'd lock the door and leave.

No sooner had the revolution ended than Saddam Hussein began to pitch rockets, missiles, and bombs into Iran from Iraq. Kobra took to sleeping fully clothed, with shoes on her feet and her identity card in her coat pocket, so that when the sirens sounded she could spring from her bed and huddle in the basement with her neighbors until the walls stopped rattling and the lights flickered back to life.

The borders were sealed, and after that the only way out of the country was by foot, or donkey, or some bandit's truck or motorcycle, over desert plains and across gorges, but still thousands of Iranians escaped, or at least contrived to send their sons out of the country.

Seven hundred and fifty thousand died that time, in that war. They died by bullets and rockets and grenades; by poisonous gases that seeped into their lungs and laid their bodies to waste; by mines that ripped flesh from bone as easily as it ripped soil from earth. Kobra would hear that somewhere in the city, in a cemetery called Zahra's Heaven, there was a fountain that ran red with martyrs' blood, and it was said that the tulips that sprang from the earth there were red, too.

Eventually Kobra cleared out our apartment. She began selling off what she could. The white leather couches had long since gone out of style and would not fetch a good price, but she managed to sell them anyway. She strung up our clothes, Lili's and Johann's and mine, on a clothesline along one wall of her bedroom, and she sold them, too, piece by piece by piece, over the course of many months. By such measures, Kobra would survive, the Lady Diola would survive, and for this she thanked God because to Kobra the *sabr*, the forbearance, God bestowed on her would always be a blessing greater than all the blessings she'd lost and would lose yet.

The war lasted eight years. In that time cousins and acquaintances carried back news of our house with its view of San Francisco, our kidney-shaped swimming pool, and the antiques Lili had piled in every room. We were rich; everyone in America was rich. "Send money," Kobra begged Lili late at night on the telephone. "Send whatever you can!" Lili bought dresses, pants, and coats and filled all the pockets with hundred-dollar bills; she stuffed the toes of shoes with toiletries and jewelry and medicine; and she packed it into two separate piles, one for Kobra and one for Sara.

When these remittances reached Iran, Kobra would open the box or the envelope, and finding their contents disturbed or gone, she'd furrow her brows and bite her lip. Voice quavering, she'd inform Lili of the losses. From then on Lili sent money and suitcases only through friends or acquaintances or relatives.

"God keep you for us," Kobra told her, "but next time could you please send more money?"

"But did you give it to her?" Lili would ask. "Did you give her what I sent?"

"Of course, of course," Kobra always assured her, but in these years Lili could be sure of nothing.

But for Lili the worst of the Iran-Iraq war were the calls that came for her late at night from Sara. Sara had no phone at her home in the countryside, but whenever she visited Tehran she'd telephone Lili. Her voice was a woman's voice by then, with a rich timbre, but it was always a child's plea that Lili heard when Sara spoke.

"Why did you leave me?"

"But the *shoolooqi*," Lili told her, "and now this war..."

"No, not now. I mean before. When I was little, when I was a baby. Why did you leave me then?"

In time Lili would tell Sara the whole of it. About Kazem and the beatings and the divorce. About her father, Sohrab, and the terrible years that had followed his death. "I was no one," she told Sara. "I had nothing...." Lili told her more than she'd ever told anyone, more even than she herself could stand to remember, but no story she could tell would ever quiet Sara. "Why did you leave me?" she'd ask each time. And: "When will you come back to Iran?"

★   ★   ★

"Where are you people from?" people would ask Lili at the Casa Buena. Each time she heard this question, she would think of the skinny Iranian boy she'd once seen on television, the one who lay huddled on the ground while a group of men took turns kicking him. "Germany," she'd answer in the most German accent she could muster, because there were dangers everywhere then and this was the way she knew to keep us safe.

She wasn't always successful.

One day a pretty blond woman drove into the parking lot in a silver BMW, swung into the office, and asked if she could look at a room before renting it. Lili shrugged and slipped her a key. Half an hour later, Lili spied the woman walking back to her car with freshly washed hair.

"Room's no good," the woman muttered when Lili caught up with her in the parking lot. Then, with a shove, she added, "God-damn spic."

Lili, for whom this slur was new and unfamiliar, staggered and fell. Before she could pull herself up, the woman fell on her and straddled her chest. Lili's backside and legs dug into the concrete. Her dress, she realized with horror, had ridden up to her waist. Lili raised her hand to strike, but despite her slight frame the woman was astonishingly strong. She gripped Lili's wrist and bit it, hard enough to break skin, then scrambled into her car and out of the parking lot.

What my mother really feared, though, was that something would happen to me. There was a small bell above the office door that rang every time someone came looking for a motel room. Whenever she heard it, she'd tell me to move farther back into the manager's suite so that no one could see me. She watched the news every night; she knew what could happen to little girls in this country. "Hide yourself!" she hissed at me in Persian whenever the bell rang at the Casa Buena.

Usually I could entertain myself by reading or making up games, but one day I wandered out of the manager's suite and walked to the far edge of the parking lot by myself. I was hunched over, inspecting a pothole, when she caught my arm, lifted me up, and slapped my face.

"You can never do that again!" she snapped. "You can't wander off by yourself, do you understand?"

Tears pricked my eyes. "Yes, *maman*," I whimpered.

"If you do it again," she said, easing her grip, "I'll go back to Iran. I'll go back to my Good Daughter."

The Good Daughter. My mother conjured her often in those days. The daughter who stayed by her mother's side, the daughter who knew not to wander off by herself. I still believed in her back then. I believed she could steal my mother away from me. The Good Daughter terrified me, and my mother counted on that terror to keep me safe. She also counted on my silence. When she dropped me off at school in the mornings, she would remind me to tell no one at school about my father's drinking, her work, or our stays at the motel. Only Americans spoke of those sorts of things, and it wasn't for such betrayals that she had left her country and her Good Daughter and brought me to this *kharab shodeh*, this awful broken-down place.

But these were not the only stories she told.

On Saturday and Sunday mornings Lili and I would go from room to room at the Casa Buena, and while she stripped beds, emptied ashtrays, and cleaned toilets I'd sit cross-legged on the floor and watch cartoons. As a treat on the days when I hadn't bothered her too much, she'd run me a bath and arrange wedges of pomegranate along the lip of the tub.

"A pomegranate," my mother told me, "is not a simple fruit. Behind its leathery hide, it draws a veil over its seeds, and when you eat it, it stains your fingers with a juice that's stubborn as ink but twice as subtle."

I loved to sit in the bathtub eating freshly quartered pomegranates and listening to Lili's stories. I'd work my way gingerly through each section, peeling away the milky white membranes to get to the fruit. Sometimes I bit straight into mounds of seeds, as if I were eating an apple, and the bitter pith mixed with the sweetness. Other times I plucked the seeds out one by one with my fingers and then ground them slowly and delicately between my teeth.

Lili would crouch beside the tub and then, as pomegranate juice dripped from my hands and my chin and the bubbles in the tub slowly turned pink, she'd tell me stories about a place she called Persia.

"Have I told you the story of my wedding? Did you know they called me Khanoom Doktor—Madame Doctor—back then?"

"Yes, *maman*," I'd say.

"And have I told you I wore no makeup at all?" she'd continue. "None at all! Just minutes before the ceremony began, my aunt Zaynab came running toward me with a stick of black kohl. Before I knew it, she'd swiped one line across each of my eyelids!"

She'd pretend to line her eyes with two flicks of the wrist.

"No other makeup at all!" She laughed. "I bought the flowers from the best florist in Tehran," she went on, "Kobra prepared the food, Zaynab and Khanoom, my grandmother, assembled the *sofreh*, the wedding spread, and my cousin Nima, who was just a scrawny boy then—but already flirting with me, if you can imagine—played the *tar* while I danced."

She'd look at me to make sure I was listening.

"Everyone, but everyone, said I was pretty as an *aroos farangi*, a foreign bride, but what they really could not believe, and still can't believe, was that when I came back from Germany I brought them a *damad farangi*, a European groom!"

By this time in the story I'd dropped the last of the pomegranate skins into a pot beside the tub. The red splotches disappeared into the bathwater, leaving not even a pink hint of my indulgence. Still smiling at the memory of her wedding, my mother would reach over and flip the drain open.

I'd forgotten home, I'd forgotten Iran, but just as some memories linger in spite of our longing to forget them, there are some loves that will take in just about any soil. When my mother Lili lined my bathtub with pomegranates, she was giving me an appetite for an unearthly fruit and the stories and secrets encased in its many-chambered heart, and this, she knew, was a pleasure from which not even a small girl could be exiled.

Ten

The Good Daughter

"Now you know there was no choice. I wanted to keep you safe. It had to be." These are my mother's last words on the tapes, but they come out with an odd inflection, like a question or even, I think, like a plea.

FOR YEARS THE WORLD seemed split between two kinds of women. The first were my mother's friends, the wives who stayed home all day, waiting for children who, as the years went on, would not answer them in Persian. In the afternoons these women dressed in pretty clothes, piled jewels around their throats and on their fingers, made up their faces, and gathered in one another's drawing rooms. They gossiped endlessly about other people's children and husbands and mothers-in-law, but they were always careful not to disclose too much about their own difficulties. If they worked, they didn't talk about it. Instead they told tales about royal ancestors and abandoned riches and took turns reading one another's fortunes in the patterns left in tiny white cups by thick potions of Turkish coffee. Each time they met, they parted with kisses, with the halting intimacy of estranged sisters.

The other kind of women were the relatives who came to stay with us for weeks and sometimes months, long enough for me to know them in ways that I would never know my mother's friends. They came between countries, marriages, and lives. Among them were wives whose husbands had found their reduced circumstances and diminished prestige in America unbearable. When their husbands left for Iran to take young wives and start new families, these women opened beauty parlors or turned their living rooms into day-care centers. One paid her son's college tuition by sewing hospital scrubs and sent him off each week with Tupperware containers marked "Herb stew, my love" and "May I die for you, rice pudding." I knew another woman who, after days spent hunched over the cash register of a small deli, stood over the bathroom sink at night, rubbing her husband's socks with a bar of soap under hot water until her hands wrinkled and the socks were restored to a virginal white.

And then there was my own mother, with her two homes and her two lives, and the unwavering pride with which she maintained the distances between them. One mother spent her days at a run-down motel along the highway answering the phone in a heavy accent and cleaning motel rooms on weekends and all the other days when the regular maid did not show up. The other wore a turquoise bathing cap and bright red lipstick when she went swimming in the backyard of our house in Tiburon. She reigned over dinner parties of fifty or a hundred guests. She coursed through rooms with marble coffee tables, gilt-framed armoires, and fields of Persian carpets. There was the woman who wrangled over motel bills with truck drivers and the woman who lined plump dates with almonds and passed them on sterling silver platters to her guests.

But just as there were two kinds of women, there were also two kinds of girls: Iranian daughters and American daughters. Iranian daughters, like The Good Daughter of my mother's stories, were shy, quiet, polite, and modest. Some, but not all, of her friends' daughters were Iranian daughters. They addressed their elders with the formal *shoma*, never *toh*. They knew how to serve a proper tea. And when they laughed, they hid their sweet smiles behind their hands.

The old ways were fading fast in America, but it was the loss of just such daughters that would reveal to Iranians the true measure of their exile.

In the mid-eighties, when Iran's borders were opened again—or opened, rather, for brief and uncertain intervals—Kobra began to visit us in California. She'd stay for six months or even as long as a year, but she never cared to stay for good. For Kobra, America was a very small place, much smaller than Iran. She didn't speak English, she didn't know how to drive, and she didn't know anyone here whom she could call or visit. She spent her days alone in the house, puttering and praying, arranging and rearranging the contents of her suitcase, and then settling into an armchair to study the actresses' hairstyles on *Days of Our Lives* until I came home from school.

Apart from television and her *namaz*, cooking was her only diversion. Some Saturdays she'd wake up as early as six in the morning, tie her hair in a kerchief, and slip into the kitchen. She steeped the day's first tea leaves with cardamom and rose essence and then she started rinsing and soaking the rice and trimming the day's vegetables and herbs. When she was not working the night shift at the Casa Buena, Lili joined Kobra at the stove and they'd settle in for a full day of cooking. I'd drift into the kitchen between cartoons to make myself some frozen waffles and find the two of them in the kitchen with all the burners on at once, frying up pounds of chopped onions, armfuls of eggplants, and mountains of marble-sized meatballs. They'd joke and bicker long into the afternoon, stopping only for a makeshift lunch of flatbread, feta cheese, and a couple of fresh walnuts, too, if those were already done soaking in salt water.

Labors of such scale, I well knew, signified just one thing: guests were coming to our house for dinner. Even a modest dinner party back then meant at least thirty or more people. The wives dressed as if for a state function and without exception only the men drank alcohol. There were always at least three kinds of stew, two types of rice with separate plates of *tahdig*, or thick crisped rice, alongside pilaf-stuffed grape leaves and bell peppers, potato cutlets, homemade yogurt, and, for dessert, bowls of a thick saffron-infused rice pudding and carefully assembled towers of fresh dates. By the time Lili and Kobra were done cooking, there'd barely be enough time for them to slip into their party dresses and swipe on some lipstick. Still, they always ushered guests to the table with apologies for the terrible simplicity of the fare.

Such parties were increasingly rare, however. With Johann gone for days and weeks at a time, Lili and Kobra spent most weekends at the motel, working side by side. I'd have no choice but to go along with them. To pass the time I'd flip on the television as we made our way through the rooms.

"For this you left your country!" Kobra would chide Lili, clucking her tongue and wringing her hands. "To be a maid!"

"I have no choice!"

"In Iran they called you Khanoom Doktor," Kobra muttered. "Why don't you come back home? Why don't you come back to your country?"

Lili lifted her chin and nodded toward me. "And how," she'd ask, "can I take her back there now?"

At this I might look up at them. "Take me where?" I'd ask my mother in English.

"You see!" Lili would say, and throw her hands into the air. "She doesn't even know where anymore!"

In the summertime they dragged blankets onto the balcony, strung up mosquito netting, and slept outside. The fog was always heaviest in the summer, but on those rare clear summer nights Lili would point toward the San Francisco skyline and ask, "Isn't it beautiful?"

"But do you remember when we slept on the rooftops in Tehran?"

"Of course," Lili answered, "but look how beautiful it is here!"

Kobra would glance, reluctantly, toward the city. "Yes, but if I stay here I will get sick," she swore, "and I will die in this place."

The sound of their voices, the roll and the lilt of Persian, and all their squabbling and confiding were never as close as when we were in the car on one of our road trips. Once a year Lili plotted a course to the relatives—the cousins and second cousins and fourth cousins once removed—who now lived scattered along the state. She'd load up the Buick (for such long journeys the Cadillac could not be trusted) and the three of us would head south toward Los Angeles.

It was a style of travel well suited to my mother and my grandmother. Iranian pop music blaring from the tape deck, they gossiped and bickered their way through pounds of sunflower seeds and pistachio nuts. "I'm bored!" I'd holler from the backseat. My mother would hand me a sheet of *lavashak,* a kind of Iranian fruit roll-up, or else a handful of pistachios and tell me to look out the window at America. I'd sulk awhile and then go back to reading a book, oblivious, then, to the imprint of their language on mine and their country on the only homeland I recognized as my own.

The summer of the salamanders, Kobra and I moved to the house in Tiburon and Lili moved into Casa Buena by herself. For some weeks—exactly how many I couldn't be sure—Lili and I went home only to grab some clothes or collect the stacks of unopened mail. But now Kobra had come from Iran to stay with us and the house was hers and mine and Johann's.

On the day of our return, I left my grandmother in the kitchen and went to the backyard by myself. The grass had grown as yellow and dry as straw and it scratched my ankles to walk through it. I slipped off my sandals and sat at the edge of the pool and looked down into the water.

Leaves had made a thick, brown carpet at the bottom of the pool, and so it took me a moment before I could see them. Dozens of salamanders, ink black, with rubbery bodies and long, thin tails, had gathered in our swimming pool. They wriggled and slipped and skidded over one another. Some lay still, as if dead.

They taught me the essence of time and of deceit, those salamanders, because all at once I understood that we must have been gone from the house for a very long time. But I was my mother's daughter; I didn't turn away. I was eleven years old and already I understood shame and secrecy, pride and resourcefulness. I stood by the edge of the pool, staring into the brackish water and considering the salamanders for a long while. Then I rummaged around the backyard until I found the long pole with a net meant to catch fallen leaves. One by one I fished all the salamanders out of our swimming pool and hurled them high over our deck and into the neighbor's yard.

Those months were the longest I'd lived with my father since we'd left Iran, but I hardly ever saw him. He spent days in his office with the door locked. "Your father's working," my grandmother would tell me when I asked after him. "Don't disturb him, *madar-joon*."

When she was busy in the kitchen or praying in her bedroom, I'd occasionally wander downstairs and linger by the band of light behind his door. He always had his radio tuned to a classical music station, but if I was very quiet I could make out the sound of a glass hitting the desk or a page rustling, and sometimes I'd hear him talking on the phone in a language that was not German and not Persian, a language I could not name, much less understand.

The police brought him home twice that summer. The first time he'd been walking home drunk on the town's main thoroughfare, a narrow, shoulderless two-lane highway with no shoulder. He stumbled to the center of the highway and sent a car swerving over the divider. It wasn't long before a policeman caught up with him, hauled him into a police car, and brought him back home to us.

"*Danke schön!*" Kobra told the policeman that night, trembling with gratitude. In her broken German and few words of English, she proceeded to ask him into the house for a cup of tea, an offer he politely but firmly refused.

Then came the day when my father staggered into the cul-de-sac, stretched his arms out, and began spinning in a circle like a dervish. One by one the neighbors came to their windows to watch. He screamed, sometimes in German, sometimes in Persian, and spun in circles, from one end of the cul-de-sac to the other, until his knees buckled and he fell, face-first, against the concrete.

When the policeman came for him that time, his forehead was wet with blood and he was weeping.

"Can't anyone cry in this country?"

"Sir," the policeman said as he led Johann out of the cul-de-sac, "you can cry all you want in your own house. But in this country nobody screams in the streets."

It was Kobra who finally saved him.

One day when I was away at school, two tall, muscled young men came to the house in Tiburon. It was nearly noon, but Johann still lay dead asleep in his office, dressed in yesterday's clothes, his pores rich with alcohol and the whole room sour with it.

Kobra murmured a quick prayer and then knelt at the side of his bed.

"You are my own dear son," she cooed. "You are a good, good man, Mr. Engineer."

He groaned.

"You love your family," she continued. "You love your daughter."

One eye opened.

"Do it for me, Mr. Engineer," Kobra pleaded.

He groaned again, turned away, and pulled the sheets over his head.

For nearly an hour Kobra sat beside him, smoothing his brow, cajoling and pleading with him until at last he let himself be taken away.

It was not called a hospital or a clinic but a rehabilitation center. A strange expression, Lili had thought when she first heard it on a TV commercial, but one that suggested homecomings. And beginnings.

Johann would spend the next eight weeks in a room with a single bed, one plastic chair, and a window that looked onto a small red-wood grove. For the first seven days he shivered and sweated and screamed, and for the next seven a succession of doctors drew his blood, held his X-rays to the light, and showed him death. His lungs had turned coal black, his arteries blocked. "You will die if you don't stop drinking and smoking," the doctors told him, and though for more than two decades Lili had told him as much, he only now beheld the proof.

For Lili there would be a revelation of another kind that year. Once a week she went to visit Johann and afterward she'd sit in a room with the other patients' wives. The women sat in a circle and one after another they told their stories. They wept openly, without shame, without apology. She had never known anyone to speak candidly of such troubles, and as she, too, wept and told her story, Lili would marvel at the honesty that is possible sometimes only among strangers.

When, at the end of two months, Johann was released from the clinic, he'd gained twenty pounds and his hair had turned completely gray, but he'd been cured of his addiction. He'd never drink again. In this same time, Lili had managed, just barely, to avert bankruptcy. She'd sold the Casa Buena, but she'd lost the house in the Tiburon hills. We had less now, by far, than we'd brought with us to

America, and no hope at all of returning to Iran. Still, what Lili saw when Johann returned to our new two-bedroom apartment on the edge of town was her shy, blue-eyed suitor in his herringbone jacket and his crooked bow tie. What I saw when he returned was the kind, bookish, soft-spoken father whose solitariness was my own.

Every time she came to visit us in America, Kobra arrived with a battered leather suitcase that smelled of mothballs and some other scent I could never place but that for me was the essence of the afternoons I had once spent with her at the Lady Diola. As soon as she got in from the airport, she'd unpack a sweater, two or three prim little house frocks, and a pair of rubber house slippers. Her fancier outfits—all her silk blouses and knockoff Chanel suits—would appear only on nights when my parents' friends came to dinner, spending the rest of their stay in America in the same suitcase in which they had arrived.

Over the next months, this suitcase would inexplicably expand to accommodate not only several more piles of girdles, sequined party dresses, and coats with matted synthetic fur collars but also huge stashes of toothpaste, razors, dish soap, shampoo, and every department store makeup sample she managed to fish out from the cabinet under my mother's bathroom sink. By the time Kobra was ready to leave, the suitcase had grown so fat that it would not close with ease. Often she and Lili would spend the day of Kobra's departure taking turns sitting on that suitcase in an effort to force its metal clasps shut. The Ritual of the Suitcase could go on for hours, and it became Kobra and Lili's way of arguing about Kobra's insistence on returning to Iran—and many other things I didn't understand.

"Why are you dragging all this back again?" my mother would start, bearing down on one corner of the suitcase while snatching vainly at its clasps. "I just don't understand you! There's nothing left back there, don't you see?"

"You don't know anything about it!" Kobra snapped.

"What are you going to do when you get really old? What am I supposed to do with you then?"

Kobra drew herself up and placed her hands on her hips. "What will I do, you ask me? Well, what did I do all through the *shoolooqi*? What did I do through the war?"

They'd spend the entire ride to the airport bickering and, in the most serious instances, swearing they would not even say good-bye to each other.

When the time came to check her suitcase, Kobra always had a tactic for evading excess baggage fees. Confronted by a man, she would bat her eyelashes and smile a schoolgirl's smile; confronted by a woman, she'd assume the pitiful posture of an invalid. She was difficult to resist in either case, and her record in evading the fees was nearly flawless.

But one year, after a particularly heated Ritual of the Suitcase, Kobra hauled her luggage onto the scale by herself and looked up hopefully at the young male attendant only to be met by a stern look.

"Thirty pounds over," he said, shaking his head and frowning.

Kobra turned to me. "What did he say?"

"He says the suitcase is too heavy," I translated. Even I could tell he would not be won by her usual strategy.

"I'm not paying it," Lili said. "I've had it with that suitcase and all the junk you keep dragging around!"

Kobra reached into the depths of her scuffed handbag and pulled out two crisp one-hundred-dollar bills to pay the excess baggage fee. This would have been enough money to buy half a year's groceries back in Iran. Nothing in her suitcase was worth that much, but she slid the bills onto the counter without flinching.

"Please take me with you!" I'd once wailed in the last minutes before she disappeared behind the gate. After months of eating her treats and listening to her stories, I could not easily let her go. I'd clutch her skirts and tell her she could just take me with her in her suitcase and no one would ever know.

My pleas would eventually become a joke between us. "I'd tuck you into my suitcase, but see how you've grown!" she'd say. Then, pinching my sides, she'd add, "Now that I've finally decided to put you in there you will never fit!"

One year we would hear of an Iranian man who had done just this to smuggle his fiancée into the United States. He had taken the precaution of punching small holes through the fabric of his suitcase, but when he opened the suitcase in America his fiancée was dead.

We could never tell our joke after that, but there was no joking at all this time at the airport. Kobra kissed me on both cheeks, whispered a prayer in my ear, and then she left America for the last time.

Whenever my parents' Iranian friends gathered for dinner parties and No Rooz celebrations, the men and women invariably parted ways just as soon as they stepped out of their cars and over the threshold of their hosts' home. As a young girl, my place had always been with the women, perfecting a pleasing muteness as they gossiped over endless rounds of bitter black tea. With each year I'd grown more eager to join my father and the other men in their earnest talk of history, politics, and mystical Persian poetry, but very few women crossed that invisible boundary in those days and in those circles of ours, and it was unthinkable that I, a young girl, should pull up a chair next to grown men. It would have been indecent.

There was so much that was indecent back then. Shorts and mini-skirts, to begin. The tweezing of eyebrows and the wearing of all but the most discreet smudge of lip gloss. Sleepovers, school dances, parties, and any event for which my mother could not serve as chaperone were out of the question as well.

To that eternal teenage wail ("But M-o-o-o-om!") I routinely added: "This isn't Iran!" This argument had no currency whatsoever with Lili. It didn't matter that we'd never go back to Iran again. Even after ten years in this country, words like "boyfriend" and "dating" were as good as obscenities in our house. Those were American words, American ideas, and not, my mother Lili gave me to understand, meant for me.

When I turned thirteen she informed me that when a girl "gave herself" to a man—the closest Persian equivalent for intercourse— she damaged herself. What's more, the damage was immediately apparent. Intercourse changed a girl's walk, her voice, her smile. And such "giving" before marriage cost a girl everything. "They use you and then..." Here her voice trailed off ominously. "Then they toss you aside like a sullied handkerchief!" Sometimes she preferred another, more distinctly Iranian metaphor: a worn and faded carpet. "Like so," she'd demonstrate, stamping her foot and then bending down to smooth the silken threads. "Afterward they think of you as nothing but the worn carpet under their feet!"

I knew that daughters of my mother's Iranian friends were growing up in a similar way, with the same exhortations and prohibitions, but it wasn't something I'd ever talk about with them. At the large public high school the Iranian girls formed cliques of their own, but at my small private school there were just three other Iranian girls and we kept to ourselves and did our best not to call attention to the Iranian parts of our lives. We did our best to pass as American. I, in any case, did my best to pass.

Once I'd tossed cucumbers and quince fruit into the trash before school started. By high school I'd learned to duck into the bathroom before classes, trade my jeans for a miniskirt, and swipe on some blush, mascara, and lipstick. It wasn't sufficient, really, to pass, and so whatever my mother forbade me I pretended to scorn. I couldn't be bothered with boys my age and I had no time for high school parties;

I'd devoted my life to higher intellectual pursuits. Said devotion mostly involved gorging myself on books. At sixteen I read all the diaries of Anaïs Nin, one volume after another, in quick, breathless, heady succession. I took to writing in my own diary. I wore black.

"What's all this?" my mother would say, throwing her hands up in the air. "Who do you think you are? Simone de Beauvoir? Can't you at least put this junk aside and read some real literature? Shakespeare, say, or some Dickens..."

I'd roll my eyes or pretend I hadn't heard her.

My father did not usually involve himself in these scenes. "Let her be," he might, however, interject on occasion. "It's perfectly harmless."

"Yes, harmless now," Lili howled, "but where, I ask you, will it end?"

Real trouble came in my senior year of high school. "Make something of yourself!" had been Lili's injunction as she hauled me from after-school class to after-school class, but what this "something" should be, and how I might become it, grew less and less clear as my graduation date approached. With the sole exception of medical school, Iranian girls did not go away to college or graduate school. They lived at home with their parents until they got married. Smart, ambitious Iranian daughters went to one of the local liberal arts colleges or else the closest public universities; the others went to community college or didn't go to college at all; and Iranian girls who left home under any other circumstances were considered members of a profession so shameful its name could not be spoken aloud.

In ten years this regimen would become ancient history, but while everyone else from my high school went away on college tours and began mailing in their applications to campuses far and wide, I sat in a café in Mill Valley (strictly off-limits, Lili warned me, for in those years there were still "hippies" in Marin), read Kierkegaard, and wrote in my journal with a fountain pen. I'd have to live at home through college or I wouldn't be able to go to college at all. It was useless to protest. I pined and ranted in my diary until the day my letter of acceptance came in from UCLA. Within weeks of its receipt, my mother packed up all our belongings and we all headed south, to Los Angeles, so that I could begin my college career.

Tehrangeles.

Some half million to a million Iranian immigrants had landed in Southern California after the 1979 revolution. From the rent-controlled apartments in Santa Monica to the high-rise condominiums on Wilshire Boulevard and the gated mansions of Beverly Hills, it was impossible to walk three paces in this part of California without seeing an Iranian face or catching a phrase of Persian. Iranian grocery stores, Iranian bookstores, and Iranian furniture stores ran the length of Westwood Boulevard, from the Westside to the East-, their signs all rendered in bold Persian script. Even the air in Los Angeles, my mother observed with obvious pleasure, smelled exactly like the air in Tehran.

I was expected home by sunset. I was not allowed to date. Still, Tehrangeles, I was determined, would have no claim on me. There were hundreds of Iranian students at UCLA and nearly all of them could be found on the southern edge of campus, poring over their organic chemistry textbooks and MCAT workbooks. I breezed past the future podiatrists, surgeons, and orthodontists and headed to North Campus, the artsy side, the side with the Romanesque architecture and landscaped lawns. From this picturesque venue I boldly declared my major: English. Fortunately, my mother approved the choice, and in this, at least, she proved more indulgent than most Iranian parents of her generation. For Lili the study of literature was permissible so long as it was cast off after the undergraduate level for a career in law.

There followed then the period in which I traveled everywhere with my *Norton Anthology*, volume 1, tucked under my arm. In the center seat of the front row of Rolfe Hall I scribbled myself into ecstasies over the poetry of Keats, Shelley, and Byron. It was not long before every one of my *Norton*'s three thousand tissue paper–thin pages was heavily annotated in ink. At night, in my parents' house and in the same canopied bed I'd slept in since I was twelve years old, I detailed the agonies of my existence in the handsome French composition books I bought in a Santa Monica stationery shop.

Between my passion for English literature and the severe restrictions on my social life, I'd manage to graduate from college in just over two years, but somewhere between the Romantics and all those tortuous journal entries I found my way into the college newsroom, and so it was with my newly minted, freshly laminated press pass swinging from my neck that I strode into the university hospital in pursuit of a story and ran into what was to me then the least likely object of desires, journalistic, intellectual, and otherwise: an Iranian doctor.

In America, good Iranian daughters became doctors, the merely pretty ones married doctors, and the very best did both. I was hopeless at math and science, so there was never any chance I'd join the ranks of Iranian American doctors. For a long time, though, I seemed destined to marry one.

I had no interest in marrying an Iranian doctor. I'd long since decided that if I ever married at all, it would be an artist—a sculptor, say, or a poet. And yet. This particular Iranian doctor possessed a vast knowledge of modern art. He'd actually *lived* in France. He wore round-rimmed glasses and he smiled a slow, lopsided smile. I was, from the very first latte he bought me in Westwood village, perfectly, lamely besotted.

Amin was thirty-one. More problematically, he'd been married before. Childhood friends raised in the same small circle of Iranian Americans, he and his wife had married in their twenties and divorced a few years later. Suitors were not supposed to have ex-wives, because Iranians didn't get divorced, so far as I'd ever heard, anyway.

"Divorced?" Lili had shrieked at the news, and clutched at her heart. "You cannot imagine I would allow you to have contact with a man who's been divorced?"

"But Mom," I whined, "this isn't Iran—"

"What exactly do *you* know about Iran?"

For weeks the situation seemed hopeless. I made protracted, enfevered productions out of my misery. Deliberations were resumed. In the end my mother's disapproval was mitigated by two factors: first, that Amin was a doctor and, second, that he could be called my suitor or *khastegari*.

According to the many rules of our courtship, he was allowed to take me out only once a week. On Saturday nights Amin would arrive at our house dressed as I would never see him otherwise—in a suit and tie—and affecting a formal manner that faded as soon as he eased into his car seat and turned to me with a conspiratorial smile.

The first night he took me to dinner in a French bistro in West LA. As votives threw shadows against the white tent he ordered chocolate soufflé in a French that would forever put my high school knowledge of that language to shame. The next week he took me to a gated white mansion in Bel Air to celebrate the birthday of a minor Saudi prince. "A patient," Amin explained coolly as I struggled to suppress my awe. At the Hollywood Bowl one July evening I sought, desperately, to find transcendence in an interminable German opera. There were, in addition, a succession of cocktail parties and dinner dates with his medical colleagues and their eminently elegant wives. "What is your opinion of García Márquez?" an impossibly tall, impossibly thin blonde asked me at one such gathering, and I, the nineteen-year-old literary critic, proceeded to deliver a pithy assessment of his oeuvre, despite never having read even one of his novels.

Summers in France had refined my suitor's ideals of female beauty. He favored darkly lined eyes, pale pink lipstick, skirts, and high heels. I took a stick of kohl to my lids, painted my lips, and adjusted my black wardrobe to include pencil skirts and pumps. One day he took me to a Westside boutique and bought me my first very expensive purse, a small boxlike number with a handle and a tiny gold clasp. "Soigné," he said as he assessed its effect on me, a word I understood to mean perfection.

"I have to go," I'd tell him, wrestling myself free at the end of the night.

He always knew enough not to ask me to stay. "But do you know where you are going, little girl?" he'd tease, catching my face in his hands and kissing me one last time before letting me go.

On the nights when I returned home after midnight, my mother would always be waiting for me in the living room, ready to take me in with a single glance.

"Can't you see that if you give yourself to him like this he'll never marry you?"

"But I don't want to get married!"

"Then he can't take you out at all!"

"But Mom, this isn't Iran!"

"Iran?" she'd say, narrowing her eyes. "You don't know anything at all about Iran!"

I'd stare dumbly at the floor, cheeks hot with shame and desperate to escape.

I would on no account have told Amin about these late-night exchanges, and if he ever wondered what happened after I closed the door to my parents' house he never asked. And if on the next day he and his parents appeared at our door, my mother—now calm and sweet—would usher them all into our living room and I would be called upon to serve everyone tea in tiny gilt-rimmed glasses.

This was the hour of the virgin. Not a single person in the room believed in my fitness for the role, but it was still necessary to play the part. I therefore dressed carefully, in pastel skirt suits and modest makeup, and I crossed my legs at the ankles whenever I sat down. During these visits, Amin and I never sat next to each other. We were careful not to look too long in each other's direction. Afterward, though, we'd laugh it all off, mocking the ridiculous customs of our parents and congratulating ourselves on yet another perfectly executed performance.

"You can leave this house," she finally told me one night.

It was two o'clock in the morning. I pulled the door closed quietly behind me. She was standing in the hallway in bare feet and a bathrobe, her arms crossed over her chest. My eyes fell to the suitcase she'd set by the door. I looked up at her, confused.

"You are not my daughter," she told me. Her voice was strangely calm. "You are not my daughter and you *should* leave this house."

In the dark she took in the whole of me—tangled hair, chapped lips, wrinkled skirt—and then she did what always scared me more than anything: she started pulling at her hair and beating her chest and tearing at her clothes.

"Look what my daughter has made herself into in this *kharab shodeh*, this broken-down place!" she wailed, turning her palms and her face up to the sky. "Leave your home and every last person who knows your name, and now...this daughter!"

I kept my eyes down. I would not cry or say even a word—I knew better than that—but later, when she'd stopping crying and screaming and had gone to sleep and the house was quiet again, I sat cross-legged on the kilim in my bedroom, tracing its rough knots and thinking of the suitcase my mother had left for me by the door.

She didn't mean, really, for me to leave home; that was still inconceivable to us both. She'd only meant I should be more clever, that I should stop "giving" myself away so easily, "giving" myself as an American girl would. That was what she'd meant with that suitcase.

Still, I couldn't put it out of my mind. Without a green card, I had no way of supporting myself. My student visa would get me as far as graduate school, but all the schools I'd applied to were far away.

Do you know where you are going, little girl?

I laughed easily whenever Amin teased me with that question, laughed as though I knew the answer and had always known. But I had no answer. And I did not know.

Every day I'd scramble out of lecture halls and seminar rooms, drive to Amin's studio by the beach, and sit cross-legged on his futon with my books while he cooked. He was a marvelous cook.

By the second year of our "courtship," I'd progressed to the second volume of the *Norton Anthology*. I traded Shelley, Keats, and Byron for Woolf, Plath, and Rich. I made my first forays into French feminist theory. While Amin stood in the kitchen stirring a pot of bouillabaisse or some such, we had epic arguments about feminism. Or rather, he cooked for us as I rehearsed my epic feminist arguments.

"Marriage," I informed him one day, "is an instrument of patriarchy."

Concurring, he gave the bouillabaisse or some such a stir.

"Unjust!" I shouted from the futon. "Unnatural!"

"Maybe so, but what exactly do you propose we do about it?"

I had no proposition as of yet, but that exchange did inspire a game of sorts.

"If you asked me to marry you...," I'd begin.

"Yes?" he'd answer, raising an eyebrow.

"I'd never, ever say yes."

"I know you wouldn't. That's exactly why I'll never, ever ask you."

We played that game a lot.

Or played it, rather, until he sensed that I was coming to hope our courtship really would end in marriage.

It was then that he began to travel. He'd take off on a day's notice and stay away for weeks. I wasn't allowed to spend more than one night a week out with him, "suitor" or not, and traveling together was out of the question. This I ascribed to my mother's ancient Iranian prohibitions and to the broader injustices of "patriarchy," but secretly I admired the casual air with which he'd set out for Berlin or Hong Kong or Buenos Aires. I coveted the financial independence and, especially, the confidence that made these decisions so natural for him. Already I was measuring the distances not only between us but also between who I was and what I wanted in these ways.

The summer after my college graduation, I drove myself back up the coast to San Francisco. It was an especially hot July day and I'd barely made it out of the San Fernando Valley when the air conditioner in my car broke down and I started to cry.

Amin had not, finally, asked me to marry him. I'd be starting law school in the fall. What I wanted and would never have asked for was to stay in Los Angeles—to be chosen, to be married—but all at once there was no choice but to go.

I drove up the I-5 that summer with all the windows down, crying the whole way, and then, slowly and clumsily, with prizes, scholarships, and all the uneasy force of the language I'd made my own in America, I began closing in on the distances that eluded me.

We met once, years later, over dinner. Amin had stayed in Los Angeles. He still lived in the same small studio on the beach. He hadn't remarried. By then I'd made my way clear across the country. I'd finished law school, practiced briefly, and then headed back to graduate school. I had a fellowship to study English at Princeton, a small living stipend, and a very small and ugly apartment of my own. When I wasn't holed up in the stacks of Firestone Library, I'd slip onto a commuter train to Manhattan and spend hours tooling around the city in a pair of thick-soled black leather boots. I was often lost those days and almost always the happier for it.

It was a lovely dinner, that last dinner with Amin, full of our old banter. Toward the end of the night, we spoke of our "courtship" in Los Angeles and with all the world-weariness of my twenty-five years I'd look back with pity at the nineteen-year-old girl I'd been.

"I was *so* young....," I groaned.

He flashed me a wry smile. "You were."

"But I wonder...," I said. I dropped my eyes to the table. "I wonder—"

"Wonder what?"

"Why didn't you ask me to marry you?"

"You wouldn't have said yes, remember?"

"But would you have asked?"

"But would you have said yes?"

A dozen coy, arch answers came to mind. Inexplicably, I told him the truth. "Yes. I would have said yes."

It was an honest but belated declaration and it belied another truth. I hadn't made a proper Iranian marriage and that had made everything else—graduate school, work, boyfriends, my daylong treks through New York—possible. I was not my mother's Good Daughter or even merely a good Iranian daughter. For days at a time no one in the world, and certainly not my mother, Lili, knew where I was. I'd go home only at school holidays, just like all my American classmates, and often not even then.

The distance was a calculated one and more hard-won than I would have admitted to anyone in those days. For all the ease with which I passed as American, I hadn't unlearned my shame or my guilt or my anger. Whenever my mother called me on the phone, we invariably bickered. Why, she'd press me, didn't I come home to California more often? This I translated as: "When will you come home and get married?" I wasn't always quick to call her back, even when I missed her and wished I could go back home, if only for a time.

Then one day she called to tell me my father was in the hospital. "Come," she told me, her voice ragged. "Please come home now."

I spent a week in my apartment in Princeton, curled up on the futon, staring at the deep green New Jersey woods and listening to my mother's tapes. I listened as she spoke of Kobra and Sohrab, of her grandmother Khanoom and her aunt Zaynab, of Kazem and of Sara. I listened with an attention I'd rarely ever given my mother's stories, but I still couldn't square the tapes with the stories or the people I knew.

Then, as my mother began to tell me about Sara and the years at the Casa Buena, my memories began to thread through hers and I began to set her stories beside my own memories. Sara. She'd been the girl who'd played with me at my grandmother's salon, the girl my grandmother had once chased from the Lady Diola with her shrieks and her cries. Sara was the daughter my mother had lost, not once but many times, until she finally became a story to tell me, her strange American daughter in a strange, broken-down place.

I skipped classes and played my mother's tapes a second and even a third time through. The thin, broken voice that I'd scarcely recognized as hers grew more familiar, for a time, than her "real" voice and more familiar, really, than even my own voice. Very slowly, I began to understand that when my mother had sheltered me so fiercely as a child and then later as a young woman it was because of this daughter, the daughter she'd left in Iran and had never been able to forget in America. The Good Daughter.

Still, there was so much I couldn't understand. I called my mother once, intending to ask her questions about Sara—how it had felt to leave her behind in Iran, whether they'd spoken in recent years, and if she wished she could see Sara again—but the truth had made us shy of each other and when we spoke on the phone afterward it was as if all her words had already been spent and she just couldn't tell me any more.

I didn't press her. I'd begun to feel a strange new tenderness toward my mother. It would make me kinder, if not always kind enough, and for now this kindness meant I'd have to make sense of the story without her.

I decided to call my grandmother in Tehran. She listened quietly as I told her about the tapes. When I finished, Kobra said, "You should come to Iran." By then my grandmother was too old to travel to America anymore. I hadn't seen her in almost ten years, and after so much time I couldn't tell the difference between sadness and old age in her voice. "You should come here," she told me that day. Sara, she continued, had a son and two daughters of her own. Her husband was kind and she was happy. "You should see your country, *madar-joon*. You should see your family."

I didn't know how to answer. It still seemed incredible that I had a sister. If I saw Sara on the streets of Tehran, I wouldn't know her from all the women there. What claim could we have to each other after all this time? What would she think of me if we met now? These thoughts overwhelmed me and I pushed them from my mind. Nearly as unsettling was my grandmother's notion that Iran was "my country," a place I could still call home. In all these years of living in America, I'd never really thought about going back to the place where I was born. "There's nothing left to see," my mother often told me when I was growing up, and I'd always believed her.

For years my Iran had been a place in California, a place made up of women and their stories. When I thought of my family's first years in America, it was mostly the sadness of these women that I remembered, the sadness that clung to them and then trailed their daughters as they made their own way in this country. That was Iran to me, and I wanted no part of that Iran.

But even if I did not want to think of it, there was always another Iran, an Iran as far away as the shrouded, angry figures on our American TV screen and as close as the sounds of my grandmother's and mother's voices waking me late at night.

Some years—like the eight years of the Iran-Iraq war—it was impossible to get a call through to Tehran. Night after night Kobra and Lili stayed up long past midnight, dialing and redialing an endless stream of numbers. When they finally managed to reach someone "over there," they always shouted—as if this were the only way their voices could be heard across such distances.

Their voices would often wake me, and I'd stumble into the living room and settle onto Kobra's lap. I'd listen as she cried into the receiver, her voice brimming. I didn't know what lay on the other side of those late-night calls, but what I could see even back then was the quiet grief that hung about my grandmother's eyes the next morning. Sitting with a glass of tea cupped between two hands or working a knife over a pile of herbs, she'd look out the window and fix her eyes on a place I couldn't see.

In the end my grandmother Kobra preferred to go back to Iran rather than to stay here looking across that emptiness. But my mother Lili was never like that. Her eyes never fell away to the distance. When her friends began making trips back to Iran in the early nineties, they'd come back invigorated by their returns and eager to tell her about their time there. My mother remained unmoved. Her eyes simply didn't look toward what she had left behind.

But now, after listening to the tapes, I began to remember other things about my mother Lili. I thought back to all the nights when the house had been completely still and I'd fumbled downstairs and found the light from her bedroom spilling out into the hallway carpet. Behind the door I'd hear her sobbing. All that time, she'd been crying for her daughter, her Good Daughter, and I had not known.

That summer, the summer after the tapes, my mother began to show me her treasures.

First came the *sheleeteh*, the flounced apricot-colored skirt her grandmother Pargol had worn the day she left her village and moved to Tehran in the early 1900s. I spread it across my lap and smoothed its pleats. The hem was frayed, the clasps were missing, and the cotton had grown thin and even transparent in places.

A few days later my mother handed me the antique Chinese bowl her father, Sohrab, had filled with honeydews and tangerines for her wedding to Kazem. More than forty years had passed, yet it was still exquisite but for a nick along its rim.

She brought me a cloth-bound journal. She lifted the cover, revealing split seams, yellowed pages, red-lettered poems, and entries written in black.

She showed me a half-gold, half-turquoise fountain pen, a gift from the boy who'd once written her beautiful letters and shaved his hair off like Yul Brynner and who now lay buried not four hundred miles away from where we were.

Next came the photographs.

"Look," she told me one day in early June. She fanned them out on the table and then she handed them to me one by one. The first was a black-and-white photograph of a girl. Hair bobbed and face in shadows, she stood on what looked to be a rooftop. At her feet, bundled in blankets, there lay a baby in a *nanoo*, a simple metal cradle. I studied the girl in that photograph. She was so young, barely fourteen years old, but already she knew everything she would need to know: how to swallow a cry before it came.

The next photograph, also black and white, showed a young woman. Her hair was long and straight with a fringe. She did not smile. My mother said nothing, but I knew her. Sara.

If my mother and I had stayed in Iran, our lives would have been folded together eventually—somehow I was sure of this—but when we came to America Sara became The Good Daughter and I became an American girl and now I wondered if I would ever know her apart from that divide.

"Look here," Lili told me, interrupting my thoughts.

The last photographs she showed me—glossy studio portraits of a bride and groom, a picture of a young man standing on a beach in a black T-shirt and aviator glasses, and a photo of a girl on a busy city street—were much more recent. "Sara's boy," Lili said with a smile as she handed me the photograph of the young man. "And that's her youngest one," Lili told me, pointing to a girl with dimples and black ringlets peeking out from her green head scarf. "They always told me she looked just like me, and I suppose there is something there...." She touched the photograph very gently, tracing the girl's face with her fingertips. "You know, she called me last year and asked my permission to marry."

"What did you tell her?"

"I wished her happiness," Lili said quietly. "What else could I do?"

She studied the photographs for another moment and then quickly cleared them from the table and shrugged her shoulders as if to say, "Enough of this, enough of the past."

I said nothing more, but the pictures of Sara and her children unsettled me. Until that moment, I'd imagined that Sara belonged to my mother's memories and not at all to me, just as I believed that Iran itself did not belong to me. Now, suddenly, I began to picture myself descending on the streets of Tehran, alone and veiled, to seek out Sara and her family. We'd find a way to each other. We would know each other after all.

But I never returned to Iran. I never sought Sara out. I told myself I was too busy with my studies and then, later, with work. I told myself I'd go just as soon as the political tensions between America and Iran eased. Really, though, I was afraid. Besides, Sara had always known about me and yet she had never tried to contact me. If I tried to find her now, I'd only be intruding on the life she had made for herself. It was childish of me to think I could feel at home with her in Iran after all this time. Still, I couldn't quite give up the possibility of returning to Iran and meeting her. *Next year*, I'd promise myself, *next year I will go back.*

Later, Lili would tell me that for thirty years, as the divide between Iran and America deepened, she had made the same promise to herself. Even when she was long past believing it, she would continue to promise herself she'd return. That promise, the occasional, strained late-night phone conversation with Sara, and a handful of pictures of the grandchildren Lili had never met had, finally, become her Iran.

The truth was that my mother Lili didn't believe the past could be recovered, no matter how much time had gone by. For years she had wanted only to forget, to make a new life in this country. In this, and so much else, I realized, we'd always been the same.

I'd wonder, though, why she'd decided to send me the tapes. No one in America, not even one of her friends here, knew about her first marriage or her daughter in Iran. Maybe, I thought, the burden of her secret had grown too heavy over the years and in telling it to me she'd hoped to free herself of its weight. Or perhaps she did it as a way of claiming me back. After all, it was just the two of us left in America after my father's death and we'd never been further apart.

That truth came out only some years later, when I at last began to make sense of my mother's stories by shaping them into my own words. I learned that she'd always meant to tell me about her life and Kobra's and Sara's, but she'd waited until she guessed I was ready to listen. Some stories, my mother taught me, only happen like that. They wait for the one who can hear them before they let themselves be told.

"Tea?" Lili asked me when she'd slipped the photographs of Sara and her children back into an album that day.

I nodded. "Yes," I answered.

When she left, I looked about the room. The old marble-topped buffet from the living room now served as a makeshift desk. It was piled high with bills. Without a proper kitchen she'd taken to burning her wild rue over a hot plate. All her fine silk Persian carpets, I saw, lay heaped atop one another, three and four deep. She'd most likely have to sell them off soon. But when she brought me a cup of tea, the scent filled the room and I knew at once that its leaves had been steeped in the old way, the Iranian way, with rose essence and cardamom pods, and I knew that whatever else she'd had to give away, she'd managed to keep her beautiful brass samovar.

My pleasure in these familiar Iranian gestures—and also in the honest, if tentative, new intimacy between us—would surprise and soothe me that summer. I felt safe in that small, crowded, makeshift house of hers. Safer than I'd felt in many years and grateful for the first time to have come back home.

"Thank you, *maman-joon*," I told her as I reached to take a cup from the tray.

She smiled gently at me. "You're welcome, *dokhtaram*, my daughter."

I tucked a sugar cube into my cheek, held the cup in two hands, and took a sip of tea. It was then that I looked out the window and noticed the flowers. All along the garden wall she'd planted vines for herself. Morning glory and honeysuckle, nasturtium and jasmine. She hadn't bothered with pots. No, my mother Lili still had too much faith in her for that. The vines would soon outgrow the pots—she'd been absolutely certain of it—and so she'd just planted the seeds straight into the ground, from one end of the garden to the other. And she'd been right. The roots had taken well, all of them. It wasn't quite summer, but already the sun had coaxed blooms from the vines and sent their beauty tumbling clear over the garden wall.

Long after they understood that Lili and I would never return to Iran, Sara and Kobra found their way to each other at last.

Once a year at the Iranian New Year, Sara brought her husband and three children to Tehran. Kobra's small apartment became so noisy with the antics of those children that she and Sara had little room left for their old quarrels. In anticipation of their visits, Kobra trekked all over her neighborhood for the children's favorite cookies and candies. For lunch she'd order two large pizzas from down the street, and for dinner they all ate kabob and cups of *dooq*, the fizzy yogurt drink she prepared herself with sprigs of fresh mint. Before they left, Kobra went to her closet, where she kept the suitcases Lili sent from America, and chose clothes and toys for Sara's children.

One year when her neighbors hadn't seen Kobra around the complex for several days, it was Sara whom they called and Sara who came for her. Kobra had suffered a stroke. Both of her legs were paralyzed. She'd been lying on the floor in the kitchen for two days, unable to move, and when Sara found her there Kobra could barely speak for dehydration.

When Kobra was released from the hospital the following week, it was again Sara who came for her. This time Sara took Kobra to the countryside where she had made her home. In the mornings Sara's son brought Kobra pots of *samanoo*—the thick germinated wheat paste that is the hard-won delicacy of every Iranian spring. Kobra ate bowl after bowl of *samanoo*, devouring it with such hunger that it seemed it was the strength of the earth she was taking into herself.

Then she began to tell her stories. She spoke of her childhood, of Sohrab and their marriage. She spoke of Lili, Sara, and of me, too, but most of all she spoke about her own mother. Pargol had died some thirty years earlier, but remembering her last years locked in a room, warbling to herself in a language of her own invention, Kobra held her hands up to her face and cried like a small child.

"If I wanted to write my life story," Kobra would tell her grandchildren the day before she died, "there wouldn't be enough paper in the world to write it on!"

The call, like all bad news from Iran, came for Lili in the middle of the night.

"Kobra died in my skirts," Sara told her. "We sprinkled rose essence on her grave for you, *maman-joon.*"

In Iran it's thought that the dead must be buried quickly or else their souls will roam between heaven and earth. But a timely burial is a mercy of another kind: it marks the borders between the living and the dead and between memory and forgetting. "Earth brings forgetfulness," Iranians say, collecting a pinch of soil from a loved one's grave and touching it to their skin to quiet their grief.

For Lili, who had not buried her father or her husband and now would not bury her mother, Kobra's death would be just another proof of how distance disfigures both love and loss. When Kobra died, Lili's grief fell around and through her, unrelentingly. Yet Sara had buried Kobra for Lili—lovingly, devotedly—and in this she'd finally find her peace.

Where there is too much distance and too many leave-takings, there are no returns, or none in which we can fully believe. Still, one love always entangles itself in another, grows unrecognizable, and survives.

ABOUT THE AUTHOR

Jasmin Darznik was born in Tehran, Iran. A former attorney, she received her Ph.D. from Princeton University. Her writing has appeared in the *New York Times, Washington Post, Los Angeles Times, San Francisco Chronicle*, and other publications. She has taught Iranian literature at the University of Virginia and is a professor of English and creative writing at Washington and Lee University. She lives in Charlottesville, Virginia.